The Istanbul Convention, Domestic Violence and Human Rights

The Convention on Preventing and Combating Violence against Women and Domestic Violence (also known as the Istanbul Convention) was adopted by the Committee of Ministers of the Council of Europe on 7 April 2011. The Convention entered into force on 1 August 2014 and has currently been ratified by 22 states. This Convention constitutes a crucial development in the movement to combat gender-based violence, as it sets new legally binding standards in this area. This book provides a detailed analysis of the Convention and its potential to make an impact in relation to the specific issue of domestic violence.

The book places the Istanbul Convention in context with regard to developments relating to domestic violence as a human rights issue. The background to the adoption of the Convention is examined, and the text of this instrument is analysed in detail. Comparative analysis is engaged in with reference to the duties that have been placed on states by other bodies such as the UN Committee on the Elimination of Discrimination against Women and the European Court of Human Rights. Comparisons are also drawn with the Inter-American Convention on the Prevention, Punishment, and Eradication of Violence against Women and with the relevant provisions of the Protocol to the African Charter on Human and Peoples' Rights on the Rights of Women in Africa. An in-depth examination of the advantages of the adoption of the Istanbul Convention by the Council of Europe is provided along with a detailed analysis of the challenges faced by the Convention. The book concludes with a number of brief reflections in relation to the question of whether the adoption of a UN convention on violence against women may be a possible development, and the potential of such an instrument, in the context of domestic violence.

Ronagh J. A. McQuigg is a Lecturer at Queen's University Belfast, UK.

Routledge Research in Human Rights Law

Available titles in this series include:

Socio-Economic Rights in Emerging Free Markets
Comparative Insights from India and China
Surya Deva

International Human Rights Law and Domestic Violence
The Effectiveness of International Human Rights Law
Ronagh J. A. McQuigg

The Right to Religious Freedom in International Law
Between Group Rights and Individual Rights
Anat Scolnicov

The ECHR and Human Rights Theory
Reconciling the Moral and the Political Conceptions
Alain Zysset

Resolving Conflicts between Human Rights
The Judge's Dilemma
Stijn Smet

The Istanbul Convention, Domestic Violence and Human Rights

Ronagh J. A. McQuigg

Routledge
Taylor & Francis Group
LONDON AND NEW YORK

First published 2017 by Routledge

2 Park Square, Milton Park, Abingdon, Oxfordshire OX14 4RN
52 Vanderbilt Avenue, New York, NY 10017

Routledge is an imprint of the Taylor & Francis Group, an informa business

First issued in paperback 2018

British Library Cataloguing in Publication Data
A catalogue record for this book is available from the British Library

Library of Congress Cataloging in Publication Data
Names: McQuigg, Ronagh J. A., author.
Title: The Istanbul Convention, domestic violence and human rights / Ronagh J.A McQuigg.
Description: Abingdon, Oxon; New York, NY: Routledge, 2017. |
Series: Routledge research in human rights law
Identifiers: LCCN 2016056461 | ISBN 9781138953673 (hbk) | ISBN 9781315652436 (ebk)
Subjects: LCSH: Family violence—Law and legislation—Europe. | International law and human rights—Europe. | Council of Europe Convention on Preventing and Combating Violence against Women and Domestic Violence (2011)
Classification: LCC KJC8385.F36 M37 2017 | DDC 344.2403/28292—dc23
LC record available at https://lccn.loc.gov/2016056461

ISBN: 978-1-138-95367-3 (hbk)
ISBN: 978-0-367-18990-7 (pbk)

Typeset in Galliard
by Keystroke, Neville Lodge, Tettenhall, Wolverhampton

Contents

Table of cases

European Court of Human Rights

European Commission of Human Rights

Inter-American Court of Human Rights

Inter-American Commission on Human Rights

Decisions of the Committee on the Elimination of Discrimination against Women under the Optional Protocol to CEDAW

United Kingdom

Table of legislation

United Kingdom

Council of Europe

Inter-American System of Human Rights

African Union

United Nations

1 Introduction

The Convention on Preventing and Combating Violence against Women and Domestic Violence (also known as the Istanbul Convention) was adopted by the Committee of Ministers of the Council of Europe on 7 April 2011. The Convention entered into force on 1 August 2014 and, at the time of writing, has been ratified by 22 states.[1] This Convention constitutes a crucial development in the movement to combat gender-based violence, as it sets new legally binding standards in this area. The aim of this book is to provide a detailed analysis of the Convention and its potential to make an impact in relation to the specific issue of domestic violence. The Convention adopts a holistic approach and covers many forms of violence against women. However, the book's specific focus on domestic violence allows the potential of the Convention with regard to this particular issue to be examined in a sufficiently in-depth and detailed manner.

In this book, the Istanbul Convention is placed in context with respect to developments relating to domestic violence as a human rights issue. The background to the adoption of the Convention is examined, and the text of this instrument is analysed in detail. In examining the Convention's provisions, comparative analysis is utilised with reference to the duties that have been placed on states by other bodies such as the UN Committee on the Elimination of Discrimination against Women (CEDAW Committee) and the European Court of Human Rights. Comparisons are also drawn with the Inter-American Convention on the Prevention, Punishment, and Eradication of Violence against Women (also known as the Convention of Belém do Pará) and with the relevant provisions of the Protocol to the African Charter on Human and Peoples' Rights on the Rights of Women in Africa (also known as the Maputo Protocol). The monitoring mechanisms of the Istanbul Convention are discussed in detail, again with the inclusion of comparative analysis. An in-depth examination of the advantages of the adoption of the Istanbul Convention by the Council of Europe is provided, as is a detailed analysis of the challenges faced by the Convention.

1 Albania, Andorra, Austria, Belgium, Bosnia and Herzegovina, Denmark, Finland, France, Italy, Malta, Monaco, Montenegro, Netherlands, Poland, Portugal, Romania, San Marino, Serbia, Slovenia, Spain, Sweden and Turkey.

The book concludes with a number of broader reflections in relation to the question of whether the adoption of a UN convention on violence against women may be a possible development, and to the potential held by such an instrument in the context of domestic violence.

Domestic violence in Europe

Domestic violence is an issue that affects vast numbers of women throughout all nations of the world, including every state within the Council of Europe. The potential held by the Istanbul Convention in relation to this particular issue therefore constitutes an important indicator of the effectiveness of the Convention as a whole. Domestic violence is an 'unseen crime' which many victims may be too frightened or too ashamed to report. It is therefore difficult, or even impossible, to produce accurate statistics on the true prevalence of this form of violence, as the number of instances reported to the police will be much lower than the number of such instances that actually occur.[2] In the Explanatory Report to the Istanbul Convention it was estimated that between 12 per cent and 15 per cent of women across Europe have been in a relationship involving domestic violence after the age of 16.[3] Many more women continue to suffer abuse from former partners even after the relationship ends.

One of the most reliable sources of statistics on the prevalence of domestic violence in the European context is now found in research carried out by the European Union Agency for Fundamental Rights, the report of which was published in March 2014.[4] Although this research was carried out only in the 28 states that are members of the European Union, as opposed to all 47 states that constitute the Council of Europe, the results of the research can nevertheless be said to be indicative of levels of domestic violence across Europe as a whole. This research is particularly informative as it is based on interviews carried out with 42,000 women across the EU, who were asked about their experiences of physical, sexual and psychological violence, including incidents of domestic violence. The survey was based on a random sample of women aged 18 to 74 years in the general population of each EU member state. Interviews were conducted face-to-face by female interviewers in the homes of the interviewees. Although the research methodology bore strong resemblances to research that has been carried out in other contexts, such as the Crime Survey for England and Wales

2 See, further, McQuigg R., *International Human Rights Law and Domestic Violence*, 2011, Routledge, Abingdon, at pp.75–6.

3 Council of Europe, 'Explanatory Report to Council of Europe Convention on preventing and combating violence against women and domestic violence', available at https://rm.coe.int/CoERMPublicCommonSearchServices/DisplayDCTMContent?documentId=09000016800d383a (accessed 18 October 2016), at para. 3.

4 European Union Agency for Fundamental Rights, 'Violence against women: an EU-wide survey', March 2014, Publications Office of the European Union, Luxembourg.

(formerly the British Crime Survey),[5] this was the first time that a comprehensive survey of this nature had been carried out in relation to violence against women across the EU. As this research goes beyond simply examining levels of reported violence, it is likely that the statistics formulated constitute a closer approximation of the true levels of gender-based violence. The research found that just over one in five women have experienced physical and/or sexual violence from a current or former partner. However, only 14 per cent of women reported their most serious incident of such abuse to the police. The report recommended that EU member states ratify the Council of Europe's Istanbul Convention, describing this Convention as 'the most comprehensive regional instrument addressing violence against women'.[6] It was also recommended that the EU itself explore the possibility of accession to this instrument.

Chapter outline

The Istanbul Convention is based upon a human rights framework. For example, Article 4(1) states: 'Parties shall take the necessary legislative and other measures to promote and protect the right for everyone, particularly women, to live free from violence in both the public and the private sphere.' Chapter 2 of this book will therefore place the Istanbul Convention in context as regards the analysis of domestic violence as a human rights issue which requires the attention of international and regional institutions, such as the United Nations and the Council of Europe. As domestic violence takes place between private individuals, it did not come within the ambit of the traditional interpretation of human rights law. Those who framed the earliest human rights treaties, such as the European Convention on Human Rights (ECHR), had no intention of encompassing issues such as violence in the home within the scope of such instruments. Instead, the main aim of those who formulated such treaties was to protect the individual from abuse perpetrated by the state itself and by state actors. The objective was essentially to ensure that there would be a sphere of activity in which the individual would be 'left alone' and with which the state would not interfere. When applied to the issue of domestic violence, such an approach is not only useless but arguably perpetuates the conditions that allow violence in the home to occur. The lack of perception of domestic violence as a human rights issue can be seen in the fact that the UN Convention on the Elimination of All Forms of Discrimination against Women (CEDAW)[7] contains no express mention of domestic violence within its provisions.

5 For further information, see www.crimesurvey.co.uk, Crime Survey for England and Wales (accessed 18 October 2016).

6 European Union Agency for Fundamental Rights, op. cit., at pp.167–8.

7 CEDAW (1249 U.N.T.S. 13) was adopted by the UN General Assembly on 18 December 1979 and entered into force on 3 September 1981.

However, there have of course been immense developments within human rights law such as the formulation of the concepts of positive obligations and state responsibility, and it is now clearly established that domestic violence constitutes a human rights issue. For example, in its General Recommendation No. 19, the CEDAW Committee interpreted CEDAW in such a manner as to encompass domestic violence within the scope of this instrument.[8] In order to place the Istanbul Convention in context, Chapter 2 will provide an analysis of such developments.

Chapter 3 will examine the background to the adoption of the Istanbul Convention. It will begin by analysing the development of domestic violence as a policy issue within the Council of Europe. Since 2007 the European Court of Human Rights has built up a substantial body of jurisprudence on domestic violence.[9] As this jurisprudence played an important role in the recognition of domestic violence as an issue that should be addressed by the Council of Europe, Chapter 3 will incorporate an analysis of this body of case law. Other developments on this issue within the context of the Council of Europe will also be examined. For example, in 1993 the third European Ministerial Conference on Equality between Women and Men focused on 'Strategies for the elimination of violence against women in society: the media and other means'. These discussions resulted in the development of an Action Plan to Combat Violence against Women. Also, in 2002 the Committee of Ministers of the Council of Europe adopted a Recommendation to states on the protection of women against violence.[10]

Chapter 3 will then proceed to analyse the events that led directly to the drafting and adoption of the Istanbul Convention. From 2006 until 2008 the Council of Europe implemented a campaign to combat violence against women. As part of this campaign, a Task Force carried out an assessment of measures that had been adopted by states in this area. It was concluded that serious gaps remained and that there was a need to ensure that levels of support and protection were

8 U.N. Doc A/47/38 (1992).

9 *Kontrova v Slovakia* (app. no. 7510/04, 31 May 2007); *Bevacqua and S. v Bulgaria* (app. no. 71127/01, 12 June 2008); *Branko Tomasic and Others v Croatia* (app. no. 46598/06, 15 January 2009); *Opuz v Turkey* (app. no. 33401/02, 9 June 2009); *E.S. and Others v Slovakia* (app. no. 8227/04, 15 September 2009); *A v Croatia* (app. no. 55164/08, 14 October 2010); *Hajduova v Slovakia* (app. no. 2660/03, 30 November 2010); *Kalucza v Hungary* (app. no. 57693/10, 24 April 2012); *E.M. v Romania* (app. no. 43994/05, 30 October 2012); *Valiuliene v Lithuania* (app. no. 33234/07, 26 March 2013); *Eremia and Others v the Republic of Moldova* (app. no. 3564/11, 28 May 2013); *B. v the Republic of Moldova* (app. no. 61382/09, 16 July 2013); *Mudric v the Republic of Moldova* (app. no. 74839/10, 16 July 2013); *N.A. v the Republic of Moldova* (app. no. 13424/06, 24 September 2013); *T.M. and C.M. v the Republic of Moldova* (app. no. 26608/11, 28 January 2014); *Rumor v Italy* (app. no. 72964/10, 27 May 2014); *Civek v Turkey* (app. no. 55354/11, 23 February 2016); *M.G. v Turkey* (app. no. 646/10, 22 March 2016); and *Halime Kılıç v Turkey* (app. no. 63034/11, 28 June 2016).

10 Recommendation Rec(2002)5.

standardised across Europe. To this end, the Task Force recommended that a Convention to combat violence against women be developed by the Council of Europe. In December 2008 the Committee of Ministers of the Council of Europe established an Ad Hoc Committee on Preventing and Combating Violence against Women and Domestic Violence with the mandate of preparing a legally binding instrument on violence against women. The draft Convention was approved by the Ad Hoc Committee in December 2010, and the finalised Convention document was adopted by the Committee of Ministers on 7 April 2011.

Chapter 4 will provide a detailed analysis of the text of the Istanbul Convention itself, with a particular focus on the provisions that relate to domestic violence. The matters discussed will include a number of definitional issues, such as the fact that the Convention repeatedly separates out domestic violence from violence against women more generally (for example, the title of the instrument is framed as 'the Convention on Preventing and Combating Violence against Women *and* Domestic Violence') and the possible rationale for such an approach. The reference within the Convention to the 'due diligence' standard will also be discussed. The obligations placed upon states parties by the Convention with regard to the issue of domestic violence will be examined in detail, and comparisons will be made with the statements and duties that have been put forward by other bodies such as the CEDAW Committee, the UN Special Rapporteur on violence against women, its causes and consequences, the UN General Assembly and the European Court of Human Rights.

The Istanbul Convention, although ground-breaking within the context of the Council of Europe, is not the first regional instrument to address the issue of violence against women. Almost 17 years prior to the Council of Europe's adoption of this Convention, the Inter-American Convention on the Prevention, Punishment, and Eradication of Violence against Women (also known as the Convention of Belém do Pará) was adopted by the General Assembly of the Organization of American States (OAS). Chapter 4 will therefore compare and contrast the approaches taken by the Istanbul Convention and the Convention of Belém do Pará to the specific issue of domestic violence. In addition, the Protocol to the African Charter on Human and Peoples' Rights on the Rights of Women in Africa (also known as the Maputo Protocol) was adopted by the African Union in 2003 and entered into force in 2005. The provisions of this Protocol that relate to gender-based violence, including domestic violence, will also be compared to those of the Istanbul Convention.

Chapter 5 will examine the monitoring procedures of the Istanbul Convention and provide an analysis of the potential held by these mechanisms. Under Article 66(1) of the Convention, the implementation of this instrument is to be monitored by a Group of Experts on Action against Violence against Women and Domestic Violence, known as 'GREVIO'. The members of GREVIO are elected by a body known as 'the Committee of the Parties' which, under Article 67(1), is to be composed of representatives of the states that are parties to the Convention. The main monitoring mechanism is a reporting procedure, with an inquiry procedure also being established. The Committee of the Parties met for the first time on 4 May 2015, and the first meeting of GREVIO took place on 21–23 September 2015.

In examining the monitoring mechanisms of the Istanbul Convention, the book will again engage in comparative analysis. For example, the Optional Protocol to CEDAW encompasses a communications mechanism, under which individuals may submit complaints concerning violations of CEDAW to the CEDAW Committee. Likewise, an individual complaints mechanism whereby petitions may be lodged with the Inter-American Commission on Human Rights is encompassed by the Convention of Belém do Pará. Such a mechanism is not included in the Istanbul Convention, and the question of whether the omission of a communications mechanism will lessen the effectiveness of this instrument will be discussed. In analysing this issue, reference will be made to communications concerning domestic violence which have been examined by the CEDAW Committee under the Optional Protocol procedure,[11] and to the relevant jurisprudence of the Inter-American Commission, such as the seminal case of *Maria da Penha Maia Fernandes v Brazil*.[12]

Chapter 6 will provide a detailed analysis of the advantages of the adoption of the Istanbul Convention by the Council of Europe. It is argued that this is certainly a very positive development, not least because of the Convention's symbolic significance. The adoption of this instrument clearly demonstrates recognition on the part of the Council of Europe of the extent of the problem of violence against women and of the urgent need for action to be taken on this issue. However, the importance of the Istanbul Convention reaches beyond symbolism. The Convention places detailed legally binding obligations on states parties as regards the measures that they must adopt in relation to violence against women, including domestic violence. The actual measures themselves are not new. Most of these have been previously articulated by UN bodies such as the CEDAW Committee and the UN Special Rapporteur on violence against women, its causes and consequences. However, in technical terms, such documents are not legally binding on states. Although CEDAW itself is of course a legally binding treaty, CEDAW contains no explicit mention of domestic violence, and it could therefore be argued that the statements of the CEDAW Committee and of the other UN bodies in this area are based on a somewhat insecure foundation. The adoption by the Council of Europe of a Convention that in effect places the recommendations that have been made by the UN human rights bodies on a legally binding footing in the context of Europe is greatly to be welcomed.

11 *AT v Hungary* (Communication No. 2/2003, 26 January 2005, CEDAW/C/32/D/2/2003); *Goekce v Austria* (Communication No. 5/2005, 6 August 2007, CEDAW/C/39/D/5/2005); *Yildirim v Austria* (Communication No. 6/2005, 1 October 2007, CEDAW/C/39/D/6/2005); *VK v Bulgaria* (Communication No. 20/2008, 17 August 2011, CEDAW/C/49/D/20/2008); *Jallow v Bulgaria* (Communication No. 32/2011, 28 August 2012, CEDAW/C/52/D/32/2011).

12 Case 12.051, Report No. 54/01 (2001).

In addition, although the European Court of Human Rights has placed clear positive obligations on states to ensure that their criminal justice systems are of a sufficient standard with regard to the issue of domestic violence, the Court has not placed duties on states in relation to other aspects of their responses. For example, it has not addressed the necessity for states to ensure that victims are provided with social support measures, despite the fact that it is often measures such as refuge accommodation and financial support that are most needed by victims.[13] Indeed, it is generally much more difficult for courts to order that affirmative programmes be put in place than it is for them to hold that certain practices be stopped. By contrast, the Istanbul Convention places detailed obligations on states parties concerning many aspects of their responses to domestic violence, including the provision of social support measures to victims.

There are also other advantages to having a Convention monitored by a reporting mechanism, as opposed to placing the onus on victims to bring cases to court. As referred to previously in this chapter, domestic violence is an 'unseen' crime. It appears therefore that alternative approaches to that of a litigation strategy may well be advantageous. Another benefit of using a strategy other than that of litigation is that a substantially more detailed approach can be adopted. Judges must confine themselves to dealing with the precise matter in the actual case that is before them, which limits the role that litigation can play in promoting change. However, in making recommendations, a body such as GREVIO is free to adopt a significantly broader approach than could a judge in dealing with a case.

Chapter 6 will also examine a number of potential difficulties that may be faced by the Istanbul Convention. These problems are mainly centred around issues relating to implementation and enforcement. Substantial difficulties with implementation affect all of the UN human rights treaties. Essentially, the implementation of international human rights law has been inconsistent, to say the least. It is very difficult to force states to comply with their obligations. The UN has no real method of compelling states to alter their policies and must instead try to persuade countries to comply with their international duties. These implementation problems have been exacerbated by difficulties surrounding the reporting procedures, which generally constitute the primary monitoring

13 In a small number of cases the European Court of Human Rights has held that in particular circumstances the state has a duty to provide resources to individuals to prevent violations of their rights. The main case in this regard is *Airey v Ireland* (app. no. 6289/73, 9 October 1979), in which the applicant alleged that her husband had subjected her to physical violence, and the issue revolved around the fact that legal aid was unavailable in Ireland for the purpose of seeking a judicial separation. The European Court found that there had been breaches of Articles 6 and 8. However, although the Court did hold that ensuring effective access to particular means of protection may in certain circumstances entail the expenditure of monetary resources, the Court did not state that civil legal aid must actually be granted in situations such as that arising in this case. The Court simply held that there must be effective access to the protective measure of a decree of judicial separation. This duty could have been fulfilled by other means – for example, by simplifying the procedures.

mechanisms for such treaties. Often states submit their reports only after long delays, and there is usually a large backlog as regards the consideration of reports by the monitoring bodies in question, which further adds to the delays. As the monitoring mechanisms of the Istanbul Convention bear strong similarities to those of UN instruments such as CEDAW, it is very possible that such problems relating to enforcement will also occur in respect of the Istanbul Convention.

The issue of how many states will actually become parties to the Convention is also of concern. As referred to above, at the time of writing, 22 of the 47 member states of the Council of Europe are parties to the Convention. It is possible that a number of states may be reluctant to ratify this instrument due to the very detailed obligations that are encompassed therein. In particular, the measures required with regard to the provision of social support measures to victims necessitate the expenditure of significant levels of monetary resources by governments. In addition, it is possible that some difficulties may arise concerning reservations – an issue that has caused considerable problems in relation to CEDAW.

Chapter 7 will summarise the key points and conclusions from the preceding discussion about the potential held by the Istanbul Convention in relation to the issue of domestic violence. In addition, the former UN Special Rapporteur on violence against women, its causes and consequences, Rashida Manjoo, has repeatedly called for the adoption of an international convention on violence against women at the UN level.[14] It is likely that the provisions of such an instrument would contain strong similarities to those of the Istanbul Convention. The chapter will therefore contain a number of brief reflections in relation to the question of whether the adoption of a UN convention on violence against women may be a possible development, and to the potential held by such an instrument in the context of domestic violence.

Terminology

Although the term 'victims' of domestic violence is used throughout this book, it is recognised that there is a debate concerning whether the term 'survivor' is more appropriate. As Burton comments, '"Survivor" does perhaps have more positive connotations than "victim"; it is suggestive of the many ways that women cope with domestic violence and the strength they show in resisting it'.[15]

14 See, for example, UN Women, 2012, 'Needed: specific international legally binding instrument on violence against women', available at www.unwomen.org/en/news/stories/2012/11/needed-specific-international-legally-binding-instrument-on-violence-against-women (accessed 11 October 2016); and Report of the Special Rapporteur on Violence against Women, its causes and consequences, Rashida Manjoo, UN.Doc.A/HRC/29/27, 10 June 2015, at paras 62–5.

15 Burton M., *Legal Responses to Domestic Violence*, 2008, Routledge-Cavendish, Abingdon, at p.124.

However, as Lewis remarks, 'many women do not feel like survivors at points in their lives, and . . . some do not survive men's violence'.[16] It is very important to remember that a number of women are in fact killed as a result of domestic violence. Although the author recognises the merits of the use of the term 'survivor', this book will nevertheless use the term 'victim' as this is the terminology used throughout the Istanbul Convention itself.

16 Lewis R., 'Making Justice Work: Effective Legal Interventions for Domestic Violence', (2004) 44 *British Journal of Criminology*, 204–24 at 204.

2 Domestic violence as a human rights issue

The Istanbul Convention is based upon a human rights framework. For example, Article 4(1) states: 'Parties shall take the necessary legislative and other measures to promote and protect the right for everyone, particularly women, to live free from violence in both the public and the private sphere.' The aim of this chapter is to place the Convention in context as regards the analysis of domestic violence as a human rights issue that requires the attention of international and regional institutions, such as the UN and the Council of Europe. As domestic violence by definition occurs between private individuals, it did not fall within the scope of the traditional interpretation of human rights law. Those who framed the earliest human rights treaties, such as the European Convention on Human Rights, did not envisage issues such as violence in the home as coming within the ambit of such instruments. The primary objective of these treaties was to protect the individual from abuse perpetrated by the state itself. The aim was essentially to ensure that there would be an area of activity in which the individual would be 'left alone' and with which the state would not interfere, thus leading to a public/private divide in human rights law. When applied to the issue of domestic violence, not only is such an approach of no benefit, but arguably it perpetuates the conditions that allow violence in the home to occur. The lack of perception of domestic violence as constituting a human rights issue at all can be viewed in the fact that the Convention on the Elimination of All Forms of Discrimination against Women (CEDAW)[1] encompasses no express mention of domestic violence.

Indeed, not only did domestic violence fall outside the ambit of the traditional interpretation of *human rights* law, but there was also a historical reluctance to view domestic violence as being an issue that required the attention of any form of law, such as the criminal law. In another formulation of the public/private dichotomy, there was a view among legal actors, such as the police, prosecutors and the courts, that domestic violence was a family matter which did not require

1 CEDAW (1249 U.N.T.S. 13) was adopted by the UN General Assembly on 18 December 1979 and entered into force on 3 September 1981.

intervention even from the criminal justice system. Given this more generalised reluctance to view domestic violence as a legal matter, it is therefore rather unsurprising that it took such a long time for domestic violence to be recognised as constituting an issue for human rights law.

However, there have been immense developments within human rights law, such as the formulation of the concepts of positive obligations and state responsibility, and it is now clearly established that domestic violence constitutes a human rights issue. For example, in its General Recommendation No. 19, the Committee on the Elimination of Discrimination against Women (CEDAW Committee) interpreted CEDAW in such a manner as to encompass domestic violence within the scope of this instrument.[2] In order to place the Istanbul Convention in context, this chapter will examine the development of domestic violence first as a legal issue, and then as an issue that requires the attention of human rights law. In analysing the recognition of domestic violence as a legal issue, particular attention will be paid to developments in the United Kingdom in order to provide a detailed example of the problems that have arisen in this respect. Many of the difficulties identified, however, also have application to a broad range of states both in Europe and around the globe. In analysing the recognition of domestic violence as an issue that falls within the ambit of human rights law, the discussion will cover developments at the UN level and also within the Inter-American and African regional systems. The developments in this sphere within the Council of Europe will not, however, be considered in this chapter as these will be discussed in detail in Chapter 3.

Difficulties with the recognition of domestic violence as a legal issue

Up until the 1970s, domestic violence was hardly viewed as a legal issue at all. As Burton comments, 'Until the 1970s there was little recognition of domestic violence as an issue that ought to be tackled by the legal system'.[3] Indeed, domestic violence was not recognised as constituting 'a significant social problem' until this time.[4] Even after it became clear in some quarters that legal intervention was crucial with regard to this issue, actors within the criminal justice system, such as police, prosecutors and courts, continued to display a reluctance to treat violence taking place in the home as being on a par with violence occurring in other circumstances. Dobash and Dobash state: 'In the early 1970s, activists discovered what battered women had long known, that the (criminal justice system) failed

2 Committee on the Elimination of Discrimination against Women, U.N. Doc A/47/38 (1992).

3 Burton M., *Legal Responses to Domestic Violence*, 2008, Routledge-Cavendish, Abingdon, at p.2.

4 Burton, op. cit., at p.11.

to protect the victim or to act against the offender.'[5] Indeed, Radford, writing in 1987, commented that solicitors would frequently discourage victims of domestic violence from seeking legal remedies. Radford was of the view that such attitudes may have been due to some solicitors being unsympathetic to victims of domestic violence and assuming that it was the victims who had precipitated any violence that had occurred.[6]

Many commentators have argued that unhelpful police attitudes constituted (and in some cases may still constitute) a very significant problem as regards domestic violence. For example, writing in 1997, Armatta stated that 'police throughout the world often fail to enforce criminal assault laws where violence occurs within an intimate relationship. Traditionally, police simply do not intervene, or intervene only to mediate on an informal basis.'[7] In 2003, Sullivan commented that police could not be relied upon to arrest the perpetrator.[8] In 2006, Hughes remarked: 'Police forces may be unresponsive to requests for assistance from women on the receiving end of domestic violence, or they may adopt a non-interventionist approach, considering that it is a "private" matter.'[9]

Research carried out in the UK during the late 1970s and early 1980s demonstrated the unhelpful attitudes of the police towards victims of domestic violence at this time. For example, in the report of research carried out by the University of Bradford in 1979, it was stated that 'a man's home is his castle, and very little short of murdering his wife will make people feel justified in violating its privacy'.[10] Essentially, violence against women taking place in the home was viewed as being unlike other types of criminal behaviour, and even not truly 'criminal' in nature. The study found that the police were extremely reluctant to violate the privacy of a perpetrator of domestic violence by intervening in the situation to protect his wife or partner. Dobash and Dobash also carried out research in 1979 into police responses to domestic violence, and they too found that responses were typified by 'animosity or at best indifference'.[11]

5 Dobash R.E. and Dobash R.P., *Women, Violence and Social Change*, 1992, Routledge, New York, at p.141.

6 Radford L., 'Legalising Woman Abuse' in J. Hanmer and M. Maynard (eds), *Women, Violence and Social Control*, 1987, Macmillan, London, 135–51. See also Burton, op. cit., at pp.33–5.

7 Armatta J., 'Getting beyond the Law's Complicity in Intimate Violence against Women', (1997) 33 *Willamette Law Review*, 774–845 at 812.

8 Sullivan C.M., 'Using the ESID Model to Reduce Intimate Male Violence against Women', (2003) 32 *American Journal of Community Psychology*, 295–303 at 296.

9 Hughes B., 'Can Domestic Violence Be Considered a Violation of Human Rights Law?', (2006) 14 *British Journal of Midwifery*, 192.

10 Bruce E., 'Attitudes of Social Workers and Police in the Select Committee Report on Violence to Women and Children', in *Women and Abused Children: Intricacies of Legal and Administrative Intervention*, 1979, Issues Publications, University of Bradford, 50–61 at 53.

11 Dobash R.E. and Dobash R.P., *Violence against Wives: A Case against the Patriarchy*, 1979, Open Books, London, at p.191.

A study carried out by the Research and Planning Unit of the Home Office in 1989 uncovered similar findings. In the report of the study it was commented that 'the single most common police response is non-intervention, that is, officers state that there is nothing they can do and leave the incident to which they have been called'.[12] The report stated that a frequent occurrence was for the victim to be told that the abuse she had suffered was a matter for the civil and not the criminal law. This was in line with general attitudes whereby domestic violence was regarded as being not truly 'criminal' in character. Other responses remarked upon by the Home Office study included attempts to defuse the situation and the removal of one of the parties from the scene for a period of time. Notably, it was often the victim who was removed.[13] Another study carried out in 1989, by Edwards, found that there was a substantial reluctance among police to record domestic violence as a crime. As with the Home Office study, Edwards found that police would frequently encourage the victim to use civil remedies, even when the victim wished for the perpetrator to be arrested.[14]

The view of domestic violence as not being criminal in nature was, as the Home Office study pointed out, based on the idea that 'domestic violence is almost exclusively a "family matter" or a "private affair" in which State intervention has no business since it would constitute not solely an intrusion into a private relationship but also an erosion of individual liberties'.[15] Edwards was of the view that inadequate police responses resulted from 'private attitudes regarding appropriate sex roles, appropriate conduct and family ideologies'.[16] Writing in 1990, Bourlet commented that 'most officers had a negative attitude towards marital violence, often feeling that they should not become involved'.[17] Goodmark asserts that, in the United States also, '[p]olice officers frequently told abusive spouses to take a walk around the block to cool down and attempted to mediate between abusers and their victims'.[18]

There was little change in police policy in the UK concerning domestic violence until the late 1980s. However, in 1987, a Metropolitan Police Force order was issued which stressed the need for positive intervention as opposed to the use of mediation in domestic violence cases and emphasised that an assault occurring in

12 Smith L.J.F., 'Domestic Violence: An Overview of the Literature', 1989, Home Office Research Study 107, p.47.
13 Smith, op. cit., at p.47.
14 Edwards S., *Policing 'Domestic' Violence: Women, the Law and the State*, 1989, Sage Publications, London.
15 Smith, op. cit., at p.55.
16 Edwards, op. cit., at p.91.
17 Bourlet A., *Police Intervention in Marital Violence*, 1990, Open University Press, Milton Keynes, p.74.
18 Goodmark L., 'Symposium: Domestic Violence & the Law: Theory, Policy, and Practice: Law is the Answer? Do We Know That for Sure? Questioning the Efficacy of Legal Interventions for Battered Women', (2004) 23 *Saint Louis University Public Law Review*, 7–48 at 13.

the home was as much a crime as one occurring in the street.[19] In 1990 a Home Office circular was distributed[20] which recommended that the police adopt pro-arrest and pro-prosecution policies in cases involving domestic violence. It also stated that domestic violence units and domestic violence liaison officer posts should be established to support victims, and that the police should engage in multi-agency initiatives on violence in the home.[21] This guidance emphasised the duty to protect victims from further attack, the need to treat domestic violence seriously, the use of the power of arrest, the dangers of mediating between the perpetrator and the victim, and the necessity of keeping complete records.[22] Burton comments: 'As a symbolic statement of the commitment to taking domestic violence more seriously the 1990 circular was important, however its practical impact was much more limited.'[23] Nevertheless, in 1993 the Association of Chief Police Officers' evidence to the Home Affairs Committee stated that 'the Police Service (had) changed its focus from one of conciliation to intervention'.[24] Another Home Office circular on domestic violence, issued in 2000, again emphasised that arrest should usually occur when an offence is committed and that charging should occur in all but exceptional cases.[25]

Nevertheless, difficulties with police responses to domestic violence still remain. Connelly and Cavanagh state that 'the attitudes of too many police officers . . . in respect of domestic abuse and the difficulties encountered in enforcing civil protection orders, are based upon stereotypes which have long been associated with domestic abuse and women who are subjected to that abuse'.[26] In September 2013 the Home Secretary commissioned Her Majesty's Inspectorate of Constabulary to conduct an inspection of the responses of police forces in England and Wales to domestic violence. The subsequent report, which was published on 27 March 2014, stated:

> The overall police response to victims of domestic violence is not good enough . . . In too many forces there are weaknesses in the service provided to victims; some of these are serious and this means that victims are put at unnecessary risk. Many forces need to take action now.[27]

19 Diduck A. and Kaganas F., *Family Law, Gender and the State*, 1999, Hart Publishing, Oxford, at p.331.
20 Home Office Circular 60/90.
21 Hague G., 'Domestic Violence Policy in the 1990s', in S. Watson and L. Doyal (eds), *Engendering Social Policy*, 1999, Oxford University Press, Oxford, 131–47 at 134.
22 Circular 60/90, at para. 11.
23 Burton, op. cit., at p.91.
24 Hale B., Pearl D., Cooke E. and Bates P., *The Family, Law and Society*, 2002, Butterworths, London, at p.401.
25 'Domestic Violence: Revised Circular to Police', Home Office Circular 19/2000.
26 Connelly C. and Cavanagh K., 'Domestic Abuse, Civil Protection Orders and the "New Criminologies": Is There Any Value in Engaging with the Law?', (2007) 15 *Feminist Legal Studies*, 259–87 at 275.
27 Her Majesty's Inspectorate of Constabulary, 'Everyone's business: Improving the police response to domestic abuse', 27 March 2014, available at www.justiceinspectorates.gov.uk/

The report also commented that '[t]ackling domestic violence too often remains a poor relation to acquisitive crime and serious organised crime'.[28]

Historically, there have also been difficulties regarding the prosecution of domestic violence. Burton comments: 'Since its inception [the Crown Prosecution Service] has struggled against the claim that it too readily discontinues domestic violence cases and fails to fully consider the options available when the victim is unwilling or unable to support the prosecution.'[29] Cretney and Davis argued in 1996: 'The difficulty about domestic assault cases lies in the frailty, as prosecutors perceive it, of the woman's commitment to the prosecution enterprise.'[30] There was a strong belief that women who said that they wished to pursue cases against their abusive partners would often drop the charges.[31] In addition, domestic violence cases were very likely to be dropped by prosecutors as they do not constitute 'the sort of successful prosecution which brings additional kudos'.[32] In 1997 Cretney and Davis remarked that domestic violence cases were 'still viewed by police, prosecutors and sentencers through the lens of "the couple" or "the family"'.[33]

In 2001, Edwards stated that the Crown Prosecution Service was particularly likely to engage in 'plea-bargaining' in cases of domestic violence.[34] Of the cases that were prosecuted, Cretney and Davis commented that the charges were often reduced from assault occasioning actual bodily harm to common assault.[35] In 2003 Hester *et al.* interviewed victims of domestic violence who had experienced the criminal justice system in the UK and found that they 'were generally bewildered and shocked by the plea-bargaining and reduction in sentences that tended to take place in court'.[36] It was also found that in cases in which the parties were back together 'the victim-witness was deemed less reliable and cases were

hmic/wp-content/uploads/2014/04/improving-the-police-response-to-domestic-abuse.pdf (accessed 12 October 2016), at p.6.

28 Her Majesty's Inspectorate of Constabulary, op. cit., at p.6. For further discussion of police responses to domestic violence, see Burton M., 'A Fresh Approach to Policing Domestic Violence', in S. Hilder and V. Bettinson (eds), *Domestic Violence: Interdisciplinary Perspectives on Protection, Prevention and Intervention*, 2016, Palgrave Macmillan, London, 37–57.

29 Burton (2008), op. cit., at p.99.

30 Cretney A. and Davis G., 'Prosecuting "Domestic" Assault', (1996) *Criminal Law Review*, 162–74 at 166.

31 Stanko E.A., *Intimate Intrusions*, 1985, Routledge & Kegan Paul, London, at p.130.

32 Stanko, op. cit., at p.130.

33 Cretney A. and Davis G., 'Prosecuting Domestic Assault: Victims Failing Courts, or Courts Failing Victims?', (1997) 36 *The Howard Journal*, 146–57 at 147.

34 Edwards S., 'New Directions in Prosecution', in J. Taylor-Browne (ed.), *What Works in Reducing Domestic Violence? A Comprehensive Guide for Professionals*, 2001, Whiting & Birch, London, 211–38 at 223.

35 Cretney and Davis (1997), op. cit., at pp.147–9.

36 Hester M., Hanmer J., Coulson S., Morahan M. and Razak A., *Domestic Violence: Making it Through the Criminal Justice System*, 2003, University of Sunderland and Northern Rock Foundation, Sunderland, at p.13.

more likely to be discontinued'.[37] In 2005 Hester and Westmarland commented: 'A lack of consistency in criminal justice practice has been found both in relation to individual professionals and in relation to geographical areas.'[38] They also stated that 'the criminal justice system often demonstrates little real understanding of domestic violence and struggles to make appropriate responses to it'.[39] Even in 2010 Hall commented:

> The difficulties of prosecuting domestic violence are well known and principally revolve around low reporting rates and the fact that, even when victims do come forward to the authorities, the perception is that complainants in such cases have a tendency to retract their initial police statement at a late stage.[40]

There have also been difficulties relating to the responses of courts to cases of domestic violence. Writing in 1987, Radford commented that when applications for injunctions were contested, frequently the bare denial of the allegation by the perpetrator was enough to constitute a viable defence, whereas the claim of the victim had to be corroborated vigorously.[41] In 1990 Barron found that the courts were overly concerned about depriving a man of his home, thus making it difficult for victims of domestic violence to obtain exclusion orders. Even where such orders were granted, the courts could afford perpetrators several weeks to leave the home. In addition, the courts tended to refuse to make exclusion orders whilst disputes over child custody were ongoing. The enforcement of injunctions was also problematic. The courts were frequently reluctant to attach powers of arrest and tended to be of the view that the order in itself was enough to prevent the reoccurrence of violence. However, Barron found that half of victims who had obtained orders or undertakings said that the perpetrator had breached these on at least one occasion, and the police and courts appeared to do little in response to such breaches.[42] It is notable that a decade after Barron's research it seemed that the approaches of the courts in this regard had not changed to any great extent. For example, in *G v G (Occupation Order: Conduct)* it was stated: 'It has been said time and time again that orders of exclusion are Draconian and only to be made in exceptional cases.'[43] Writing in 1999, Thomas commented that

37 Hester, Hanmer, Coulson, Morahan and Razak, op. cit., at p.9.

38 Hester M. and Westmarland N., 'Tackling Domestic Violence: Effective Interventions and Approaches', 2005, Home Office Research Study 290, at p.43.

39 Hester and Westmarland, op. cit., at p.56.

40 Hall M., 'The Relationship between Victims and Prosecutors: Defending Victims' Rights?', (2010) *Criminal Law Review*, 31–45 at 40.

41 Radford, op. cit.

42 Barron J., *'Not Worth the Paper . . . ?' The Effectiveness of Legal Protection for Women and Children Experiencing Domestic Violence*, 1990, Women's Aid Federation England, Bristol. See also Burton (2008), op. cit., at pp.35–6.

43 [2000] 2 FLR 36 at 41.

'judges from every region demonstrate a dangerous unwillingness to understand the causes and consequences of domestic violence and to enforce the laws against it'.[44] Again the difficulty was that violence against women in the home was viewed as being less serious than violence between strangers.

Also writing in 1999, Diduck and Kaganas commented that in the UK charges in domestic violence cases were often reduced and bind-overs were frequently used. Reduced sentences tended to be handed down if the perpetrator was not viewed as a danger to the public; and if the couple had not separated, the perpetrator was less likely to be convicted.[45] In 2000 Miles stated that conditional bail and remand were not always used efficiently by police and courts in order to protect victims from intimidation before trial.[46] In 2001 Edwards commented that 'when defendants are proceeded against and convicted at the sentencing stage magistrates and judges continue to pass derisory sentences'.[47] Also in 2001, Hague *et al.* found that the courts were one of the organisations least likely to respond appropriately to domestic violence.[48] In 2003 Hester *et al.* found that victims 'felt particularly let down by the court process and the frequently inadequate outcomes'.[49] In 2008 Burton commented: 'The substantive criminal law sometimes appears to be context blind when it comes to domestic violence; judges are either unable or unwilling to adapt the law to accommodate the experiences of victims of domestic violence.'[50]

The public/private dichotomy in international human rights law

Given the very substantial difficulties that surrounded the recognition of domestic violence as being an issue worthy of the attention of criminal justice systems, it is unsurprising that it is only relatively recently that violence against women in the home began to be regarded as an issue for international human rights law. In addition to the problems surrounding the recognition of domestic violence as a

44 Thomas C., 'Domestic Violence', in K.D. Askin and D.M. Koenig (eds), ***Women and International Human Rights Law***, Vol. 1, 1999, Transnational Publishers, New York, 219–56 at 219.

45 Diduck and Kaganas, op. cit., at p.333.

46 Miles J., 'Domestic Violence', in J. Herring (ed.), *Family Law: Issues, Debates, Policy*, 2001, Willan Publishing, Devon, 78–124 at 93.

47 Edwards (2001), op. cit., at p.212.

48 Hague G., Mullender A., Aris R. and Dear W., 'Abused Women's Perspectives: Responsiveness and Accountability of Domestic Violence and Inter-Agency Initiatives', 2001, Report to the ESRC, at p.13.

49 Hester, Hanmer, Coulson, Morahan and Razak, op. cit., at p.13.

50 Burton (2008), op. cit., at p.86. For further discussion of the difficulties regarding the responses of the criminal justice system to cases involving domestic violence, see McQuigg R., *International Human Rights Law and Domestic Violence*, 2011, Routledge, Abingdon, at pp.19–30.

legal issue at all, there were additional difficulties involved in the recognition of domestic violence as falling within the ambit of international human rights law.

The main problem in this respect was found in the way in which the rights themselves were formulated. As Thomas and Beasley comment, 'The concept of human rights developed largely from Western political theory of the rights of the individual to autonomy and freedom.'[51] International relations are founded upon the concept of the liberal state. Romany remarks that '[l]iberalism constructs a social and political order which seeks to emancipate the individual from the oppression of political structures'.[52] International law therefore has its basis in the liberal social contract theory, whereby states are viewed as individuals which should have equality, independence and freedom. Inherent to this theory is the concept of negative rights ensuring individual freedom. This idea is therefore embedded deeply in the discourse of international law, and subsequently human rights law.[53] Essentially, the concept of 'negative rights' means that the state cannot interfere with an individual in certain aspects of his or her life.[54] As Fredman remarks, 'Human rights have long been understood as providing protection for individual freedom against an intrusive State.'[55] Another main principle of international law is that in general only states can be subject to this body of law.

The concept of negative rights ensuring individual freedoms emerged again during the fight against totalitarianism, which constituted an important catalyst in the development of human rights law. Human rights evolved to protect the rights of the individual from encroachment by the state. As Thomas and Beasley comment, 'States are bound by international law to respect the individual rights of each and every person and are thus accountable for abuses of those rights.'[56] However, the rights norms that emerged were generally formulated in a negative way, whereby the state was obliged only to refrain from breaching the rights in question. There were no duties on the state to adopt positive measures to ensure that the rights of the individual were not violated. In addition, the 'neo-liberal commitment to minimal state intervention'[57] resulted in the situation whereby the state was not obliged to protect the rights of the individual from violation by another private party.

51 Thomas D.Q. and Beasley M.E., 'Symposium on Reconceptualizing Violence against Women by Intimate Partners', (1995) 58 *Albany Law Review*, 1119–47 at 1121.

52 Romany C., 'Women as Aliens: A Feminist Critique of the Public/Private Distinction in International Human Rights Law', (1993) 6 *Harvard Human Rights Journal*, 87–125 at 90.

53 Romany, op. cit., at pp.89–98.

54 For historical arguments on rights, see Harvey C., 'Talking about Human Rights', (2004) *European Human Rights Law Review*, 500–16.

55 Fredman S., *Human Rights Transformed: Positive Rights and Positive Duties*, 2009, Oxford University Press, Oxford, at p.1.

56 Thomas and Beasley, op. cit., at p.1121.

57 Hirschl R., '"Negative" Rights vs. "Positive" Entitlements: A Comparative Study of Judicial Interpretations of Rights in an Emerging Neo-Liberal Economic Order', (2000) 22 *Human Rights Quarterly*, 1060–97 at 1063.

Rights therefore developed in such a way as to create a public/private divide by which human rights norms were upheld in the public sphere where the state was involved, but were not applied in the private sphere. The public/private dichotomy may be formulated in several ways. Cook highlights two possibilities.[58] First, the public sphere can be viewed as the area that is regulated by law and politics, and the private sphere as the area where regulation is seen as inappropriate. Second, the public realm can be viewed as the state and its agents, whereas the private arena is constituted by non-state activities. With regard to the first formulation of the public/private dichotomy, it is true that many would be of the view that there are certain areas that should remain unregulated, in order to respect the right to privacy. However, the public/private divide has been applied to the issue of domestic violence in a manner that is extremely problematic. As Burton comments, 'In the classic public/private dichotomy intimate relationships are seen as part of the "private" sphere not suitable for public regulation'.[59] Indeed, it has been attitudes such as this that have created such immense difficulties historically regarding the responses of actors within the criminal justice system, such as police, prosecutors and courts, to cases of domestic violence, as discussed earlier in the chapter.

The second formulation of the public/private divide, as outlined by Cook, is equally problematic when applied to the issue of domestic violence. As Ewing comments, 'The public/private distinction in international law . . . places many forms of violence against women beyond the protective scope of human rights instruments'.[60] The rights of women often come into conflict with powers other than that of the state. These powers generally emanate from the private arena, such as from within the family unit.[61] Knop states that 'women are more vulnerable than men to serious harm, injustice, and discrimination in the private sphere, and the public/private distinction has prevented the law from remedying the situation'.[62] Women all around the globe suffer from human rights abuses occurring in the private sphere, such as domestic violence, female genital mutilation and dowry killing.[63] Under traditional principles, such abuses did not come within

58 Cook R.J., 'Women's International Human Rights Law: The Way Forward', in R.J. Cook (ed.), *Human Rights of Women: National and International Perspectives*, 1994, University of Pennsylvania Press, Philadelphia, 3–36 at 6.

59 Burton (2008), op. cit., at p.7. See also Lacey N., *Unspeakable Subjects*, 1998, Hart Publishing, Oxford, at pp.71–97.

60 Ewing A.P., 'Establishing State Responsibility for Private Acts of Violence against Women under the American Convention on Human Rights', (1995) 26 *Columbia Human Rights Law Review*, 751–800 at 753.

61 Rishmawi M., 'The Developing Approaches of the International Commission of Jurists to Women's Human Rights', in R.J. Cook (ed.), *Human Rights of Women: National and International Perspectives*, 1994, University of Pennsylvania Press, Philadelphia, 340–8 at 341.

62 Knop K., 'Introduction', in K. Knop (ed.), *Gender and Human Rights*, 2004, Oxford University Press, Oxford, 1–12 at 6.

63 Rishmawi, op. cit., at p.341.

the scope of human rights law as they are not inflicted directly by the state. As Isa remarks, 'international human rights law and the set of international legal norms it encompasses has developed in such a way that it reflects the experiences of men, excluding those of women'.[64] Van Leeuwen comments that 'abuses, exclusions and constraints that are more typical of women's lives are neither recognised nor protected by mainstream human rights instruments'.[65] Charlesworth states that the main impact of the public/private dichotomy has been 'to muffle, and often completely silence, the voices of women'.[66]

However, the public/private divide does not now pose an insurmountable problem with regard to the recognition of domestic violence as an issue for human rights law. Various ways have been developed in which human rights may now enter into the private sphere. In particular, the concept of state responsibility has been developed, under which positive obligations can be placed directly on the state to ensure that human rights standards are upheld in situations involving only private individuals. For example, the United Nations human rights bodies frequently refer to the state's duties to respect, protect, promote and fulfil rights. At the regional level, the judicial branches of both the Inter-American and Council of Europe systems have been extremely instrumental in developing the concepts of state responsibility and positive obligations. As will be discussed

64 Isa F.G., 'The Optional Protocol for the Convention on the Elimination of All Forms of Discrimination against Women: Strengthening the Protection of Women's Human Rights', (2003) 20 *Arizona Journal of International and Comparative Law*, 291–322 at 293.

65 Van Leeuwen F., *Women's Rights Are Human Rights*, 2010, Intersentia, Antwerp, at p.9.

66 Charlesworth H., 'What are "Women's International Human Rights"?', in R.J. Cook (ed.), *Human Rights of Women: National and International Perspectives*, 1994, University of Pennsylvania Press, Philadelphia, 58–84 at 68. For further discussion of the public/private dichotomy in international human rights law, see McQuigg, op. cit., at pp.3–8. For discussion of the rights of women in international human rights law, see Johnstone R.L., 'Feminist Influences on the United Nations Human Rights Treaty Bodies', (2006) 28 *Human Rights Quarterly*, 148–85; Charlesworth H. and Chinkin C., *The Boundaries of International Law: A Feminist Analysis*, 2000, Manchester University Press, Manchester; Binion G., 'Human Rights: A Feminist Perspective', (1995) 17 *Human Rights Quarterly*, 509–26; Fraser A.S., 'Becoming Human: The Origin and Development of Women's Human Rights Law', (1999) 21 *Human Rights Quarterly*, 853–906; Charlesworth H., Chinkin C. and Wright S., 'Feminist Approaches to International Law', (1991) 85 *American Journal of International Law*, 613–45; Bond J.E., 'International Intersectionality: A Theoretical and Pragmatic Exploration of Women's International Human Rights Violations', (2003) 52 *Emory Law Journal*, 71–186; Bunch C., 'Women's Rights as Human Rights: Towards a Re-Visioning of Human Rights', (1990) 12 *Human Rights Quarterly*, 486–98; O'Hare U., 'Realising Women's Human Rights', (1999) 21 *Human Rights Quarterly*, 364–402; Lacey N., 'Feminist Legal Theory and the Rights of Women', in K. Knop (ed.), *Gender and Human Rights*, 2004, Oxford University Press, Oxford, 13–55; and Gaer F.D., 'And Never the Twain Shall Meet? The Struggle to Establish Women's Rights as International Human Rights', in C.E. Lockwood, D.B. Magraw, M.F. Spring and S.I. Strong (eds), *The International Human Rights of Women: Instruments of Change*, 1998, American Bar Association, Washington, DC, 1–89.

in Chapter 4, the Inter-American Court of Human Rights is credited with one of the earliest formulations of the principle of state responsibility in the case of *Velasquez Rodriguez v Honduras.*[67]

In the context of the Council of Europe, the European Court of Human Rights has used the doctrine of positive obligations in a particularly effective manner in order to overcome the problems that were once posed by the public/private divide. As Schriver comments, 'The express provisions of the (European Convention on Human Rights) do not require the European Court to impose affirmative duties.'[68] In fact, most of the rights contained in the Convention are couched in very negative terms. For example, although Article 8 prevents an interference with the exercise of the right to private and family life, it does not state that a right to privacy is guaranteed to individuals. A similar analysis could be carried out regarding the majority of the rights found in the Convention. Nevertheless, in certain circumstances, positive obligations can be placed on states to protect the rights of individuals from threats posed by other private parties. The European Court has essentially derived this principle from three sources. First, under Article 1 of the Convention, states parties have a duty to secure the rights to everyone within their jurisdictions. This appears to indicate that states are obliged to take positive steps to ensure that private individuals are able to enjoy their rights freely. Second, it is assumed that rights should be effective, as opposed to being simply theoretical.[69] As Mowbray remarks, 'Passive non-interference by governmental authorities with persons' Convention rights is not sufficient to ensure that many of those rights are fully and effectively respected.'[70] Third, under Article 13 of the Convention, states parties must provide effective remedies for breaches of rights.[71] Again this provision serves to impose positive obligations on states parties. The positive duties that may be placed on states parties are wide-ranging. Indeed, Starmer explains that the European Court has recognised five main categories of obligations that can be imposed: a duty to establish a legal framework providing effective rights protection; an obligation to prevent breaches of rights; a duty to provide information relevant to the rights violation; an obligation to respond to breaches; and a duty to provide resources to individuals to prevent violations of their rights.[72] The use of the concepts of state responsibility and positive obligations by the judicial branches of the Inter-American and

67 Judgment of 29 July 1988, Inter-Am. Ct. H.R., (Ser. C) No. 4.

68 Schriver T., 'Establishing an Affirmative Governmental Duty to Protect Children's Rights: The European Court of Human Rights as a Model for the United States Supreme Court', (2000) 34 *University of San Francisco Law Review*, 379–408 at 400.

69 Starmer K., *European Human Rights Law, the Human Rights Act 1998 and the European Convention on Human Rights*, 1999, LAG, London, at p.194.

70 Mowbray A.R., *The Development of Positive Obligations under the European Convention on Human Rights by the European Court of Human Rights*, 2004, Hart Publishing, Oxford, at p.221.

71 Starmer, op. cit., at p.194.

72 Starmer, op. cit., at p.196.

Council of Europe regional systems in cases involving domestic violence will be discussed in Chapter 3.[73]

Developments within the United Nations regarding domestic violence

None of the UN human rights treaties make any express reference to domestic violence. However, the UN human rights bodies have now brought the issue of domestic violence within their scope through the use of provisions such as the right to life; the right not to be subjected to torture or other cruel, inhuman or degrading treatment or punishment; the right to equality; the right to liberty and security of person; the right to equal protection under the law; the right to be free from all forms of discrimination; and the right to the highest standard attainable of physical and mental health.[74] Various categories of recommendations have been made to states as regards their responses to domestic violence. These include the adoption of measures relating to improving their criminal justice systems; improving measures of civil protection; providing social support measures for victims; increasing awareness within society regarding issues surrounding domestic violence; increasing awareness of professionals who may be particularly likely to come into contact with victims; and developing programmes for perpetrators.

Instruments that are relevant to the issue of domestic violence include CEDAW, General Recommendation No. 19 of the CEDAW Committee,[75] resolutions of the UN General Assembly, including the UN Declaration on the Elimination of Violence against Women,[76] reports of the Special Rapporteur on violence against women, its causes and consequences, and resolutions of the Commission on Human Rights. Of these instruments, in strict legal terms, only CEDAW is binding on states. This Convention was adopted by the UN General Assembly in 1979 and came into force in 1981.[77] Article 1 of this instrument prohibits

73 For further discussion of the concept of positive obligations as developed by the European Court of Human Rights, see McQuigg, op. cit., at pp.43–6.

74 General Assembly Resolution 48/104 (1993) Article 3.

75 Committee on the Elimination of Discrimination against Women, U.N. Doc A/47/38 (1992).

76 General Assembly Resolution 48/104 (1993).

77 For discussion of CEDAW generally, see Chinkin C. and Freeman M.A., 'Introduction', in M.A. Freeman, C. Chinkin and B. Rudolf (eds), *The UN Convention on the Elimination of All Forms of Discrimination against Women: A Commentary*, 2012, Oxford University Press, Oxford, 2–33; and Byrnes A., 'The Convention on the Elimination of All Forms of Discrimination against Women' in W. Benedek, E.M. Kisaakye and G. Oberleitner (eds), *Human Rights of Women: International Instruments and African Experiences*, 2002, Palgrave, New York, 119–72.

> any distinction, exclusion or restriction made on the basis of sex which has the effect or purpose of impairing or nullifying the recognition, enjoyment or exercise by women, irrespective of marital status, on the basis of equality between men and women, of human rights or fundamental freedoms in the political, economic, social, cultural, civil or any other field.

At the time of writing, 189 states are parties to CEDAW. This means that it is one of the most widely ratified of the UN treaties. However, it is important to note that this instrument contains no express mention of domestic violence, or indeed of violence against women more generally, within its provisions. At first glance, the omission of gender-based violence from a treaty that focuses on the rights of women may seem somewhat surprising. As Rehman remarks, 'A serious criticism of the Women's Convention has been the absence of specific provisions condemning violence against women, an omission which is unacceptable in the light of everyday instances of violence against women in every region of the world.'[78] However, this omission can be explained by the fact that CEDAW was adopted in 1979, and, as explained earlier in the chapter, it was only in the 1970s that domestic violence began to be viewed as an issue that merited the attention of any form of law, let alone international human rights law.

However, in 1992 the CEDAW Committee issued its General Recommendation No. 19. This was an immensely important development as this General Recommendation officially interpreted CEDAW as prohibiting violence against women in both the public and private contexts. As Chinkin comments, 'General Recommendation 19 has been the basis of the Committee's work on violence against women.'[79] It is worth noting that in 1989 the CEDAW Committee had referred to the issue of violence against women in its General Recommendation No. 12.[80] This Recommendation was, however, very brief and simply asserted that states parties should include in their periodic reports to the Committee information concerning the legislation in force to protect women against the incidence of all kinds of violence in everyday life, including sexual violence, abuses in the family and sexual harassment at the work place;[81] other measures adopted to eradicate this violence;[82] the existence of support services for women who are the victims of aggression or abuses;[83] and statistical data on the incidence of violence of all kinds against women and on women who are the victims of violence.[84]

78 Rehman J., *International Human Rights Law*, 2nd edn, 2010, Pearson Education, Harlow, at p.551.
79 Chinkin and Freeman, op. cit., at p.473.
80 Committee on the Elimination of Discrimination against Women, U.N. Doc. A/44/38 (1989).
81 At para. 1.
82 At para. 2.
83 At para. 3.
84 At para. 4.

In particular, General Recommendation No. 12 did not explain how CEDAW actually encompassed violence against women.[85]

General Recommendation No. 12 was thus superseded three years later by General Recommendation No. 19,[86] which was a much more detailed document. General Recommendation No. 19 stated clearly: 'The full implementation of the Convention required States to take positive measures to eliminate all forms of violence against women.'[87] Chinkin remarks that 'General Recommendation 19 provides the first holistic international law definition of gender-based violence against women'.[88] The General Recommendation asserted:

> The definition of discrimination includes gender-based violence, that is, violence that is directed against a woman because she is a woman or that affects women disproportionately. It includes acts that inflict physical, mental or sexual harm or suffering, threats of such acts, coercion and other deprivations of liberty. Gender-based violence may breach specific provisions of the Convention, regardless of whether those provisions expressly mention violence.[89]

The General Recommendation stated that gender-based violence may breach *inter alia* the right to life; the right not to be subject to torture or to cruel, inhuman or degrading treatment or punishment; and the right to liberty and security of person.[90] It emphasised that:

> discrimination under the Convention is not restricted to action by or on behalf of Governments . . . Under general international law and specific human rights covenants, States may be responsible for private acts if they fail to act with due diligence to prevent violations of rights or to investigate and punish acts of violence, and for providing compensation.[91]

In this way the concept of state responsibility was used to great effect to transcend the public/private dichotomy. The General Recommendation also stated:

> Family violence is one of the most insidious forms of violence against women. It is prevalent in all societies. Within family relationships women of all ages

85 Šimonović D., 'Global and Regional Standards on Violence against Women: The Evolution and Synergy of the CEDAW and Istanbul Conventions', (2014) 36 *Human Rights Quarterly*, 590–606 at 600.

86 Committee on the Elimination of Discrimination against Women, U.N. Doc A/47/38 (1992).

87 At para. 4.

88 Chinkin C., 'Violence against Women' in M.A. Freeman, C. Chinkin and B. Rudolf (eds), *The UN Convention on the Elimination of All Forms of Discrimination against Women: A Commentary*, 2012, Oxford University Press, Oxford, 443–74 at 452.

89 At para. 6.

90 At para. 7.

91 At para. 9.

> are subjected to violence of all kinds, including battering, rape, other forms of sexual assault, mental and other forms of violence, which are perpetuated by traditional attitudes.[92]

The General Recommendation asserted that measures necessary to overcome family violence included 'criminal penalties where necessary', and that 'states parties should ensure that laws against family violence and abuse . . . give adequate protection to all women, and respect their integrity and dignity'.[93] In this document, the CEDAW Committee recognised that '[e]ffective legal measures, including . . . civil remedies'[94] were necessary to protect women from violence occurring in the private sphere. It has been argued that the provision of social support measures to victims of domestic violence is the state response that is most needed by victims.[95] The necessity for such provision was recognised by the CEDAW Committee and it was recommended that states parties provide '[p]rotective measures, including refuges, counselling, rehabilitation and support services for women who are the victims of violence or who are at risk of violence'.[96] The Committee also recommended that states provide public education programmes to change attitudes concerning the status of men and women,[97] and stated that gender-sensitive training of judicial and law enforcement officers and other public officials was essential for the effective implementation of the Convention.[98] In addition, the Committee recommended that states parties provide rehabilitation programmes for perpetrators,[99] and asserted that they 'should encourage the compilation of statistics and research on the extent, causes and effects of violence, and on the effectiveness of measures to prevent and deal with violence'.[100]

In addition, it is worth noting that the CEDAW Committee has now considered a number of complaints regarding the responses of states to domestic violence which have been taken under the Optional Protocol procedure.[101] The Optional Protocol to CEDAW, which entered into force in December 2000,

92 At para. 23.
93 At para. 24.
94 At para. 24.
95 Schneider E., *Battered Women and Feminist Lawmaking*, 2000, Yale University Press, Connecticut, at pp.196–7.
96 U.N. Doc A/47/38 (1992), at para. 24(t)(iii).
97 At para. 24(t)(ii).
98 At para. 24(b).
99 At para. 24(r)(iv).
100 At para. 24(c).
101 *AT v Hungary* (Communication No. 2/2003, 26 January 2005, CEDAW/C/32/D/2/2003); *Goekce v Austria* (Communication No. 5/2005, 6 August 2007, CEDAW/C/39/D/5/2005); *Yildirim v Austria* (Communication No. 6/2005, 1 October 2007, CEDAW/C/39/D/6/2005); *VK v Bulgaria* (Communication No. 20/2008, 17 August 2011, CEDAW/C/49/D/20/2008); *Jallow v Bulgaria* (Communication No. 32/2011, 28 August 2012, CEDAW/C/52/D/32/2011).

allows individuals or groups to submit claims of violations of the Convention to the CEDAW Committee. Essentially, the Protocol gives to every woman in states that have ratified it an opportunity to go to the CEDAW Committee and argue that the state has failed to protect her rights under the Convention. Communications relating to the responses of states parties to domestic violence will be considered in depth in Chapter 5.

Following the World Conference on Human Rights held in Vienna in 1993,[102] a Special Rapporteur on violence against women, its causes and consequences was appointed by the UN Commission on Human Rights. Gaer describes the appointment of the Special Rapporteur as being '[p]erhaps the most important single action in the post-Vienna time period to fulfill the goals of the women's human rights movement'.[103] The Special Rapporteur's mandate is to:

> [s]eek and receive information on violence against women, its causes and consequences, from Governments, treaty bodies, specialized agencies, other special rapporteurs...[and] [r]ecommend measures, ways and means, at the national, regional and international level to eliminate violence against women and its causes, and to remedy its consequences.[104]

It has been remarked that the Special Rapporteur on violence against women has 'brought international consciousness to a new level'.[105] Radhika Coomaraswamy was appointed to the post in 1994 and in 1996 she produced a framework for model legislation on domestic violence.

The framework for model legislation dealt in a fairly detailed manner with how a state's criminal justice system should respond to cases of domestic violence. For example, in relation to complaint mechanisms it stated:

> The law shall provide for victims, witnesses of domestic violence, family members and close associates of victims, State and private medical service providers and domestic violence assistance centres to complain of incidents of domestic violence to the police or file action in court.[106]

According to the Special Rapporteur, the law should provide that police officers must respond to every request for assistance in cases of alleged domestic

102 The Vienna Declaration and Programme of Action can be found at www.ohchr.org/EN/ProfessionalInterest/Pages/Vienna.aspx, Office of the High Commissioner for Human Rights (accessed 12 October 2016).

103 Gaer, op. cit., at p.37.

104 U.N. Commission on Human Rights, Resolution 1994/45, paras 7(a) and (b).

105 Stark B., 'Symposium on Integrating Responses to Domestic Violence', (2001) 47 *Loyola Law Review*, 255–82 at 265.

106 Report of the Special Rapporteur on violence against women, its causes and consequences – A framework for model legislation on domestic violence, E/CN.4/1996/53/Add.2, 2 February 1996, at para. 12.

violence.[107] Also, police officers should not regard calls concerning alleged domestic abuse as being of a lower priority than calls alleging violence by strangers.[108] The offender should be removed from the home or, if this is not possible and the victim remains in danger, the offender should be arrested.[109] In addition, the police officer must provide the victim with a written statement outlining all the legal procedures available to her.[110] Essentially, the police must take all reasonable measures to ensure that the victim is safe.[111] The Special Rapporteur also laid down proper practice for prosecutors and courts in cases involving violence against women in the home. For example, if a court dismisses criminal charges, the specific reasons for dismissal should be recorded.[112] During the course of the trial, the defendant should have no unsupervised contact with the plaintiff,[113] and clear sentencing guidelines should be established.[114]

In addition, the report of the Special Rapporteur detailed the restraining orders and protection orders that should be made available by states.[115] Such orders should have the capacity *inter alia* to compel the offender to vacate the family home, regulate the offender's access to dependent children, restrain the offender from contacting the victim and compel the offender to pay the victim's medical bills. In another report issued in 1996, the Special Rapporteur gave detailed consideration to the issue of child contact in cases involving domestic violence. This report asserted:

> In cases of domestic violence, women should be granted full custody of the children. In cases of woman-battering, the batterer should not be granted visitation . . . In cases in which visitation rights are granted, visitation should be supervised and arranged in a way so as not to cause the woman any contact with the batterer.[116]

The report of the Special Rapporteur containing the framework for model legislation detailed the services that states should provide for victims of domestic violence, such as emergency services including immediate transport from the victim's home to a medical centre, shelter or other place of safety, emergency legal counselling and crisis counselling.[117] States should also provide services to assist

107 At para. 13.
108 At para. 14.
109 At para. 17(h).
110 At para. 21(e).
111 At para. 21(d).
112 At para. 45.
113 At para. 49.
114 At para. 55.
115 At paras 26–43.
116 Report of the Special Rapporteur on violence against women, its causes and consequences, E/CN.4/1996/53, 5 February 1996, at para. 142(k).
117 Report of the Special Rapporteur on violence against women, its causes and consequences, E/CN.4/1996/53/Add.2, 2 February 1996, at para. 60.

in the rehabilitation of victims through counselling and job training.[118] In addition, the Special Rapporteur stated: 'Recognizing the nexus between domestic violence and homelessness, priority should be given to victim-survivors of domestic violence in State-sponsored housing.'[119]

The Special Rapporteur also asserted that states should take steps to raise societal awareness of violence against women. For example, one of her reports from 1996 referred to the need for 'demystifying domestic violence',[120] and in 2003 the Special Rapporteur recommended 'the adoption of a societal project to delink masculinity from an association with oppressive uses of power'.[121] In addition to raising the awareness of society generally regarding domestic violence, it has been commented that it is also necessary to provide particular educational programmes for those who may regularly come into contact with victims in a professional capacity, such as healthcare professionals, lawyers, judges and social workers.[122] In the report of the Special Rapporteur containing a framework for model legislation on domestic violence, it was stated that one of the aims of the draft legislation was to:

> [t]rain judges to be aware of the issues relating to child custody, economic support and security for the victims in cases of domestic violence by establishing guidelines for protection orders and sentencing guidelines which do not trivialize domestic violence.[123]

The report also laid out details for the training of police officers in dealing with cases involving domestic violence. Police should be educated in '[t]he nature, extent, causes and consequences of domestic violence'[124] and the legal rights, services and facilities available to victims.[125] In addition, the need to educate other professionals has been recognised by the Special Rapporteur in other documents. For example, a 2002 report asserted that '[s]tates should train all public officials in the administration of justice, education and health sectors to be sensitive and energetic with regard to issues relating to violence against women'.[126]

118 At para. 61(a).
119 Report of the Special Rapporteur on violence against women, its causes and consequences, E/CN.4/1996/53, 5 February 1996, at para. 142(m).
120 Report of the Special Rapporteur on violence against women, its causes and consequences, E/CN.4/1996/53, 5 February 1996, at para. 141.
121 Report of the Special Rapporteur on violence against women, its causes and consequences, E/CN.4/2004/66, 26 December 2003, at para. 58.
122 Smith, op. cit., at pp.97–8.
123 Report of the Special Rapporteur on violence against women, its causes and consequences, E/CN.4/1996/53/Add.2, 2 February 1996, at para. 2(k).
124 At para. 62(a).
125 At paras 62(b) and (c).
126 Report of the Special Rapporteur on violence against women, its causes and consequences, E/CN.4/2002/83, 31 January 2002, at para. 128.

The 1996 report of the Special Rapporteur outlining a framework for model legislation recommended that states deliver services to assist in the rehabilitation of abusers.[127] The report asserted: 'The law shall mandate counselling programmes for perpetrators as a supplement to and not as an alternative to the criminal justice system.'[128] Such programmes should be designed to assist the perpetrator in taking responsibility for his violence and making a commitment not to inflict further violence[129] and they should educate him on the illegality of violence.[130] However, the report stressed that funding for perpetrator programmes should not be taken from resources that are assigned to assist victims.[131]

The UN General Assembly has also made recommendations relating to states' responses to domestic violence. For example, even as far back as 1985 the General Assembly urged member states to take action 'in order to prevent domestic violence and to render the appropriate assistance to the victims thereof';[132] to adopt specific measures with a view to making criminal and civil justice systems more sensitive in responding to domestic violence;[133] and to ensure coordination of social welfare and criminal justice measures in relation to domestic violence.[134] In 1990 the General Assembly again urged states:

> to begin or continue to explore, develop and implement multidisciplinary policies, measures and strategies, within and outside of the criminal justice system, with respect to domestic violence in all its facets, including legal, law enforcement, judicial, societal, educational, psychological, economic, health-related and correctional aspects.[135]

In 1993 the General Assembly issued its important Declaration on the Elimination of Violence against Women (DEVAW). As a General Assembly Resolution, the Declaration is not a legally binding instrument; however, '[t]he fact that the Resolution was adopted without a vote, but by consensus amongst States, has added to its weight and authority'.[136] In this Declaration, the General Assembly asserted that states 'should pursue by all appropriate means and without delay a policy of eliminating violence against women'.[137] For example, they should '[d]evelop penal, civil, labour and administrative sanctions in domestic legislation

127 Report of the Special Rapporteur on violence against women, its causes and consequences, E/CN.4/1996/53/Add.2, 2 February 1996, at para. 61(b).
128 At para. 70.
129 At para. 71(i).
130 At para. 71(ii).
131 At para. 72.
132 General Assembly Resolution 40/36 (1985) at para. 2.
133 At para. 7.
134 At para. 7(j).
135 General Assembly Resolution 45/114 (1990) at para. 1.
136 Rehman, op. cit., at p.552.
137 General Assembly Resolution 48/104 (1993), Article 4.

to punish and redress the wrongs caused to women who are subjected to violence'.[138] States should also '[d]evelop, in a comprehensive way, preventive approaches and all those measures of a legal, political, administrative and cultural nature that promote the protection of women against any form of violence'.[139] States were urged to:

> [w]ork to ensure, to the maximum extent feasible in the light of their available resources and, where needed, within the framework of international cooperation, that women subjected to violence and, where appropriate, their children have specialized assistance, such as rehabilitation, assistance in child care and maintenance, treatment, counselling, and health and social services, facilities and programmes, as well as support structures, and should take all other appropriate measures to promote their safety and physical and psychological rehabilitation.[140]

The Declaration also urged states to '[c]onsider the possibility of developing national plans of action to promote the protection of women against any form of violence . . . taking into account . . . such cooperation as can be provided by non-governmental organizations'.[141] As Rehman comments, the Declaration 'has had a considerable impact in developing the law relating to women's rights and has provided substantial ammunition to CEDAW to scrutinise practices which contravene the provisions of the Declaration'.[142]

The Fourth World Conference on Women was held in 1995 in Beijing. The Beijing Platform for Action urged states to adopt a wide range of measures regarding violence against women, including domestic violence, and asserted that states should:

> [p]rovide women who are subjected to violence with access to the mechanisms of justice and, as provided for by national legislation, to just and effective remedies for the harm they have suffered and inform women of their rights in seeking redress through such mechanisms.[143]

The Platform for Action emphasised the need for measures to be adopted to increase societal awareness of domestic violence. It stated that governments should support initiatives of women's organisations to raise awareness of the issue of violence against women[144] and that they should organise and fund community-based campaigns to raise awareness about violence against women as a human

138 Article 4(d).
139 Article 4(f).
140 Article 4(g).
141 Article 4(e).
142 Rehman, op. cit., at p.552.
143 Beijing Platform for Action, U.N. Doc.A/CONF.177/20 (1995), at para. 124(b).
144 At para. 125(d).

rights violation.[145] States should also '[p]rovide well-funded shelters and relief support for girls and women subjected to violence, as well as medical, psychological and other counselling services and free or low-cost legal aid, where it is needed, as well as appropriate assistance to enable them to find a means of subsistence'.[146]

In addition, the UN Commission on Human Rights also issued statements relevant to domestic violence. For example, in 2001 the Commission on Human Rights issued a resolution on the elimination of violence against women in which it called upon states *inter alia* to condemn violence against women;[147] to take action to investigate and punish persons who perpetrate acts of violence against women;[148] to support initiatives undertaken by women's organisations and non-governmental organisations on the elimination of violence against women;[149] and to consider undertaking campaigns about violence against women.[150] Similar statements were also made by the Commission in a 2004 resolution on the elimination of violence against women.[151] In 2006, the Commission on Human Rights was superseded by the Human Rights Council,[152] and in 2010 the latter also issued a resolution on 'accelerating efforts to eliminate all forms of violence against women' which again urged states to adopt a range of measures with regard to this issue.[153]

The Convention of Belém do Pará

The growing recognition of domestic violence as constituting an issue for human rights law is not of course confined to the UN system. With the adoption of the Istanbul Convention, the Council of Europe has taken the important step of adopting a legally binding instrument that addresses the issue of violence against women; however, it is not the first of the regional human rights systems to do so. Indeed, almost 17 years prior to the Council of Europe's adoption of the Istanbul Convention, the Inter-American Convention on the Prevention, Punishment, and Eradication of Violence against Women (also known as the Convention of Belém

145 At para. 125(e).
146 At para. 125(a).
147 Commission on Human Rights Resolution 2001/49, at para. 9(b).
148 At para. 10(c).
149 At para. 10(d).
150 At para. 10(e).
151 Commission on Human Rights Resolution 2004/46, at para. 15(j).
152 Pursuant to General Assembly Resolution 60/251 of 15 March 2006, all mandates, mechanisms, functions and responsibilities of the Commission on Human Rights were assumed, as of 19 June 2006, by the Human Rights Council.
153 Human Rights Council Resolution 14/12, 30 June 2010. For further discussion of developments at the UN level, see McQuigg, op. cit., at pp.78–98. See also Meyersfeld B., *Domestic Violence and International Law*, 2010, Hart, Oxford, at pp.24–78; and Hasselbacher L., 'State Obligations Regarding Domestic Violence: The European Court of Human Rights, Due Diligence, and International Legal Minimums of Protection', (2010) 8 *Northwestern Journal of International Human Rights*, 190–215 at 191–200.

do Pará) was adopted by the General Assembly of the Organization of American States (OAS). In addition, the Protocol to the African Charter on Human and Peoples' Rights on the Rights of Women in Africa (also known as the Maputo Protocol) was adopted by the African Union in 2003. The next part of this chapter will provide an introduction to these instruments, the provisions of which will be compared with those of the Istanbul Convention in Chapter 4.[154]

The OAS constitutes the world's oldest regional organisation. The origins of the OAS system date back to the First International Conference of American States which was held in Washington, DC, from October 1889 until April 1890. International Conferences of American States were held periodically thereafter, and at the Ninth International Conference, which was held in Bogotá, Colombia, in 1948, the Charter of the Organization of American States, the American Treaty on Pacific Settlement and the American Declaration on the Rights and Duties of Man were adopted. The OAS was established, as stated in Article 1 of the Charter, in order to achieve among its member states 'an order of peace and justice, to promote their solidarity, to strengthen their collaboration, and to defend their sovereignty, their territorial integrity, and their independence'. All 35 independent states of the Americas are now members of the OAS, which is based upon the pillars of democracy, human rights, security and development.[155]

The American Declaration on the Rights and Duties of Man was also adopted in Bogotá in 1948. The Inter-American Commission on Human Rights was created in 1959 and held its first session in 1960. In 1961 the Commission began to carry out on-site visits to observe the general human rights situations in states or to investigate particular situations, and in 1965 it was expressly authorised to examine complaints regarding specific cases of human rights breaches. The American Convention on Human Rights was adopted in 1969 and entered into force in 1978. In addition to listing the rights that states parties must respect and ensure, the Convention also created the Inter-American Court of Human Rights and defines the functions and procedures of both the Commission and the Court.

The Convention of Belém do Pará was drafted by the Inter-American Commission of Women (CIM). Established in 1928, CIM was the first intergovernmental agency established to ensure recognition of the human rights of women. The Convention of Belém do Pará was adopted by the OAS General Assembly on 9 June 1994 at its 24th session in Belém do Pará, Brazil. This Convention entered into force on 5 March 1995. The adoption of the Convention

154 It is notable that the ASEAN (Association of Southeast Asian Nations) Intergovernmental Commission on Human Rights (AICHR) adopted a Declaration on the Elimination of Violence against Women and Elimination of Violence against Children in ASEAN on 9 October 2013. This document can be found at www.ohchr.org/Documents/Issues/Women/WG/ASEANdeclarationVaW_violenceagainstchildren.pdf (accessed 12 October 2016). This Declaration is not, however, a legally binding instrument. For further information on the AICHR, see http://aichr.org (accessed 12 October 2016).

155 See further www.oas.org/en/about/who_we_are.asp, Organization of American States (accessed 12 October 2016).

of Belém do Pará was certainly an innovative development within the OAS system, as seen when viewed against the backdrop of developments in this area at the UN level. It was not until 1992 that the CEDAW Committee issued its General Recommendation No. 19 which officially interpreted CEDAW as prohibiting violence against women in both the public and private contexts.[156] The UN General Assembly adopted the Declaration on the Elimination of Violence against Women in 1993,[157] and it is noteworthy that the Convention of Belém do Pará was adopted only one year later. This instrument was certainly a pioneering development, given that it constituted the first regional instrument to address the issue of violence against women.

The Maputo Protocol

The concept of drafting a document establishing a human rights protection mechanism in Africa was first discussed in the early 1960s. At the first Congress of African Jurists, held in Lagos in Nigeria in 1961, the Congress adopted a declaration, known as the 'Law of Lagos', which called on African governments to adopt an African convention on human rights with a court and a commission. However, at this time the idea received little support from the governments of African states. The Organisation of African Unity (OAU) was established on 25 May 1963. It was disbanded on 9 July 2002 and replaced by the African Union (AU). The Charter that established the OAU imposed no explicit obligations on member states concerning the protection of human rights. This document merely required states parties to have due regard for human rights standards, as set out in the Universal Declaration of Human Rights, in their international relations. Despite the absence of a clear human rights mandate, however, the OAU took steps to address a number of human rights issues such as decolonisation, racial discrimination, environmental protection and refugee problems. Nevertheless, the OAU prioritised socio-economic development, territorial integrity and state sovereignty over human rights protection, and supported the principle of non-interference in the internal affairs of member states.[158]

At the first Conference of Francophone African Jurists, held in Dakar in Senegal in 1967, discussion again arose regarding the need for an instrument to provide regional protection of human rights in Africa. Following the Conference, the Dakar Declaration was adopted, in which the International Commission of Jurists was asked to consider, in consultation with other relevant African organisations, the possibility of creating a regional human rights mechanism. A series of seminars and conferences on this issue took place in a number of African countries and were facilitated by the UN. The UN Human Rights Commission also set up an ad hoc

156 U.N. Doc A/47/38 (1992), at para. 9.

157 General Assembly Resolution 48/104, 20 December 1993.

158 See further www.achpr.org/instruments/achpr/history, African Commission on Human and Peoples' Rights (accessed 12 October 2016).

working group. However, the process then stalled. In 1979 the Assembly of Heads of States and Government of the OAU, at a meeting held in Monrovia in Liberia, unanimously requested the Secretary General of the OAU to convene a committee of experts to draft a regional human rights instrument for Africa. A conference of 20 experts presided over by Judge Kéba M'baye subsequently took place in 1979 in Dakar, during which an initial draft of a human rights charter was prepared. Two Ministerial Conferences were convened in Banjul in Gambia, where the draft charter was adopted and subsequently submitted to the OAU Assembly. The African Charter on Human and Peoples' Rights was finally adopted by the OAU Assembly on 28 June 1981, in Nairobi in Kenya. The Charter came into force on 21 October 1986, and by 1999 it had been ratified by all the member states of the OAU. The African Commission on Human and Peoples' Rights (ACHPR), which was established in 1987 and which is now based in Banjul, has the tasks of overseeing and interpreting the Charter. A Protocol to the Charter was adopted in 1998 as regards the establishment of an African Court on Human and Peoples' Rights. This Protocol came into effect on 25 January 2005.[159]

The Maputo Protocol was adopted by the AU in 2003 in Maputo in Mozambique, and entered into force in November 2005. It was recognised that inadequate protection was afforded to women by the African Charter on Human and Peoples' Rights. Although the African Charter states that '[e]very individual shall be entitled to the enjoyment of the rights and freedoms recognised and guaranteed in the present Charter without distinction of any kind such as . . . sex',[160] and that '[e]very individual shall be equal before the law',[161] it does not articulate specific violations of women's rights that result from discrimination.[162] A meeting organised by Women in Law and Development in Africa, which took place in March 1995 in Lomé in Togo, called for the development of a protocol to the African Charter to focus on the rights of women. In June 1995, the ACHPR was given a mandate by the Assembly of the OAU to develop such a protocol. A first draft of the Protocol was subsequently developed by an expert group of members of the ACHPR, representatives of non-governmental organisations and international observers. This draft was submitted to the ACHPR in October 1997, and then circulated for comments to other NGOs. In April 1998 the ACHPR endorsed the appointment of Julienne Ondziel Gnelenga as the first Special Rapporteur on Women's Rights in Africa, and gave her a mandate to work

159 Protocol to the African Charter on Human and Peoples' Rights on the Establishment of an African Court on Human and Peoples' Rights. See further www.achpr.org/instruments/achpr/history, African Commission on Human and Peoples' Rights (accessed 12 October 2016).

160 African Charter on Human and Peoples' Rights, Article 2.

161 Article 3(1).

162 See further www.achpr.org/instruments/achpr/subsequent-standards, African Commission on Human and Peoples' Rights (accessed 12 October 2016).

towards the adoption of the draft Protocol. The draft was submitted to the OAU Secretariat in 1999, and in 2000 this draft document was combined with a draft Convention on Traditional Practices in a joint session of the ACHPR and the Inter-African Committee. Following some delay, the finalised document was officially adopted by the AU on 11 July 2003 and came into effect on 25 January 2005. Ocran remarks that the speed of the 15 ratifications that were necessary to bring the Maputo Protocol into force is 'a sign that, more and more, the male-dominated African governments are becoming conscious of the importance of securing women's human rights, or at the very least, would like to be perceived as championing this cause'.[163] Writing in 2006, Banda commented that 'the adoption and coming into force of the African Protocol on Women's Rights is . . . a strong indicator of the normative acceptance of the idea that human rights are women's rights'.[164]

It is important to note that the Maputo Protocol is not focused solely on violence against women. Instead, it covers a wide range of rights, encompassing civil and political rights; economic, social and cultural rights; and group rights. Issues that are addressed in the Protocol include violence against women, harmful traditional practices, child marriage, polygamy, inheritance, economic empowerment, women's political participation, education, and women in armed conflict. The Protocol recognises that certain women may suffer multiple forms of discrimination and therefore particular provisions for elderly women, widows and women with disabilities are included.[165] Writing in 2007, Ocran commented: 'The Protocol is a pioneering and legally binding instrument, which marks a new beginning in the promotion and protection of women's human rights on the African continent.'[166]

Conclusion

The aim of this chapter has been to place the Istanbul Convention in context with regard to the analysis of domestic violence as a human rights issue that necessitates the attention of international and regional institutions. As has been discussed, there was a historical reluctance to view domestic violence as an issue that required the attention of any form of law, let alone human rights law. Given this reluctance even to view domestic violence as a legal matter, the slowness in recognition of domestic violence as being a human rights issue is unsurprising.

163 Ocran C., 'The Protocol to the African Charter on Human and Peoples' Rights on the Rights of Women in Africa', (2007) 15 *African Journal of International and Comparative Law*, 147–52 at 147–8.

164 Banda F., 'Blazing a Trail: The African Protocol on Women's Rights Comes into Force', (2006) 50 *Journal of African Law*, 72–84 at 84.

165 See www.achpr.org/instruments/achpr/subsequent-standards, African Commission on Human and Peoples' Rights (accessed 12 October 2016).

166 Ocran, op. cit., at p.147.

The public/private dichotomy in international human rights law undoubtedly created immense difficulties as regards the application of human rights law to the issue of domestic violence. However, there have been major developments within human rights law such as the formulation of the concepts of positive obligations and state responsibility, and it is now clearly established that domestic violence constitutes a human rights issue. As has been discussed, UN bodies such as the CEDAW Committee have now made detailed statements relevant to violence against women and, more specifically, to domestic violence. These developments have not been limited to the UN level. As has been seen, the Inter-American system has had a Convention on violence against women for the past two decades, and the African system also includes a women's rights instrument which encompasses violence against women. It is against the background of these developments that the Istanbul Convention must be analysed. The next chapter will now turn to the examination of the immediate events that led up to the adoption of the Istanbul Convention itself.

3 The background to the adoption of the Istanbul Convention

The aim of this chapter is to examine the background to the adoption of the Istanbul Convention. The chapter will begin by analysing the development of domestic violence as a policy issue within the Council of Europe. Since 2007 the European Court of Human Rights has built up a substantial body of jurisprudence on domestic violence.[1] As this jurisprudence played an important role in the recognition of domestic violence as an issue that should be addressed by the Council of Europe, this body of case law will be examined. However, attention has been paid to the issue of domestic violence within the context of the Council of Europe since long before 2007. For example, as far back as 1985 the Committee of Ministers issued a Recommendation on Violence in the Family,[2] and in 1990 it passed another Recommendation relating to violence within the family, this time focusing on social measures.[3] In addition, the third European Ministerial Conference on Equality between Women and Men, which took place in Rome in October 1993, focused on 'strategies for the elimination of violence against

1 *Kontrova v Slovakia* (app. no. 7510/04, 31 May 2007); *Bevacqua and S. v Bulgaria* (app. no. 71127/01, 12 June 2008); *Branko Tomasic and Others v Croatia* (app. no. 46598/06, 15 January 2009); *Opuz v Turkey* (app. no. 33401/02, 9 June 2009); *E.S. and Others v Slovakia* (app. no. 8227/04, 15 September 2009); *A v Croatia* (app. no. 55164/08, 14 October 2010); *Hajduova v Slovakia* (app. no. 2660/03, 30 November 2010); *Kalucza v Hungary* (app. no. 57693/10, 24 April 2012); *E.M. v Romania* (app. no. 43994/05, 30 October 2012); *Valiuliene v Lithuania* (app. no. 33234/07, 26 March 2013); *Eremia and Others v the Republic of Moldova* (app. no. 3564/11, 28 May 2013); *B. v the Republic of Moldova* (app. no. 61382/09, 16 July 2013); *Mudric v the Republic of Moldova* (app. no. 74839/10, 16 July 2013); *N.A. v the Republic of Moldova* (app. no. 13424/06, 24 September 2013); *T.M. and C.M. v the Republic of Moldova* (app. no. 26608/11, 28 January 2014); *Rumor v Italy* (app. no. 72964/10, 27 May 2014); *Civek v Turkey* (app. no. 55354/11, 23 February 2016); *M.G. v Turkey* (app. no. 646/10, 22 March 2016); and *Halime Kılıç v Turkey* (app. no. 63034/11, 28 June 2016). There are also a number of cases pending before the European Court of Human Rights that involve domestic violence: *Camarasescu v Romania* (app. no. 49645/09); *Munteanu v Moldova* (app. no. 34168/11); and *D.M.D. v Romania* (app. no. 23022/13).

2 Recommendation No. R (85) 4 on Violence in the Family.

3 Recommendation No. R (90) 2 on Social Measures concerning Violence within the Family.

women in society: the media and other means'. The issue of violence against women, including domestic violence, gained increased momentum with the adoption in 2002 by the Committee of Ministers of Recommendation Rec(2002)5 on the protection of women against violence. These developments will be analysed in this chapter.

The chapter will then proceed to examine the events that led directly to the drafting and adoption of the Istanbul Convention, such as the establishment in 2006 of a Task Force to Combat Violence against Women, including Domestic Violence, and the creation in 2008 of an Ad Hoc Committee on Preventing and Combating Violence against Women and Domestic Violence. A 2007 report of the European Committee on Crime Problems (CDPC) concerning a feasibility study regarding a convention on domestic violence was also of substantial importance in this respect.

Committee of Ministers Recommendation No. R (85) 4 on Violence in the Family

Domestic violence is certainly a major problem throughout Europe. No comprehensive data exists for prevalence rates for Europe as a whole, but it is estimated that between 12 per cent and 15 per cent of women have been in a relationship involving domestic violence after the age of 16. Many more women continue to suffer abuse from former partners even after the relationship ends.[4] The Explanatory Report to the Istanbul Convention states:

> One of the primary concerns of the Council of Europe, representing 47 member states and their 800 million citizens, is to safeguard and protect human rights. Violence against women, including domestic violence, undermines the core values on which the Council of Europe is based.[5]

Nevertheless, it was not until the 1990s, more than 40 years after its formation, that the Council of Europe took substantive steps in relation to domestic violence.[6] This again emphasises the fact, as discussed in Chapter 2, that it is only relatively recently that domestic violence was recognised as being an issue of social and legal concern, let alone an issue falling within the ambit of human rights law that should be addressed by a body such as the Council of Europe. It is worth noting, however, that in 1985 the Committee of Ministers of the Council of Europe passed a Recommendation on Violence in the Family.[7] This instrument

4 Council of Europe, 'Explanatory Report to Council of Europe Convention on preventing and combating violence against women and domestic violence', available at https://rm.coe.int/CoERMPublicCommonSearchServices/DisplayDCTMContent?documentId=09000016800d383a (accessed 18 October 2016), at para. 3.

5 At para. 7.

6 The Council of Europe was founded on 5 May 1949.

7 Recommendation No. R (85) 4 on Violence in the Family.

advised that the governments of member states take steps to alert public opinion as to 'the extent, seriousness and specific characteristics of violence in the family with a view to obtaining its support for measures aimed at combating this phenomenon', and stated that they should 'promote the dissemination among families of knowledge and information concerning social and family relations, early detection of potentially conflictual situation and the settlement of interpersonal and intra-family conflicts'. According to this Recommendation, member states should also provide appropriate training for professionals responsible for intervening in cases of violence in the family, and 'arrange for and encourage the setting up, and support the work, of agencies, associations or foundations whose aim is to help and assist the victims of violent family situations, with due respect for the privacy of others'. In addition, governments should 'set up administrative departments or multidisciplinary boards with the task of looking after victims of violence in the family and with powers to deal with such cases'. Steps should be taken to ensure that, following acts of violence within the family, appropriate measures can be quickly taken to protect the victim and to prevent similar incidents from occurring in the future.

It should be noted, however, that there are elements of this Recommendation that may be viewed as being problematic. For example, it was stated that 'criminal measures should be taken only as a last resort'. It was also recommended that member states ensure that 'the prosecuting authority or the court is able to propose or take measures other than criminal ones, especially when the suspect or accused agrees to submit [to] the supervision of the competent social, medico-social or probation authorities'. The inclusion of such statements seems to indicate some reluctance as regards the use of criminal law measures in cases of family violence.

Committee of Ministers Recommendation No. R (90) 2 on Social Measures concerning Violence within the Family

However, since the 1990s, the Council of Europe, and in particular the Steering Committee for Equality between Women and Men, has undertaken a series of initiatives to promote the protection of women from violence. In 1990 the Committee of Ministers of the Council of Europe passed another Recommendation on violence within the family, this time focusing on social measures.[8] This Recommendation stated: 'Women who are victims of violence within the family should be given co-ordinated and comprehensive assistance, including, if necessary, financial assistance in accordance with national legislation.' It was also recommended that in situations in which the victim of violence was financially dependent on the perpetrator, financial assistance should be made available to enable the victim to become independent. The Recommendation stated:

> There should be general and sufficient provision of possibilities of finding accommodation in a hostel for battered women (shelter). The aim of shelters

8 Recommendation No. R (90) 2 on Social Measures concerning Violence within the Family.

> for battered women is to provide rapid help for women and children in danger. Before being provided with accommodation in a hostel for battered women, the persons concerned should, where possible, be given counselling.

In addition, it was asserted that when a victim of domestic violence has been admitted to a shelter, she should, if she so wishes, receive adequate assistance from social workers, psychologists, lawyers and other qualified persons.

Third European Ministerial Conference on Equality between Women and Men

The third European Ministerial Conference on Equality between Women and Men, which took place in Rome in October 1993, focused on 'strategies for the elimination of violence against women in society: the media and other means'. This conference resulted in a 'Declaration on Policies for Combating Violence against Women in a Democratic Society'.[9] In this document it was affirmed that 'the effective enjoyment of fundamental rights and freedoms by women on an equal footing with men is an essential principle of democratic societies',[10] and that 'violence against women constitutes an infringement of the right to life, security, liberty, dignity, and integrity of the victim and, consequently, a hindrance for the functioning of a democratic society, based on the rule of law'.[11] The document also noted that the responsibility of states may be engaged with regard to private acts of violence 'if the State does not take action with sufficient diligence to prevent the violation of rights or investigate acts of violence, to sanction them and provide support for the victims'.[12] The ministers of the states participating in the conference therefore resolved to work towards combating violence against women 'wherever it occurs, in the family, at the place of work, or in society, and irrespective of whether or not it is perpetrated or tolerated by public officials' by the implementation of a Plan of Action using political, judicial, administrative, educational, cultural and other means.[13] An Action Plan to Combat Violence against Women was subsequently developed which constituted a policy framework for governments.

Committee of Ministers Recommendation Rec(2002)5 on the protection of women against violence

In 2002 the Committee of Ministers adopted Recommendation Rec(2002)5 to member states on the protection of women against violence. The Explanatory Report to the Istanbul Convention states that this document 'represent[ed] a

9 Council of Europe, 1993, Strasbourg, MEG-3(93) 22.
10 At para. 4.
11 At para. 6.
12 At para. 18.
13 At para. 22.

milestone in that it propose[d], for the first time in Europe, a comprehensive strategy for the prevention of violence against women and the protection of victims in all Council of Europe member states'.[14] As regards domestic violence specifically, the Recommendation noted with concern the extent of violence against women in the family and recommended that states '[r]ecognise that [they] have an obligation to exercise due diligence to prevent, investigate and punish acts of violence, whether those acts are perpetrated by the state or private persons, and provide protection to victims'.[15] A substantial list of recommendations to states regarding steps that should be taken to combat violence against women was appended to the Recommendation. Paragraph 3 of the Appendix stated:

> Member states should introduce, develop and/or improve where necessary, national policies against violence based on:
>
> (a) maximum safety and protection of victims;
> (b) empowerment of victimised women by optimal support and assistance structures which avoid secondary victimisation;
> (c) adjustment of the criminal and civil law including the judicial procedure;
> (d) raising of public awareness and education of children and young persons;
> (e) ensuring special training for professionals confronted with violence against women;
> (f) prevention in all respective fields.

With regard to domestic violence specifically, the document recommended that member states classify all forms of violence within the family as criminal offences,[16] and revise and increase the penalties, where necessary, for deliberate assault and battery committed within the family.[17] States should also preclude adultery as an excuse for violence.[18] Paragraph 58 of the Appendix recommended that member states 'envisage the possibility' of taking measures in order to:

> (a) enable police forces to enter the residence of an endangered person, arrest the perpetrator and ensure that he or she appears before the judge;
> (b) enable the judiciary to adopt, as interim measures aimed at protecting the victims, the banning of a perpetrator from contacting, communicating with or approaching the victim, residing in or entering certain defined areas;
> (c) establish a compulsory protocol for operation so that the police and medical and social services follow the same procedure;

14 Council of Europe, 'Explanatory Report to Council of Europe Convention on preventing and combating violence against women and domestic violence', at para. 9.
15 At para. 11.
16 At para. 55 of the Appendix.
17 At para. 56 of the Appendix.
18 At para. 57 of the Appendix.

(d) promote pro-active victim protection services which take the initiative to contact the victim as soon as a report is made to the police;
(e) ensure smooth co-operation of all relevant institutions, such as police authorities, courts and victim protection services, in order to enable the victim to take all relevant legal and practical measures for receiving assistance and taking actions against the perpetrator within due time limits and without unwanted contact with the perpetrator;
(f) penalise all breaches of the measures imposed on the perpetrators by the authorities.

In addition, under paragraph 59, member states should consider granting immigrant women who have been or who are the victims of domestic violence an independent right to residence in order to allow them to leave their violent husbands without having to leave the host state.

A monitoring framework relating to implementation by member states of this Recommendation was established in 2005. The monitoring cycles demonstrate that although much has been done by states to improve the responses of their criminal justice systems to violence against women, many gaps nevertheless remain, particularly in the area of the provision of services for victims.[19]

Parliamentary Assembly Resolution 1582 on domestic violence against women

In 2002 the Parliamentary Assembly of the Council of Europe adopted Resolution 1582 on domestic violence against women.[20] This Resolution stated:

> Domestic violence is the most common form of violence against women and its consequences affect many areas of the lives of victims – housing, health, education and the freedom to live their lives without fear and in the way they wish. This widespread phenomenon is common to all European countries and is not limited to any particular social group or class. Domestic violence can take a number of forms such as physical assault, sexual abuse and rape, threats and intimidation and should be recognised as a crime.[21]

The Resolution went on to assert that 'domestic violence should be treated as a political and public problem, and a violation of human rights'.[22] The Parliamentary Assembly therefore called on member states to 'recognise that they have an obligation to prevent, investigate and punish all acts of domestic violence and to provide protection to its victims'.[23] Member states should thus implement effective

19 Council of Europe, 'Explanatory Report to Council of Europe Convention on preventing and combating violence against women and domestic violence', at para. 9.
20 Adopted on 27 September 2002.
21 Parliamentary Resolution 1582 on domestic violence against women, at para. 1.
22 At para. 2.
23 At para. 4.

awareness-raising policies and campaigns to inform and educate their citizens in relation to this issue.[24] As regards measures that should be taken in relation to victims of domestic violence, the Assembly called on member states to provide victims with free legal advice and to assist them by opening residential centres where they could receive psychological support. States should also provide financial support to welfare associations and emergency services, and ensure effective protection for victims after the violent incident and during the whole legal procedure. Particular financial support should be given to non-governmental organisations and women's associations who work with victims of domestic violence. In addition, member states were called upon to promote the training of health personnel and professionals working with young people, to identify victims of violence and children and adolescents growing up in violent homes. Also, immigrant women who were victims of domestic violence should be granted an independent right of residence.[25]

With regard to measures that should be taken in relation to the prevention of domestic violence, the Parliamentary Assembly called upon member states to develop partnerships between the authorities responsible for the protection of women's rights and regional and local authorities in order to increase the availability of shelters and rehabilitation centres for women victims. Continuing cooperation and understanding between the police, government departments and non-governmental organisations should be encouraged, and action plans should be developed in order to create a climate where domestic violence is rejected. States should also implement, through the media, national awareness campaigns against domestic violence and organise sufficient training for professionals who deal with victims of domestic violence, such as police and social workers. Education on gender equality and non-violent behaviour should begin at a very early stage and adequate training should be provided for teachers on issues surrounding domestic violence and gender equality. Citizens should be encouraged, through educational programmes, 'to accept their responsibilities, and take positive steps to reduce and prevent domestic violence in society'. In addition, states should increase funding to support social services dealing with domestic violence, and encourage the media to cover the issue of domestic violence in a non-biased and objective manner. According to the Resolution, women should be encouraged to learn self-defence techniques, and member states should also develop programmes specifically for perpetrators of violence against women. In addition, special information programmes for men should be implemented with the aim of preventing domestic violence.[26]

In terms of legal measures to be adopted, the Parliamentary Assembly stated:

> [N]ational legislation should prohibit all forms of domestic violence and introduce effective legal provisions, including the immediate removal of the

24 At para. 5.
25 At para. 7.
26 At para. 7.

> violent partner from the common household and the environment of the woman and her children, without prior evidence of violence, and on the first complaint without waiting for the court order.[27]

In addition, the concept of domestic violence should be defined in national legislation in such a manner that it is treated as a serious offence, and the police and law enforcement agencies should be granted the authority to carry out investigations and to lodge complaints on behalf of victims of domestic violence.[28]

Stocktaking study of 2006

In 2006 a report entitled 'Combating Violence against Women: Stocktaking study on the measures and actions taken in Council of Europe member states'[29] was published. This report highlighted a number of positive developments as regards the responses of member states of the Council of Europe to the issue of domestic violence. The report stated that 'a large proportion of member states have recognised domestic violence as a grave problem which has to be dealt with on a solid legal foundation'.[30] The report also found that '[t]here is an overall trend towards broadening legal protection measures and establishing both a protective and punitive path of dealing with the problem'.[31] However, it was stated:

> Despite the increased attention to violence against women throughout the world, and many positive developments in policy and practices, campaigns and activities to combat violence against women and services to support and protect the victims, violence against women in its various forms is still widespread in all European countries.[32]

It was found that '[t]he guiding principle of empowerment of the victim seems to depend on the extent to which specialised women's advocacy services are established'.[33] The report stated that 'major deficits' were to be found in the implementation of criminal laws regarding domestic violence, 'both in factors that discourage reporting and in high attrition rates for reported violations'.[34] Another major deficit was constituted by 'the failure to co-ordinate criminal sanctions with protective measures that may be founded in civil or administrative law, police law or family law'. The report stated: 'As a result, different segments of the justice

27 At para. 7.
28 At para. 7.
29 Council of Europe, 2006, Directorate of Human Rights, Strasbourg.
30 At p.40.
31 At p.40.
32 At p.7.
33 At p.40.
34 At p.41.

system and policing can act at cross-purposes or contravene each other in their interventions. There is an urgent need for co-ordination.'[35]

Task Force to Combat Violence against Women, including Domestic Violence

In May 2005 the Heads of State and Government of the member states of the Council of Europe decided at their Third Summit, held in Warsaw, to implement a large-scale campaign on the issue of violence against women. Chapter II.4 of the Action Plan adopted during this Summit[36] stated:

> The Council of Europe will take measures to combat violence against women, including domestic violence. It will set up a task force to evaluate progress at national level and establish instruments for quantifying developments at pan-European level with a view to drawing up proposals for action. A pan-European campaign to combat violence against women, including domestic violence, will be prepared and conducted in close co-operation with other European and national actors, including NGOs.

A Task Force to Combat Violence against Women, including Domestic Violence, was subsequently established in early 2006. The aims of this body were to evaluate the effectiveness of the measures for preventing and combating violence against women that had been adopted at national and international level; to make proposals for the revision of these measures or for the adoption of new measures; to develop a method of assisting member states in adopting practical policies for combating violence against women; to assess the results of the monitoring framework which aimed to evaluate progress in the implementation of Recommendation Rec(2002)5 on the protection of women against violence; to further identify possible roles of men in the context of family violence, not just as perpetrators of violence but as victims, as well as their role in both preventing violence within the family and protecting victims of such violence; and to prepare a blueprint for the Council of Europe campaign and identify the main subjects to be highlighted in preventing and combating violence against women during the campaign as well as the activities to be conducted.[37]

Based on the blueprint developed by the Task Force and approved by the Committee of Ministers on 21 June 2006, the Council of Europe Campaign to Combat Violence against Women, including Domestic Violence, was launched on 27 November 2006 in Madrid. The campaign, which was carried out from 2006

35 At p.41.

36 Available at www.coe.int/t/dcr/summit/20050517_plan_action_en.asp, Council of Europe (accessed 13 October 2016).

37 As stated at www.coe.int/t/dg2/equality/domesticviolencecampaign/Intro_Task_Force_EN.asp, Council of Europe (accessed 13 October 2016).

until 2008, was conducted at the intergovernmental, parliamentary and local levels. Member states were asked to make significant progress in four key aspects: legal and policy measures; support and protection for victims; data collection; and awareness-raising. States were also asked to implement national campaigns to lobby for improved implementation of Recommendation Rec(2002)5 on the protection of women against violence.[38] Essentially, states were invited to assess their national approaches to preventing and combating domestic violence and identify any existing gaps, which should then be filled by appropriate measures. The campaign aimed to spread the messages that combating domestic violence calls for joint public action; that domestic violence is a human rights violation; that domestic violence seriously injures women and damages the whole of society, including future generations; and that domestic violence calls for men's active participation to combat violence against women. During the campaign, the relevant bodies of the Council of Europe carried out a series of regional information and awareness-raising seminars; activities involving national parliaments; and the publication of studies on violence against women. The Council of Europe also provided campaign material which was widely disseminated in member states. More than half of all member states carried out national awareness-raising campaigns, and many others reviewed their policies and legislation or implemented other measures. Many national parliaments placed the issue of domestic violence on their agenda through parliamentary debates, hearings or tabling amendments to the law.[39]

The assessment of national measures to address violence against women which was carried out by the Task Force demonstrated the necessity for harmonised legal standards and the collection of relevant data to ensure that victims across Europe were given the same levels of protection and support. The Task Force therefore recommended in its Final Activity Report, issued in 2008,[40] that the Council of Europe develop a human rights convention to prevent and combat violence against women. The report stated:

> There is a clear need for a European Convention to prevent and combat violence against women and to protect its victims. The Council of Europe has a unique opportunity to lead the process in the preparation of the first European human rights treaty to prevent and combat violence against women.[41]

The report proceeded to comment that with the creation of such a treaty the measures and standards found in Recommendation Rec(2002)5 on the protection

38 Council of Europe, 'Explanatory Report to Council of Europe Convention on preventing and combating violence against women and domestic violence', at para. 11.

39 As stated at www.coe.int/t/dg2/equality/domesticviolencecampaign/Fact_Sheet_en.asp, Council of Europe (accessed 13 October 2016).

40 EG-TFV (2008) 6, available at www.coe.int/t/dg2/equality/domesticviolencecampaign/Source/Final_Activity_Report.pdf, Council of Europe (accessed 13 October 2016).

41 At p.79.

of women against violence would become legally binding for states parties to the Convention. The report pointed out that the European Convention on Human Rights is a general human rights treaty and does not provide for specific protection to female victims of gender-based violence. Mention was made of the Inter-American Convention on the Prevention, Punishment, and Eradication of Violence against Women (Convention of Belém do Pará), and it was stated that '[t]he fact that this is the most widely ratified convention within the Inter-American system demonstrates the strong political will to set common legally binding standards in this field'.[42] The report also referred to the call for the protection of women from violence in both private and public life that is found in the Protocol to the African Charter on Human and Peoples' Rights on the Rights of Women in Africa (Maputo Protocol), as a form of protection of the right to life, integrity and security of the person. The Task Force's report stated that 'it could be considered that the agreement among Council of Europe member states to prepare a new legally binding human rights instrument will demonstrate their strong commitment to eradicating violence against women'.[43]

The Task Force 'strongly recommended that a future Council of Europe Convention to prevent and combat violence against women should be a human rights instrument containing justiciable rights in relation to the protection of the rights of victims'.[44] The report therefore stated:

> Any future Council of Europe legally binding instrument to combat violence against women should be a comprehensive human rights treaty and its paramount objectives should be the prevention of gender-based violence, the protection of victims and the prosecution of the perpetrators.[45]

As regards the underlying principle of such a convention, the report stated:

> It is important to recognize the gendered nature of the phenomenon of domestic violence and the structural causes of violence against women. Women are disproportionately subjected to many forms of violence and they are subjected to this violence because they are women . . . This gender-based violence is a human rights violation which results from an imbalance of power between women and men and is an obstacle to achieving gender equality.[46]

The Task Force was of the view that such an instrument should comprise all forms of gender-based violence perpetrated against women throughout their lifetimes, and should therefore include girls, as '[r]estricting its application to women who

42 At p.79.
43 At p.79.
44 At p.79.
45 At p.79.
46 At p.79.

have reached the age of majority would limit the scope and effectiveness of such an instrument'.[47] The report stated that a convention should encompass *inter alia* physical violence, sexual violence and psychological violence. The Task Force also highlighted the fact that the definition of violence against women used in the Maputo Protocol[48] covered not only all acts causing physical, sexual and psychological harm, but also economic harm, and that this definition therefore went beyond the scope of violence against women encompassed by General Recommendation No. 19 of the Committee on the Elimination of Discrimination against Women (CEDAW Committee)[49] or the Convention of Belém do Pará.[50] According to the Task Force, a future convention should encompass the prevention of violence, the protection of victims and the punishment of perpetrators, and should contain a comprehensive set of measures covering these three areas.

In relation to the monitoring mechanism to be attached to a future convention, the report stated:

> It is generally recognised that the effectiveness of international instruments can be measured by the effectiveness of their monitoring mechanism. Therefore any future convention should be equipped with an effective and independent monitoring mechanism . . . The monitoring body of such a convention should be composed of independent and highly qualified experts capable of monitoring implementation of the obligations contained therein.[51]

The Task Force was of the view that in determining the composition and competences of such a monitoring mechanism, it would be appropriate to examine existing human rights treaty bodies or monitoring mechanisms such as the monitoring mechanism of the Council of Europe Convention on Action against Trafficking in Human Beings, the CEDAW Committee and the Mechanism to Follow Up on the Implementation of the Convention of Belém do Pará.[52]

The report stated that the group in charge of drafting such a human rights instrument should be multidisciplinary and should encompass experts with professional experience in violence against women, gender equality, human rights, criminal law and civil law, including experts from non-governmental organisations. The Task Force therefore proposed that a new ad hoc committee be established to encompass such expertise. In December 2008 the Committee of Ministers of the Council of Europe subsequently established an Ad Hoc

47 At p.80.
48 At Article 1(b) of the Maputo Protocol.
49 Committee on the Elimination of Discrimination against Women, U.N. Doc A/47/38 (1992), at para. 6.
50 At Article 1 of the Convention of Belém do Pará.
51 EG-TFV (2008) 6, at p.80.
52 This follow-up mechanism to the Convention of Belém do Pará, known as MESECVI, was created in 2004. For further information on MESECVI, see www.oas.org/en/mesecvi/about.asp, Organization of American States (accessed 13 October 2016).

Committee on Preventing and Combating Violence against Women and Domestic Violence (abbreviated to 'CAHVIO'). The Committee's mandate was to prepare a legally binding instrument 'to prevent and combat domestic violence including specific forms of violence against women, other forms of violence against women, and to protect and support the victims of such violence as well as prosecute the perpetrators'.[53] The Committee began negotiations on a Convention on Preventing and Combating Violence against Women and Domestic Violence, and published an Interim Report on 27 May 2009.[54] This report made it abundantly clear that a future convention should be placed very much within a human rights framework, and stated:

> In opting for a convention on the elimination of violence against women with, if appropriate, possible additional legally binding instruments, including protocols, the Committee places the future convention squarely within the wider context of achieving substantive equality between women and men and the full enjoyment of human rights by women. In line with other existing legal instruments and declarations, the Committee considers violence against women a human rights violation and an obstacle in achieving full equality between women and men. Recognising the fact that violence against women is the result of an imbalance of power between women and men, the purpose of the convention is thus to guarantee the full enjoyment of women's human rights such as the right to life, the right to liberty and security of the person, and the right to health. Consequently, the provisions of the future convention will put into effect the obligation of the state to prevent violence against women, protect victims of such violence and investigate and appropriately sanction all acts of violence against women – the due diligence standard now widely accepted in international human rights law.[55]

In the report, the Committee addressed a number of issues surrounding the coverage of a future convention with regards to gender. For example, the report stated:

> The Committee is of the opinion that the focus of the future convention should be on the elimination of violence against women. Furthermore, the future convention should deal with domestic violence which affects women disproportionately. The convention should also allow for the application of its provisions to all victims of domestic violence.[56]

53 Council of Europe, 'Explanatory Report to Council of Europe Convention on preventing and combating violence against women and domestic violence', at para. 19.

54 Ad Hoc Committee on Preventing and Combating Violence against Women and Domestic Violence Interim Report (2009) 4 FIN.

55 At para. IIB(8).

56 At para. IIA(6).

The report went on to state:

> The Committee has agreed that the gender dimension should be duly taken into account in the convention. It agreed to identify the ways in which to integrate the gender dimension in the provisions of the convention, notably in relation to the prevention of violence and the protection of victims, while always taking into consideration the different aspects of the instrument and the requirements, as far as possible of gender neutral criminal provisions.[57]

It also stated:

> The Committee recognised that violence against women is a manifestation of historically unequal power relations between men and women, which have led to domination over and discrimination against women by men. This violence is thus both a cause and a consequence of the inequality between women and men, linked to a certain perception of their roles in the family and in society.[58]

The report outlined the types of measures that the Committee believed should be encompassed in a future convention on violence against women, all of which are included in the Istanbul Convention itself. The provisions of the Convention are discussed in Chapter 4 of this book. With regard to monitoring mechanisms, the Committee stated in its interim report that it was of the view that 'a strong, independent and adequately resourced monitoring mechanism is needed to assess states' willingness to efficiently implement the provisions contained in the future instrument(s) and identify good practices in order to assist states to implement the obligations of the convention'.

The monitoring mechanisms that were eventually included in the Istanbul Convention will be discussed in detail in Chapter 5.

Following the publication of this report, the Committee began its drafting work on a convention, and carried this out during a number of subsequent meetings which took place in November 2009, March 2010, June 2010 and October 2010. Between one and four government representatives from each of the Council of Europe member states took part in these meetings. In addition, the Committee included many observers, such as representatives from non-governmental organisations and representatives from other organisations, in particular the European Union. Various steering committees and bodies of the Council of Europe, such as the Commissioner for Human Rights and the Congress of Local and Regional Authorities were also represented. The drafting process was closely monitored by the Parliamentary Assembly, which actively contributed to the negotiations on

57 At para. IIB(9).
58 At para. IIB(10).

the text. In May 2010 the Committee published an information leaflet entitled 'The Council of Europe – Working towards a convention on preventing and combating violence against women and domestic violence'. In this leaflet the Committee stated: 'The future convention will fill a significant gap in human rights protection for women and will also extend its protection to male victims of domestic violence.' It also stated:

> The work on the future convention demonstrates that international consensus on the importance of preventing and combating violence against women is growing the world over. It ties in with efforts in Europe and other regions of the world to remove inequalities between women and men and enhance the protection of the human rights of women.

Interestingly, although this publication stated that the Convention would enter into force following the ratification or accession of five parties, it was subsequently decided that the finalised instrument would not enter into force until it had been ratified by ten parties.

The text of the draft convention was approved by CAHVIO in December 2010, and was then transmitted to the Committee of Ministers for submission to the Parliamentary Assembly. The Assembly gave its opinion on 11 March 2011, and the finalised document was adopted by the Committee of Ministers on 7 April 2011.

European Committee on Crime Problems (CDPC) feasibility study regarding a convention on domestic violence

Given the specific focus of this book on domestic violence in the context of the Istanbul Convention, it is noteworthy that there was some debate regarding the merits of a convention focusing solely on domestic violence. In October 2006 the European Ministers of Justice decided during their 27th Conference, held in Yerevan in Armenia, to assess the need for a Council of Europe legal instrument on domestic violence, noting that such violence can be based on discriminatory prejudices in terms of inequalities resulting from gender and economic dependency.[59] The European Committee on Crime Problems (CDPC) carried out a feasibility study regarding a convention on domestic violence, the report of which was published on 12 June 2007.[60] As domestic violence is the aspect of violence against women that is focused on specifically by this book, it is worth examining this report in some detail. The report recommended that 'the effort to curb domestic violence would benefit from a comprehensive form of

59 Council of Europe, 'Explanatory Report to Council of Europe Convention on preventing and combating violence against women and domestic violence', at para. 15.

60 European Committee on Crime Problems, 'Feasibility study for a convention against domestic violence', 12 June 2007, Council of Europe, Strasbourg, CDPC (2007)09 rev.

international legislation encompassing both criminal and non-criminal dimensions and solutions (which) would serve as a general framework and reference point for the Council of Europe member states'.[61]

The recommendations of this report related to a convention to address domestic violence only, as opposed to a convention on violence against women generally including domestic violence, such as the Istanbul Convention. Nevertheless, a number of the recommendations made in this report are very relevant to the provisions on domestic violence which became part of the Istanbul Convention. For example, in relation to defining domestic violence, the report stated that its focus was on 'interpersonal partner – or ex-partner – related violence in male–female relationships',[62] as opposed to violence taking place in the home more generally. The focus would not therefore be upon, for example, violence against children. The reason given for this approach was that the dynamics underpinning various forms of abuse taking place in the home differ greatly. In particular, the forms of violence differ in respect of gender. There is no clear correlation with gender as regards abuse against children, or against parents or grandparents. However, the report asserted that domestic violence between adults is distinctly gendered. According to the report:

> It disproportionately victimises women more than men, whilst men are over-represented as perpetrators. It is also strongly related to socially determined power differentials between men and women. Although the debate resurfaces now and then about the reliability of prevalence data on women's physical abuse of male partners, the leading researchers and policymakers increasingly agree that such violence, however prevalent, is far *less serious* on average than partner violence against women. Equally if not more important, violent abuse of men by a female partner is not known to continue systematically after separation, in contrast to partner violence against women. A substantial proportion of the latter (stalking or outright physical violence by the ex-partner) is perpetrated during separation and continues thereafter, particularly when the break was initiated by the victim. That period also carries the highest risk of *lethal* violence for the (female) victim, and to a lesser extent for the male perpetrator as well.[63]

This focus on domestic violence as inter-partner violence perpetrated by men against women is replicated in the Istanbul Convention itself, as will be seen from the discussion in Chapter 4 of this book. The Istanbul Convention is primarily an instrument that addresses violence against women, including domestic violence, and therefore the model of domestic violence focused on by the Convention is very much that of inter-partner violence perpetrated by men against women.

61 At p.3.
62 At p.5.
63 At p.4, original italics.

As will be seen in Chapter 4, although the Convention encourages states parties to apply its provisions on domestic violence to male victims as well as to female victims, the focus remains essentially on the prevention of violence against women, encompassing *inter alia* such violence that takes place in the home.

One of the issues considered by the CDPC report was how a convention on domestic violence would operate relative to the various international instruments in this area, as outlined in the previous chapter of this book. As discussed in Chapter 2, a large number of statements and recommendations have been made by various UN bodies on the issue of domestic violence. However, technically these documents are not legally binding on states. The Convention on the Elimination of All Forms of Discrimination against Women (CEDAW)[64] itself is of course a legally binding treaty; however, the difficulty is that CEDAW contains no express mention of violence against women, let alone domestic violence more specifically. This may have been due to the fact that CEDAW was drafted in the 1970s, at a time when violence against women was not recognised as being an issue falling within the scope of international human rights law. As discussed in Chapter 2, during this time domestic violence was barely even recognised as being an issue that required the intervention of any form of law. If violence against women had been expressly included in CEDAW, this may well have jeopardised the acceptance of this treaty by many states. However, domestic violence has now been recognised as an issue falling within the ambit of international human rights law, as demonstrated by the proliferation of statements and recommendations made by the UN bodies on this matter. There have indeed been calls for the adoption of a UN treaty on violence against women in order to place such recommendations on a firm legally binding footing, as will be discussed briefly in Chapter 7 of this book. In relation to the existing UN documents, the CDPC report stated:

> On the one hand, it is important not to underestimate the value of the existing international recommendations and resolutions which address domestic violence indirectly and sometimes directly. Recommendations often have a powerful moral force, as well as giving practical guidance to member states in their conduct. Such instruments are valuable because they are recognised and accepted by a large number of states and, even without legally binding effect, they may be seen as declaratory of broadly accepted goals and principles within the international community . . . Hence, even though soft law norms may lack formal legal consequences, states still often aspire to comply with them.[65]

64 CEDAW (1249 U.N.T.S. 13) was adopted by the UN General Assembly on 18 December 1979 and entered into force on 3 September 1981.

65 European Committee on Crime Problems, 'Feasibility study for a convention against domestic violence', 12 June 2007, Council of Europe, Strasbourg, CDPC (2007)09 rev, at p.10.

The report also went on to state: 'Adopting legally binding documents does not automatically induce countries to adapt their national legislation, create the necessary infrastructures to effectuate those rights, or enforce compliance.'[66] This is of course very true, as evidenced by the substantial difficulties in relation to implementation and enforcement that surround all of the UN human rights treaties, and which will be discussed further in Chapter 6.

Nevertheless, despite these considerations, the CDPC report put forward four arguments to support the development of a legally binding instrument on domestic violence within the context of the Council of Europe. The first of these arguments was that no international legally binding document exists that deals with penal and non-penal aspects of domestic violence in a comprehensive and specific manner. The report highlighted the somewhat fragmented and highly divergent approaches taken towards the issue of domestic violence by the member states of the Council of Europe, and asserted that a convention could serve to promote uniformity.[67] The second argument put forward by the report was that increased migration in member states had brought 'specific vulnerabilities into the foreground which involve[d] the violent victimisation of women',[68] and that there had been an increase in forced marriages and so-called 'honour killings' in some ethnic minority communities. The report stated: 'In the context of the ongoing debate on cultural diversity in relation to political unity, it is crucial to establish regulation which allows for cultural differences without jeopardizing the protection of victims of domestic violence.'[69]

Third, it was asserted by the report that the adoption of a convention on domestic violence by the Council of Europe would 'imply an unequivocal recognition of the rights of domestic violence victims'.[70] Essentially:

> The social and psychological empowerment that could emanate from such a measure must not be underestimated, given the scope of the problem. In view of the specific characteristics of the violence and the special types of legal and social measures that are necessary to effectively address this specifically domestic form of victimization, a specific instrument to support victims of domestic violence would be of added benefit above and beyond general instruments in support of victims and victim rights.[71]

The fourth argument put forward by the report in support of a convention on domestic violence was that such an instrument would enable the creation of a monitoring mechanism which could play a vital role in the promotion of

66 At p.10.
67 At p.11.
68 At p.11.
69 At p.11.
70 At p.11.
71 At p.11.

implementation and compliance. According to the report, 'A supervisory body of independent experts will be needed which can employ a set of robust monitoring methods.'[72] Such a monitoring mechanism was indeed included in the Istanbul Convention, and will be discussed in Chapter 5 of this book. It should be noted, however, that the effectiveness of treaty monitoring bodies of this nature is a matter which is somewhat open to debate. As stated above, there are major implementation problems surrounding all of the UN human rights treaties, instruments that generally rely on a reporting mechanism as their main monitoring measure. Further discussion of these difficulties can be found in Chapter 6.

The CDPC report also commented:

> In accordance with its human rights-based approach, a Council of Europe convention on domestic violence would provide a link to the European Convention on Human Rights by placing a positive obligation on each party to protect its citizens against these particular human rights violations (notably, of the right to respect for private and family life, the right to liberty and security, and the torture prohibition).[73]

It is notable that the CDPC report was published prior to the development of the case law of the European Court of Human Rights on domestic violence. Such positive obligations have now been placed on all member states of the Council of Europe through this body of jurisprudence, which is discussed later in this chapter. It is noteworthy, however, that the positive duties that have been placed upon states by this case law are largely restricted to ensuring that criminal justice responses to domestic violence are adequate. The European Court has not placed positive obligations on states as regards other aspects of their responses to domestic violence, such as the provision of social support measures to victims. The Istanbul Convention, however, places very detailed duties on states parties to this instrument with regard to matters such as the provision of social support measures to victims and the raising of awareness within society as a whole of issues relating to violence against women. This point will be further discussed in Chapter 6.

According to the CDPC report, a Council of Europe convention on domestic violence could also 'provide a basis for other international instruments', and could act as 'a ready-made model that could inspire developments globally'.[74] It is interesting to note that attention is currently being paid within the international human rights community to the merits of adopting a UN convention on violence against women. These developments will be considered briefly in Chapter 7. The Istanbul Convention is certainly acting as an inspiration and catalyst to such developments, given that this instrument is so comprehensive in its approach, as will be discussed in Chapter 4.

72 At p.11.
73 At pp.11–12.
74 At p.12.

As regards the specific content of a Council of Europe convention on domestic violence, the CDPC report drew attention to the fact that although a minority of states within the Council of Europe had begun to develop action plans on violence against women generally, or on domestic violence specifically, much more needed to be done. According to the report, a convention would constitute an important opportunity to provide guidelines to states on the drawing up of national action plans on domestic violence, which were necessary in order to ensure a multisectoral approach that engages professionals from all the relevant fields. The report stated that a convention on domestic violence should have four main purposes: preventing and combating domestic violence in all its forms; protecting the rights of victims; ensuring sanctions for perpetrators and encouraging the bringing about of behavioural change to prevent recidivism and revictimisation; and promoting international cooperation in combating transnational aspects of domestic violence, such as forced marriages and killings in the name of honour. These four purposes are all found in the Istanbul Convention, as will be discussed further in Chapter 4. According to the CDPC report:

> In establishing the scope of a convention, the starting point is that it should be comprehensive, providing for a complete set of policies to prevent violence, restrain and punish perpetrators, and help the victims by providing both legal assistance and immediate and long-term psychological and social support.[75]

This is certainly the approach taken by the Istanbul Convention, as will be seen in Chapter 4.

Interestingly, the CDPC report states:

> Even though the majority of victims are women, a convention would preferably use gender-neutral terminology. That would not preclude a gender-based analysis of the underlying problem, nor a gender-sensitive implementation of the convention. Furthermore, it would provide the tools to address male victimisation in domestic violence when necessary.[76]

By contrast, this approach differs substantially from that adopted by the Istanbul Convention. As referred to earlier in this chapter, the language of the Convention is certainly not gender-neutral, and this instrument is heavily focused upon a model of domestic violence in which the victim is female and the perpetrator is male. This divergence in approach may be explained by the fact that the focus of the Istanbul Convention is on violence against women, with domestic violence being viewed as one aspect of this phenomenon. The focus of the CDPC report,

75 At p.13.
76 At p.13.

however, was on the perceived need for a convention on domestic violence, of which men can of course be victims.

This raises the question of whether a convention focusing solely on domestic violence would have been advantageous, as compared with a convention in which domestic violence is subsumed within violence against women in a general sense. It is arguable that simply including domestic violence in a convention on violence against women devalues the issue of domestic violence perpetrated against male victims.[77] As noted above, although states are encouraged to apply the provisions of the Istanbul Convention on domestic violence to male victims, the focus remains primarily on the prevention of violence against women, encompassing *inter alia* such violence that takes place in the home. This approach thus leaves male victims with little protection under this instrument. Conversely, however, violence against women in all of its forms constitutes a widespread human rights violation in all states. It would therefore be difficult to argue that the Council of Europe should not have adopted a convention to address violence against women, and an instrument on violence against women that did not include domestic violence would be very strange indeed. The fact that domestic violence is repeatedly separated out from violence against women more generally within the provisions of the Istanbul Convention itself, as demonstrated even by the full title of the Convention (the Council of Europe Convention on Preventing and Combating Violence against Women and Domestic Violence), has indeed met with criticism (as will be discussed in Chapter 4). It is extremely probable therefore that the adoption of two completely separate conventions – an instrument on forms of violence against women apart from domestic violence and a gender-neutral instrument on domestic violence – would have been severely criticised and would in fact have been very unlikely to have survived the drafting process.

An alternative option may have been to have formulated an instrument on violence against women which would also include domestic violence when the victims are women, and an additional, gender-neutral, instrument on domestic violence. Two conventions incorporating the issue of domestic violence would, however, have the potential to prove to be very unwieldy and difficult to operate in practice, particularly if the duties that each instrument placed on states as regards domestic violence differed. Such an approach would also create an additional burden for states as it might entail presenting reports to two monitoring bodies, instead of one. The other option would have been to have included domestic violence against male victims within the scope of the Istanbul Convention in exactly the same manner as domestic violence against female victims. This would have been a more workable approach, but this too gives rise to difficulties. It is arguable that the social dynamics relating to domestic violence when men are

77 For discussion of domestic violence against men, see, for example, Martin L., 'Debates of Difference: Male Victims of Domestic Violence and Abuse', in S. Hilder and V. Bettinson (eds), *Domestic Violence: Interdisciplinary Perspectives on Protection, Prevention and Intervention*, 2016, Palgrave Macmillan, London, 181–201.

the victims differ significantly from the dynamics involved when men are the perpetrators and women are the victims, and that situations involving the latter tend to be linked much more to the concepts of power and control that are relevant to gender-based violence more generally. It appears that including domestic violence against men in the Istanbul Convention in precisely the same manner as domestic violence against women and other forms of gender-based violence may therefore also have proven to be problematic. It seems fair to say, however, that one of the reasons why domestic violence is repeatedly separated out from violence against women more generally in the terminology used in the Istanbul Convention is the fact that attention had previously been paid to the issue of the adoption of a convention on domestic violence only, as evidenced by the CDPC report.

The definition of domestic violence used in the CDPC report was 'any act of violence between partners or ex-partners which results in (or is likely to result in) physical, sexual or psychological harm or suffering, including threats of such acts, coercion, or arbitrary deprivation of liberty'.[78] This includes 'physical and mental aggression, emotional and psychological abuse and sexual violence'.[79] As will be discussed in Chapter 4, under Article 3(b) of the Istanbul Convention, 'domestic violence' is defined as meaning 'all acts of physical, sexual, psychological or economic violence that occur within the family or domestic unit or between former or current spouses or partners, whether or not the perpetrator shares or has shared the same residence with the victim'. The definition of domestic violence incorporated in the Istanbul Convention is therefore broadly similar to that used by the CDPC report, with the important addition of 'economic violence'. The fact that this form of abuse is included in the Istanbul Convention, but not in the definition of domestic violence used in the CDPC report, may simply be evidence of an increased understanding of domestic violence developing even in the four-year period between the publication of the CDPC report in 2007 and the adoption of the Istanbul Convention by the Council of Europe in 2011. As Mullender and Morley comment, 'Although we normally think of domestic violence as physical, commonly the physical is but one aspect of a pattern of abuse which also includes sexual, emotional, and material abuses.'[80]

According to the CDPC report, a Council of Europe convention on domestic violence should place duties on states to:

> [e]nsure that criminal law provides that any act of physical or sexual violence against spouses, ex-spouses, regular or occasional partners or cohabitants

78 European Committee on Crime Problems, 'Feasibility study for a convention against domestic violence', 12 June 2007, Council of Europe, Strasbourg, CDPC (2007)09 rev, at p.13.

79 At p.13.

80 Mullender A. and Morley R., 'Context and Content of a New Agenda', in A. Mullender and R. Morley (eds), *Children Living with Domestic Violence*, 1994, Whiting & Birch, London, 2–16 at 6.

> constitutes a violation of that person's physical, psychological and/or sexual freedom and integrity, and not solely a violation of morality, honour or decency.[81]

Sexual violence and psychological violence should be penalised, and it should be ensured that 'cultural and/or religious traditions justifying violence against or the killing of a family member, particularly women, cannot be accepted as mitigating circumstances or so-called cultural defences'.[82] The criminal laws of states should also provide options for the treatment of perpetrators of domestic violence as part of legally based sanctioning regimes. Essentially, it was deemed necessary that 'an eventual convention on domestic violence call for appropriate measures and sanctions in national legislation, thus enabling swift, effective action to restrain perpetrators and to redress the wrongs done to victims'.[83] This should entail affording victims of domestic violence the right to respect and recognition at all stages of the criminal proceedings; the right to receive information about the progress of the case; the right to provide information to officials responsible for decisions relating to the offender; the right to have legal counsel available, regardless of the means of the victim; the right to protection of victims' privacy and their physical safety; the right to compensation from the offender and the state for any pecuniary, physical, psychological, moral and social damage suffered; and the right to receive victim support. Training on the issues involved in domestic violence should be given to police, prosecutors and members of the judiciary, and adequate advocacy support for victims should also be developed. Cases involving domestic violence should be systematically recorded by police forces. The report also stated that international cooperation in investigations was particularly important in cases of forced marriages and so-called honour killings.

As regards the civil law, the report stated that judicial protection orders for victims of domestic violence should be available in national legal systems. Provision should therefore be made for allowing victims to have the perpetrator temporarily barred from the premises shared by the victim and perpetrator; for allowing protection of a victim's privacy (such as through protection orders and non-contact orders); and for taking the victim's and the children's safety into full consideration in deciding on custody and visiting arrangements following divorce or separation. According to the report, a convention on domestic violence should also contain provisions relating to the implementation of awareness-raising campaigns regarding domestic violence, to provide information to victims and also to educate the wider social community. Information on domestic violence should be incorporated into the curriculum in both primary and secondary

81 European Committee on Crime Problems, 'Feasibility study for a convention against domestic violence', 12 June 2007, Council of Europe, Strasbourg, CDPC (2007)09 rev, at p.14.

82 At p.14.

83 At p.14.

schools. With regard to social support measures for victims, states should provide shelters, telephone helplines and support for children who have been traumatised by witnessing the abuse. In addition to criminal justice-based treatment programmes, the report stated that perpetrators of domestic violence should also be offered treatment programmes that they can attend on a voluntary basis. As will be seen in the discussion in Chapter 4, provisions concerning all of these matters are now found in the Istanbul Convention.

The CDPC report also stated that even though the opinions put forward by the monitoring body of a Council of Europe convention on domestic violence may be non-binding, they could nevertheless be used by other bodies such as the European Court of Human Rights in future case law.[84] It will indeed be interesting to observe how the European Court of Human Rights will make use of the statements and opinions of the monitoring body of the Istanbul Convention in its future jurisprudence concerning domestic violence.

Case law of the European Court of Human Rights on domestic violence

In an explanatory document produced by the Council of Europe, it is stated that 'the drafting process [of the Istanbul Convention was] inspired by case-law from the European Court of Human Rights and jurisprudence of the United Nations Committee on the Elimination of Discrimination against Women on violence against women'.[85] Until 2007 domestic violence had not been directly addressed substantively by the European Court of Human Rights. However, since 2007 the Court has directly addressed this issue in a series of cases involving violence against women in the home. These cases are *Kontrova v Slovakia*;[86] *Bevacqua and S v Bulgaria*;[87] *Branko Tomasic and Others v Croatia*;[88] *Opuz v Turkey*;[89] *E.S. and Others v Slovakia*;[90] *A v Croatia*;[91] *Hajduova v Slovakia*;[92] *Kalucza v Hungary*;[93] *E.M. v Romania*;[94] *Valiuliene v Lithuania*;[95] *Eremia and Others v the Republic of Moldova*;[96] *B. v the Republic of Moldova*;[97] *Mudric v*

84 At p.16.
85 Council of Europe, 'Working towards a Convention on preventing and combating violence against women and domestic violence.'
86 App. no. 7510/04, 31 May 2007.
87 App. no. 71127/01, 12 June 2008.
88 App. no. 46598/06, 15 January 2009.
89 App. no. 33401/02, 9 June 2009.
90 App. no. 8227/04, 15 September 2009.
91 App. no. 55164/08, 14 October 2010.
92 App. no. 2660/03, 30 November 2010.
93 App. no. 57693/10, 24 April 2012.
94 App. no. 43994/05, 30 October 2012.
95 App. no. 33234/07, 26 March 2013.
96 App. no. 3564/11, 28 May 2013.
97 App. no. 61382/09, 16 July 2013.

the Republic of Moldova;[98] *N.A. v the Republic of Moldova*;[99] *T.M. and C.M. v the Republic of Moldova*;[100] *Rumor v Italy*;[101] *Civek v Turkey*;[102] *M.G. v Turkey*;[103] and *Halime Kılıç v Turkey*.[104] Violations of the European Convention on Human Rights were found in all of these cases, with the exception of *Rumor v Italy*. It has thus now been established that domestic violence can breach the right to life, as found in Article 2; the right to be free from torture and from inhuman or degrading treatment, as enshrined in Article 3; the right to respect for one's private and family life (which has been held to encompass bodily integrity),[105] as found in Article 8; and the Article 14 equality provision.

It certainly seems likely that the very important developments in both the case law of the European Court of Human Rights and the jurisprudence of the CEDAW Committee exerted a heavy influence on the process of formulating the Istanbul Convention. Indeed, it is noteworthy that Article 21 of the Convention provides that 'Parties shall ensure that victims have information on and access to applicable regional and international individual/collective complaints mechanisms'. Such complaints mechanisms include both taking a case before the European Court of Human Rights and submitting a complaint to the CEDAW Committee.

As domestic violence appears to constitute a clear violation of four articles of the European Convention on Human Rights, it is rather surprising that until 2007 domestic violence had not been directly addressed substantively by the European Court. Up until that point there had only been one admissibility decision of the European Commission of Human Rights which dealt with this issue. *Myszk v Poland*[106] involved an applicant who had attempted to commit suicide. After she left hospital, she moved in with her mother. Her two children remained with her husband in the family home, and she sought access to them. Although access was granted by the national courts, the applicant's husband nevertheless consistently refused to abide by the orders that had been made. The applicant argued that the state's response to her situation was insufficient to protect her rights. One of her submissions was that her husband was violent and that her family needed regular therapy. She argued that the state did not provide effective prevention programmes in relation to domestic violence, and that this constituted a violation of her Article 8 right to respect for her private and family life. The applicant also

98 App. no. 74839/10, 16 July 2013.
99 App. no. 13424/06, 24 September 2013.
100 App. no. 26608/11, 28 January 2014.
101 App. no. 72964/10, 27 May 2014.
102 App. no. 55354/11, 23 February 2016.
103 App. no. 646/10, 22 March 2016.
104 App. no. 63034/11, 28 June 2016.
105 See, for example, *Y.F. v Turkey*, app. no. 24209/94, 22 July 2003.
106 App. no. 28244/95, 1 July 1998.

claimed that the domestic courts did not treat domestic violence as seriously as they should. In response, the Commission stated:

> [T]he notion of 'respect' enshrined in Article 8 is not clear-cut. Especially where the positive obligations implicit in that concept are concerned, its requirements will vary considerably from case to case according to the practices followed and the situations obtaining in the Contracting States.

The Commission noted that the applicant complained that the state did not provide an adequate framework for families experiencing difficulties to obtain family counselling. However, the applicant had not specified the precise nature of the problems in question, except for the fact that her husband tended to be violent. She also had not stated if she had attempted to obtain counselling. The Commission commented that 'the positive obligations of the State inherent in an effective "respect" for family life within the meaning of Article 8 of the Convention do not encompass an obligation to provide ex officio effective family counselling to families with problems'. The Commission therefore decided that this part of the application was manifestly ill-founded. The application was thus held to be inadmissible due to the lack of information provided by the applicant.

However, in 2007 the European Court directly and substantively addressed the issue of domestic violence for the first time in *Kontrova v Slovakia*.[107] In this case the applicant had been subjected to domestic violence by her husband, who had then killed himself and their two children. The applicant alleged that the police had failed to take appropriate action to protect her children's lives under Article 2 of the European Convention on Human Rights, and also her own private and family life under Article 8 of the Convention, despite knowing of her husband's abusive behaviour.

In examining the case under Article 2, the European Court stated that this provision:

> enjoins the State not only to refrain from the intentional and unlawful taking of life, but also to take appropriate steps to safeguard the lives of those within its jurisdiction . . . It also extends in appropriate circumstances to a positive obligation on the authorities to take preventive operational measures to protect an individual whose life is at risk from the criminal acts of another individual.[108]

However, the Court went on to comment:

> Bearing in mind the difficulties in policing modern societies, the unpredictability of human conduct and the operational choices which must be made

107 App. no. 7510/04, 31 May 2007.
108 At para. 49.

> in terms of priorities and resources, the scope of the positive obligation must be interpreted in a way which does not impose an impossible or disproportionate burden on the authorities. Not every claimed risk to life, therefore, can entail for the authorities a Convention requirement to take operational measures to prevent that risk from materialising. For a positive obligation to arise, it must be established that the authorities knew or ought to have known at the time of the existence of a real and immediate risk to the life of an identified individual from the criminal acts of a third party and that they failed to take measures within the scope of their powers which, judged reasonably, might have been expected to avoid that risk.[109]

In applying these principles to the case in question, the Court observed that the situation in the applicant's family had been known to the local police department. Under national law in Slovakia, the police had various specific duties, such as accepting and registering the applicant's complaint, launching a criminal investigation and commencing proceedings against the applicant's husband immediately. However, they had failed to comply with any of these obligations. The Court held therefore that there had been a violation of Article 2 in respect of the deaths of the applicant's two children.

Although the applicant had additionally alleged that the violation of Article 2 constituted a violation of her own right to respect for private and family life under Article 8, the Court nevertheless held that in the light of the finding of a violation of Article 2 it was unnecessary to examine the case under Article 8 also. In this instance therefore, although the Court found a breach of the Convention in a situation involving domestic violence, it should be noted that the violation was found in relation to the right to life of the children. The abuse suffered by the applicant herself was not directly addressed. However, the following year another case involving domestic violence came before the Court – that of *Bevacqua and S v Bulgaria*.[110] In this case the Court held that there had been a violation of Article 8 of the Convention, in respect of the actual abuse suffered by a victim of domestic violence due to failures of the Bulgarian criminal justice system to provide sufficient protection.

In 2009 the European Court considered the case of *Branko Tomasic and Others v Croatia*,[111] in which an individual referred to in the Court's judgment as M.M. had killed himself, his wife (referred to in the judgment as M.T.) and their daughter (referred to as V.T.), after having made numerous threats to do so. The applicants in the case were the wife's parents and siblings. They alleged that the state was in violation of Article 2 of the Convention, due to a failure to comply with its positive obligations in order to prevent the deaths of M.T. and V.T., and also due to a failure to conduct a thorough investigation into the

109 At para. 50.
110 App. no. 71127/01, 12 June 2008.
111 App. no. 46598/06, 15 January 2009.

possible responsibility of agents of the state for the deaths of M.T. and V.T. The Court found that the relevant domestic authorities had failed to take all necessary and reasonable steps in the circumstances of the present case to afford protection to the lives of M.T. and V.T. There had therefore been a violation of Article 2. However, the Court stated that having found a breach of the substantive aspect of Article 2, it was unnecessary to examine the case under the procedural aspect. Also in 2009, the European Court considered the very important case of *Opuz v Turkey*,[112] which is perhaps the best-known and most frequently cited of the Court's cases on the issue of domestic violence. In this case the applicant alleged that the authorities had failed to protect her and her mother from domestic violence on the part of the applicant's husband, which had resulted in the death of her mother and her own ill-treatment. She complained that the authorities had failed to safeguard the right to life of her mother under Article 2 of the Convention. In examining this argument, the Court stated that 'the legislative framework then in force . . . fell short of the requirements inherent in the State's positive obligations to establish and apply effectively a system punishing all forms of domestic violence and providing sufficient safeguards for the victims'.[113] The Court also stated:

> [I]n the light of the State's positive obligation to take preventive operational measures to protect an individual whose life is at risk, it might have been expected that the authorities, faced with a suspect known to have a criminal record of perpetrating violent attacks, would take special measures consonant with the gravity of the situation with a view to protecting the applicant's mother.[114]

However, the authorities failed to take such measures. The Court therefore concluded that 'the national authorities cannot be considered to have displayed due diligence',[115] and that they had therefore failed to fulfil their positive obligations to protect the right to life of the applicant's mother under Article 2. The Court held that:

> The criminal law system, as applied in the instant case, did not have an adequate deterrent effect capable of ensuring the effective prevention of the unlawful acts committed by [the applicant's husband]. The obstacles resulting from the legislation and failure to use the means available undermined the deterrent effect of the judicial system in place and the role it was required to play in preventing a violation of the applicant's mother's right to life as enshrined in Article 2 of the Convention.[116]

112 App. no. 33401/02, 9 June 2009.
113 At para. 145.
114 At para. 148.
115 At para. 149.
116 At para. 153.

The applicant also argued that although she had been subjected to violence, injury and death threats, the authorities had been negligent towards her situation, which caused her pain and fear in violation of Article 3 of the Convention. She alleged that the injuries she had suffered amounted to torture within the meaning of Article 3. The Court held that the violence suffered was sufficiently serious to amount to ill-treatment within the meaning of Article 3, although it did not state whether it amounted to torture, as opposed to inhuman or degrading treatment. The Court was of the view that it could not be said that the local authorities 'displayed the required diligence to prevent the recurrence of violent attacks against the applicant, since the applicant's husband perpetrated them without hindrance and with impunity to the detriment of the rights recognised by the Convention'.[117] Indeed, 'the response to the conduct of the applicant's former husband was manifestly inadequate to the gravity of the offences in question'.[118] The Court thus held that there had been a violation of Article 3 'as a result of the State authorities' failure to take protective measures in the form of effective deterrence against serious breaches of the applicant's personal integrity by her husband'.[119] This case therefore represented another crucial development in the Court's case law in this area, in that it had now established that domestic violence can constitute a violation of Article 3.

In addition, the applicant claimed that she and her mother had been discriminated against on the grounds of their gender, and that there had thus been a violation of Article 14 of the Convention, taken in conjunction with Articles 2 and 3. This argument was also upheld by the Court. The alleged discrimination at issue resulted from the general attitude of the local authorities, such as the manner in which the women were treated at police stations when they reported domestic violence. The applicant demonstrated through statistical data that domestic violence affected mainly women, and established that judicial passivity in Turkey led to a climate that was conducive to domestic violence. The Court therefore stated:

> Bearing in mind . . . that the general and discriminatory judicial passivity in Turkey, albeit unintentional, mainly affected women, the Court considers that the violence suffered by the applicant and her mother may be regarded as gender-based violence which is a form of discrimination against women.[120]

The finding of a violation of Article 14 in a case involving domestic violence again constituted another important milestone in the Court's jurisprudence on domestic violence.[121]

117 At para. 169.
118 At para. 170.
119 At para. 176.
120 At para. 200.
121 For further discussion of *Opuz v Turkey*, see Burton M., 'The Human Rights of Victims of Domestic Violence: *Opuz v Turkey*', (2010) 22 *Child and Family Law Quarterly*, 131–40.

A short time after its judgment in *Opuz v Turkey*, the European Court considered another case involving domestic violence – that of *E.S. and Others v Slovakia*.[122] In this case the applicants were a mother and her three children. All four applicants had suffered abuse from the first applicant's husband, who was the father of the three children. The Court held that the Article 3 and Article 8 rights of all four applicants had been breached due to the failure of the state authorities to protect them in an adequate manner from the treatment to which they had been subjected.

The following year, the Court considered the case of *Hajduova v Slovakia*,[123] in which the applicant's husband had attacked her both physically and verbally. He had also threatened to kill the applicant, as well as several other persons. Criminal proceedings were brought against him and he was subsequently convicted. However, as he was suffering from a severe personality disorder, the court decided not to impose a prison sentence on him and held that he should undergo psychiatric treatment. He was then transported to a hospital, but the required treatment was not implemented, and the domestic court did not order the hospital in question to carry out the treatment. On his release from the hospital, the applicant's husband repeatedly threatened both the applicant and her lawyer. The applicant argued that there had therefore been a violation of her rights under Article 8 of the Convention. In examining the case, the Court stated that although threats following the release of the applicant's husband from hospital did not actually materialise into concrete acts of physical violence, nevertheless, given his history of physical abuse and menacing behaviour, any threats made by him would arouse in the applicant a well-founded fear that they might be carried out. In the Court's opinion, this would be enough to affect the applicant's psychological integrity and well-being to a sufficient extent as to engage Article 8. The Court stated that it was the national authorities' inactivity and failure to ensure that the applicant's husband was detained for psychiatric treatment that enabled him to continue to threaten both the applicant and her lawyer. In addition, 'owing to the particular vulnerability of victims of domestic violence . . . the domestic authorities should have exercised an even greater degree of vigilance in the present case'.[124] There had thus been a violation of the state's positive obligations under Article 8 of the Convention to secure respect for the applicant's private life.

Although only a selection of the European Court's case law on domestic violence has been discussed in this chapter, it is worth noting that violations of

For discussion of *Opuz v Turkey* and also of *Bevacqua and S v Bulgaria*, see Hasselbacher L., 'State Obligations Regarding Domestic Violence: The European Court of Human Rights, Due Diligence, and International Legal Minimums of Protection', (2010) 8 *Northwestern Journal of International Human Rights*, 190–215 at 203–15.

122 App. no. 8227/04, 15 September 2009.

123 App. no. 2660/03, 30 November 2010.

124 At para. 50.

the Convention have also been found in a range of other cases on this issue.[125] It is certainly likely that the earlier part of this jurisprudence exerted a substantial influence on the drafting process of the Istanbul Convention. Overall, it can be seen from these cases that states clearly have positive obligations to ensure that their criminal justice systems are of a certain standard in dealing with domestic violence. These cases undoubtedly constitute an extremely important development in the response of human rights law to this issue. Nevertheless, problems with the case law still remain. These difficulties will be discussed in Chapter 6.[126]

Decisions of the CEDAW Committee on domestic violence

As referred to earlier in this chapter, an explanatory document produced by the Council of Europe stated that the drafting process was also inspired by the jurisprudence of the CEDAW Committee on violence against women.[127] The CEDAW Committee has now dealt substantively with a number of communications on the issue of domestic violence made using the Optional Protocol to CEDAW. The Optional Protocol, which came into force in December 2000, allows individuals or groups of individuals who are victims of any breaches of CEDAW to submit complaints to the Committee. Communications may also be submitted on behalf of individuals with their consent. The first communication involving domestic violence was *AT v Hungary*,[128] in which the views of the CEDAW Committee were adopted in January 2005. Other communications that have been considered by the Committee on this issue are *Goekce v Austria*[129] and *Yildirim v Austria*,[130] in which the views of the Committee were adopted in August 2007;

125 *A v Croatia* (app. no. 55164/08, 14 October 2010); *Kalucza v Hungary* (app. no. 57693/10, 24 April 2012); *E.M. v Romania* (app. no. 43994/05, 30 October 2012); *Valiuliene v Lithuania* (app. no. 33234/07, 26 March 2013); *Eremia and Others v the Republic of Moldova* (app. no. 3564/11, 28 May 2013); *B. v the Republic of Moldova* (app. no. 61382/09, 16 July 2013); *Mudric v the Republic of Moldova* (app. no. 74839/10, 16 July 2013); *N.A. v the Republic of Moldova* (app. no. 13424/06, 24 September 2013); *T.M. and C.M. v the Republic of Moldova* (app. no. 26608/11, 28 January 2014); *Civek v Turkey* (app. no. 55354/11, 23 February 2016); *M.G. v Turkey* (app. no. 646/10, 22 March 2016); and *Halime Kılıç v Turkey* (app. no. 63034/11, 28 June 2016).

126 For further discussion of Articles 3 and 8 of the European Convention on Human Rights in the context of domestic violence, see Choudhry S. and Herring J., 'Righting Domestic Violence', (2006) 20 *International Journal of Law, Policy and the Family*, 95–119. It should, however, be noted that this article was published prior to the development of the jurisprudence of the European Court of Human Rights on domestic violence.

127 Council of Europe, 'Working towards a Convention on preventing and combating violence against women and domestic violence'.

128 Communication No. 2/2003, views adopted 26 January 2005, CEDAW/C/32/D/2/2003.

129 Communication No. 5/2005, views adopted 6 August 2007, CEDAW/C/39/D/5/2005.

130 Communication No. 6/2005, views adopted 6 August 2007, CEDAW/C/39/D/6/2005.

VK v Bulgaria,[131] in which the views of the Committee were adopted in July 2011; and *Jallow v Bulgaria*,[132] in which the views of the Committee were adopted in July 2012. These decisions will be discussed in detail in Chapter 5.

Conclusion

It can be seen that domestic violence has a relatively long history in constituting an issue of concern within the Council of Europe. Attention has been paid to this issue since as far back as 1985 and, more substantively, since the 1990s. These developments then gained added momentum with the adoption in 2002 by the Committee of Ministers of Recommendation Rec(2002)5 on the protection of women against violence. The establishment in 2006 of the Task Force to Combat Violence against Women, including Domestic Violence, constituted another important milestone in this regard, as did the creation in 2008 of the Ad Hoc Committee on Preventing and Combating Violence against Women and Domestic Violence. The 2007 report of the European Committee on Crime Problems (CDPC) concerning its feasibility study regarding a convention on domestic violence was also of immense significance. Chapter 4 will turn to an examination of the provisions of the Istanbul Convention itself.

131 Communication No. 20/2008, views adopted 25 July 2011, CEDAW/C/49/D/20/2008.

132 Communication No. 32/2011, views adopted 23 July 2012, CEDAW/C/52/D/32/2011.

4 The provisions of the Istanbul Convention

The aim of this chapter is to provide a detailed analysis of the text of the Istanbul Convention itself, with a particular focus on the provisions that relate to domestic violence. The chapter will begin by discussing a number of definitional issues. The question of how domestic violence should be defined has no easy answer, and the experience of England and Wales will be discussed briefly in order to illustrate the difficulties that can arise as regards this issue. The approach adopted by the Istanbul Convention to defining domestic violence will then be analysed in detail. Of particular note is the fact that the Convention repeatedly separates out domestic violence from violence against women more generally (for example, the title of the instrument is framed as 'the Convention on Preventing and Combating Violence against Women *and* Domestic Violence') and the possible rationale for such an approach will be examined. The reference within the Convention to the 'due diligence' standard will also be discussed. The substantive obligations placed upon states parties by the Convention in relation to domestic violence will be examined in detail, and comparisons will be drawn with the statements that have been made by other bodies such as the UN Committee on the Elimination of Discrimination against Women (CEDAW Committee), the UN Special Rapporteur on violence against women, its causes and consequences, the UN General Assembly and the European Court of Human Rights in relation to this issue.

As discussed in Chapter 2, the Istanbul Convention is not the first regional instrument to address the issue of violence against women. Almost 17 years prior to the Council of Europe's adoption of this Convention, the Inter-American Convention on the Prevention, Punishment, and Eradication of Violence against Women (the Convention of Belém do Pará) was adopted by the General Assembly of the Organization of American States (OAS). The chapter will therefore compare and contrast the approaches taken by the two Conventions to the issue of domestic violence.[1] In addition, the Protocol to the African Charter on Human

1 Some comparative analysis of the Istanbul Convention and the Convention of Belém do Pará can also be found in McQuigg R., 'A Contextual Analysis of the Council of Europe's

and Peoples' Rights on the Rights of Women in Africa (the Maputo Protocol) was adopted by the African Union in 2003 and entered into force in 2005. The provisions of this Protocol that relate to gender-based violence, including domestic violence, will also be compared with those of the Istanbul Convention.

Definitional issues

Prior to discussing the substantive provisions of the Istanbul Convention that relate to domestic violence, it is necessary to examine the interesting and rather unusual approach that the Convention adopts to the issue of defining domestic violence. The question of how domestic violence should be defined is a difficult and controversial issue. For example, in England and Wales until very recently there was no specific criminal offence relating to domestic abuse. Although an offence of exertion of controlling and coercive behaviour in intimate relationships has now been enacted,[2] the physical aspects of domestic abuse must still be prosecuted under the more general criminal legislation, such as the Offences Against the Person Act 1861. Under this statute, the perpetrator may be held to have committed common assault,[3] aggravated assault,[4] assault occasioning actual bodily harm[5] or grievous bodily harm,[6] or unlawful wounding.[7] However, the lack of a specific offence of domestic violence meant that agencies such as the police and the Crown Prosecution Service (CPS) had to produce their own definitions of domestic violence in order to identify instances in which their emerging policies on this issue should be applied. Government departments also put forward definitions of domestic violence for use with regard to the development of policy.[8] These definitions varied in scope, which could result in confusion. In 2003 the Home Office issued a definition of domestic violence as being '[a]ny violence between current and former partners in an intimate relationship, wherever and whenever the violence occurs. The violence may include physical, emotional and financial abuse.' In 2004 this definition was widened to encompass:

> [a]ny threatening behaviour, violence or abuse between adults who are or have been in a relationship, or between family members. It can affect anybody, regardless of their gender or sexuality. The violence can be psychological,

Convention on Preventing and Combating Violence against Women', (2012) 1 *International Human Rights Law Review*, 367–81.

2 Serious Crime Act 2015, section 76.

3 Offences Against the Person Act 1861, section 42.

4 Section 43.

5 Section 47.

6 Section 18.

7 Section 20.

8 Burton M., *Legal Responses to Domestic Violence*, 2008, Routledge-Cavendish, Abingdon, at p.2.

> physical, sexual or emotional. It can include honour based violence, female genital mutilation, and forced marriage.

This definition was therefore broader than the previous definition in that it included abuse carried out against family members other than current or former partners.

However, on 31 March 2013 a new cross-government definition of domestic violence and abuse, which remains in force at the time of writing, was adopted by the Home Office.[9] Under this definition, 'domestic violence and abuse' is constituted by:

> any incident or pattern of incidents of controlling, coercive, threatening behaviour, violence or abuse between those aged 16 or over who are, or have been, intimate partners or family members regardless of gender or sexuality. The abuse can encompass, but is not limited to psychological, physical, sexual, financial [and] emotional.

It is noteworthy that the phrase 'between those aged 16 or over' is included in this definition. Previously, the definition of domestic violence applied only to adults – that is, those aged 18 or over. In addition, the new definition incorporates the idea of coercive control. 'Controlling behaviour' is defined as:

> a range of acts designed to make a person subordinate and/or dependent by isolating them from sources of support, exploiting their resources and capacities for personal gain, depriving them of the means needed for independence, resistance and escape, and regulating their everyday behaviour.

'Coercive behaviour' is constituted by 'an act or pattern of acts of assault, threats, humiliation, intimidation or other abuse that is used to harm, punish, or frighten their victim. This includes so called "honour" based violence, female genital mutilation (FGM) and forced marriage.'[10]

9 See www.gov.uk/guidance/domestic-violence-and-abuse, UK Government (accessed 14 October 2016).

10 For discussion of the concept of coercive control, see Bettinson V. and Bishop C., 'Is the Creation of a Discrete Offence of Coercive Control Necessary to Combat Domestic Violence?', (2015) 66 *Northern Ireland Legal Quarterly*, 179–97; Kuennen T.L., 'Analyzing the Impact of Coercion on Domestic Violence Victims: How Much is Too Much?', (2007) 22 *Berkeley Journal of Gender, Law and Justice*, 2–30; Stark E., 'Rethinking Coercive Control', (2009) 15 *Violence Against Women*, 1509–25; Hanna C., 'The Paradox of Progress: Translating E. Stark's Coercive Control into Legal Doctrine for Abused Women', (2009) 15 *Violence Against Women*, 1458–76; and Williamson E., 'Living in the World of the Domestic Violence Perpetrator: Negotiating the Unreality of Coercive Control', (2010) 16 *Violence Against Women*, 1412–23.

Nevertheless other agencies such as the CPS have used different definitions of domestic violence. For example, in 2005 the CPS stated that the term 'domestic violence' meant '[a]ny criminal offence arising out of physical, sexual, psychological, emotional or financial abuse by one person against a current or former partner in a close relationship, or against a current or former family member'.[11] This definition was in a sense more limited than the then existing Home Office definition in that the CPS definition focused on criminal offences. Although emotional and financial abuse were encompassed by the CPS definition, these types of abuse were much more difficult to fit into the UK's criminal law system than was physical violence. Nevertheless, the Protection from Harassment Act 1997 could be used in some such cases. This Act contains both criminal law and civil law provisions, and section 1 prohibits any person from engaging in a course of conduct which he knows, or ought reasonably to know, constitutes harassment. Section 7 states that 'harassment' includes alarming or causing distress to a person and may take the form of words or conduct. A 'course of conduct' involves conduct on at least two occasions. In addition, in *R v Ireland and R v Burstow*[12] it was held that a recognisable psychiatric illness could constitute 'bodily harm' for the purposes of sections 18, 20 and 47 of the Offences Against the Person Act. Nevertheless, states of mind which are not supported by medical evidence of psychiatric injury are still not encompassed by the 1861 legislation and, as Burton commented, 'The insistence upon a clinically recognized condition may perhaps be unduly restrictive in domestic violence cases.'[13] This proposition was supported by the case of *R v D*[14] in which the husband of a victim of domestic abuse who had committed suicide was prosecuted for unlawful act manslaughter. In order for the defendant to be convicted, the prosecution had to prove that there had been an unlawful and dangerous act. The prosecution's case was that the defendant had inflicted serious psychological injury on the victim contrary to section 20 of the Offences Against the Person Act, through repeated psychological abuse and some physical abuse. However, two of the three psychiatric experts who were consulted by the prosecution could not make a diagnosis of a psychiatric illness and the prosecution was therefore unsuccessful.[15]

Due to such concerns, on 20 August 2014 the government announced its plans to consult on reconciling the criminal law in England and Wales with the Home Office definition of domestic violence by criminalising coercive

11 See www.cps.gov.uk/publications/equality/domestic_violence.html, Crown Prosecution Service (accessed 14 October 2016).

12 [1997] 4 All ER 225.

13 Burton, op. cit., at p.61.

14 (2006) 2 Cr App R 24.

15 See Burton, op. cit., at p.62. For further discussion of the concept of 'bodily harm', see Bishop C., 'Domestic Violence: The Limitations of a Legal Response', in S. Hilder and V. Bettinson (eds), *Domestic Violence: Interdisciplinary Perspectives on Protection, Prevention and Intervention*, 2016, Palgrave Macmillan, London, 59–79 at 70–1.

control.[16] This consultation process closed on 15 October 2014. Eighty-five per cent of respondents agreed that the law did not currently provide sufficient protection to victims, and 55 per cent said that a new offence was needed to strengthen and clarify the law on coercive and controlling behaviour in intimate relationships.[17] On 18 December 2014 the government announced that there would be a new domestic abuse offence of coercive and controlling behaviour. The government stated: 'The new law will help protect victims by outlawing sustained patterns of behaviour that stop short of serious physical violence, but amount to extreme psychological and emotional abuse.'[18] Under section 76(1) of the Serious Crime Act 2015, a person commits an offence if he repeatedly or continuously engages in behaviour towards another person that is controlling or coercive; the two individuals involved are personally connected (defined as including intimate personal relationships);[19] the behaviour has a serious effect on the victim;[20] and the perpetrator knows or ought to know that the behaviour will have such an effect. Under section 76(11), the offence carries a maximum penalty of five years' imprisonment and a fine.[21]

As regards the approach adopted by the Istanbul Convention to defining domestic abuse, it should first be noted that in the terminology used throughout the Convention domestic violence is repeatedly separated out from violence against women more generally. The most obvious example of this can be found in the actual title of the Convention itself – 'the Council of Europe Convention on preventing and combating violence against women *and* domestic violence' [italics added]. Other clear examples of this approach can be seen in the purposes of the Convention, as stated in Article 1. These purposes include to 'protect women against all forms of violence, and prevent, prosecute and eliminate violence against women *and* domestic violence';[22] to 'design a comprehensive framework,

16 Home Office, 'Strengthening the Law on Domestic Abuse – A Consultation', August 2014, available at www.gov.uk/government/uploads/system/uploads/attachment_data/file/344674/Strengthening_the_law_on_Domestic_Abuse_-_A_Consultation_WEB.PDF (accessed 14 October 2016).

17 Home Office, 'Strengthening the Law on Domestic Abuse Consultation – Summary of Responses', December 2014, available at www.gov.uk/government/uploads/system/uploads/attachment_data/file/389002/StrengtheningLawDomesticAbuseResponses.pdf (accessed 14 October 2016).

18 Home Office, Press Release, 'Government to create new domestic abuse offence', 18 December 2014, available at www.gov.uk/government/news/government-to-create-new-domestic-abuse-offence (accessed 14 October 2016).

19 Serious Crime Act 2015, section 76(2).

20 Under section 76(4), the behaviour will be regarded as having a 'serious effect' on the victim if it causes the victim to fear, on at least two occasions, that violence will be used, or it causes the victim serious alarm or distress which has a substantial adverse effect on her usual day-to-day activities.

21 For further discussion of section 76 of the Serious Crime Act 2015, see Bishop, op. cit., at pp.71–2.

22 Istanbul Convention, Article 1(a).

policies and measures for the protection of and assistance to all victims of violence against women *and* domestic violence';[23] to 'promote international co-operation with a view to eliminating violence against women *and* domestic violence';[24] and to 'provide support and assistance to organisations and law enforcement agencies to effectively co-operate in order to adopt an integrated approach to eliminating violence against women *and* domestic violence'[25] [italics added].

The approach of repeatedly separating out domestic violence from violence against women more generally has received some criticism. For example, in a publication produced by the European Women's Lobby Centre on Violence against Women, it was commented that 'such an approach poses a real danger that domestic violence be regarded as a separate issue, unrelated to the structural problem of all forms of male violence against women'.[26] It appears, however, that the approach adopted by the Istanbul Convention serves two purposes. First, it highlights the importance that the Istanbul Convention places on combating domestic abuse, an aim that is certainly praiseworthy. Second, it is recognised in this instrument that men as well as women may be the victims of such abuse.

The question of whether a gender-neutral approach should be adopted to the issue of domestic violence (as is the case of the Home Office's definition) or whether a gendered approach is necessary has raised a great deal of debate in the relevant literature. Burton remarks, 'Contradictory views about whether women are as likely as men to perpetrate violence against an intimate partner abound in the literature.'[27] However, Dobash and Dobash are of the view that women's violence against men differs substantially from men's violence against women in terms of the context and the consequences.[28] Women's violence often takes place in the context of self-defence and the consequences of women's violence against men are less severe. Essentially, 'Women's violence towards male intimate partners does not occur with the same frequency or ferocity as men's violence towards female intimate partners.'[29] Dobash and Dobash are thus of the view that in formulating policies, priority should be accorded to those that tackle men's violence against women.[30] Likewise, Chinkin comments that 'while men also experience domestic violence, it is more frequently inflicted upon women and has

23 Article 1(c).
24 Article 1(d).
25 Article 1(e).
26 European Women's Lobby Centre on Violence against Women, 'Towards a Strong Convention on All Forms of Violence against Women', at p.8, available at www.edf.org.uk/blog/wp-content/uploads/2010/06/EWL-Lobbying-Kit-Convention-of-CoE-on-VAW.pdf (accessed 14 October 2016).
27 Burton, op. cit., at p.5.
28 Dobash R.P. and Dobash R.E., 'Women's Violence to Men in Intimate Relationships: Working on a Puzzle', (2004) 44 *British Journal of Criminology*, 324–49.
29 Burton, op. cit., at p.6.
30 Dobash and Dobash, op. cit.

disparate economic and social consequences'.[31] Kimmel goes so far as to state that '[w]hen sexual violence and violence by ex-spouses are considered, the evidence is overwhelming that gender asymmetry in domestic violence remains in full effect'.[32]

With regard to the approach that is adopted by the Istanbul Convention to this issue, the starting point can be found in Article 3(b) which defines domestic violence in a gender-neutral manner as encompassing 'all acts of physical, sexual, psychological or economic violence that occur within the family or domestic unit or between former or current spouses or partners, whether or not the perpetrator shares or has shared the same residence with the victim'.[33] However, although Article 2(2) asserts that '[p]arties are encouraged to apply this Convention to all victims of domestic violence', this provision also emphasises that '[p]arties shall pay particular attention to women victims of gender-based violence in implementing the provisions of this Convention'. In addition, it is stated in Article 2(1): 'This Convention shall apply to all forms of violence against women, including domestic violence, which affects women disproportionately.' Therefore, although states are 'encouraged' to apply the provisions of the Convention to male victims of domestic abuse, the focus remains primarily on the prevention of violence against women, encompassing *inter alia* such violence that takes place in the home.

The approach of the Istanbul Convention to defining domestic violence is notably different to the approaches to this question adopted in previous human rights instruments. The UN documents that address the issue of domestic violence are based on a gendered perspective whereby domestic violence is situated essentially in the frameworks of violence against women or discrimination against women. For example, as discussed in Chapter 2, in analysing the response of the UN to the issue of domestic violence, one of the key documents is General Recommendation No. 19 of the CEDAW Committee, which interpreted the Convention on the Elimination of All Forms of Discrimination against Women

31 Chinkin C., 'Addressing Violence against Women in the Commonwealth within States' Obligations under International Law', (2014) 40 *Commonwealth Law Bulletin*, 471–501 at 475.

32 Kimmel M.S., '"Gender Symmetry" in Domestic Violence: A Substantive and Methodological Research Review', (2002) 6 *Violence Against Women*, 1332–63 at 1359. For further discussion of arguments surrounding 'gender symmetry' as regards domestic violence, see Johnson M.P., 'Conflict and Control: Gender Symmetry and Asymmetry in Domestic Violence', (2006) 12 *Violence Against Women*, 1003–18. For further discussion of domestic violence as a gendered phenomenon, see Bishop, op. cit., at pp.61–2.

33 It is noteworthy that this is the first time that domestic violence has been defined in a treaty. As will be seen later in the chapter, under the Convention of Belém do Pará, domestic violence is simply viewed as a facet of violence against women more generally, and no actual definition of domestic violence was therefore included in this instrument. The term 'domestic violence' is not used in the Maputo Protocol, under which this form of violence is again subsumed in violence against women as a whole.

(CEDAW)[34] as prohibiting violence against women in both the public and private domains.[35] This document states:

> The definition of discrimination includes gender-based violence, that is, violence that is directed against a woman because she is a woman or that affects women disproportionately. It includes acts that inflict physical, mental or sexual harm or suffering, threats of such acts, coercion and other deprivations of liberty. Gender-based violence may breach specific provisions of the Convention, regardless of whether those provisions expressly mention violence.[36]

As regards violence taking place in the private sphere, such as domestic violence, General Recommendation No. 19 asserts that:

> discrimination under the Convention is not restricted to action by or on behalf of Governments . . . Under general international law and specific human rights covenants, States may be responsible for private acts if they fail to act with due diligence to prevent violations of rights or to investigate and punish acts of violence, and for providing compensation.[37]

The General Recommendation also states:

> Family violence is one of the most insidious forms of violence against women. It is prevalent in all societies. Within family relationships women of all ages are subjected to violence of all kinds, including battering, rape, other forms of sexual assault, mental and other forms of violence, which are perpetuated by traditional attitudes.[38]

It can be seen therefore that in General Recommendation No. 19, the issue of domestic violence is simply framed as a form of gender-based violence, which in turn is analysed as discrimination against women. As Chinkin comments, the CEDAW Committee has therefore rejected the view that domestic violence 'can be described in gender-neutral language that conceals the gender-based quality of violence against women'.[39]

34 CEDAW (1249 U.N.T.S. 13) was adopted by the UN General Assembly on 18 December 1979 and entered into force on 3 September 1981.

35 As discussed in Chapter 2, CEDAW itself contains no express reference to violence against women.

36 Committee on the Elimination of Discrimination against Women, U.N. Doc A/47/38 (1992), at para. 6.

37 At para. 9.

38 At para. 23.

39 Chinkin C., 'Violence against Women' in M.A. Freeman, C. Chinkin and B. Rudolf (eds), *The UN Convention on the Elimination of All Forms of Discrimination against Women: A Commentary*, 2012, Oxford University Press, Oxford, 443–74 at 452.

Another of the key documents regarding the response of the UN to domestic violence is the Declaration on the Elimination of Violence against Women, which was issued by the UN General Assembly in 1993.[40] Article 1 of this document states:

> [T]he term 'violence against women' means any act of gender-based violence that results in, or is likely to result in, physical, sexual or psychological harm or suffering to women, including threats of such acts, coercion or arbitrary deprivation of liberty, whether occurring in public or in private life.

Article 2(a) of the Declaration asserts that '[v]iolence against women shall be understood to encompass . . . physical, sexual and psychological violence occurring in the family'. In this document the General Assembly asserted that states had a duty to '[e]xercise due diligence to prevent . . . acts of violence against women, whether these acts are perpetrated by the State or by private persons'.[41] Again, domestic violence is approached simply as a facet of violence against women. As was discussed in Chapter 2, other key documents on domestic abuse in the UN context include the framework for model legislation on domestic violence which was produced in 1996 by the Special Rapporteur on violence against women, its causes and consequences,[42] and the 1995 Beijing Platform for Action which emerged from the Fourth World Conference on Women.[43] Again, such documents clearly frame domestic violence as simply an aspect of violence against women more generally.

A similar approach to that of the UN can also be viewed in regional instruments that encompass the issue of domestic violence. For example, the actual term 'domestic violence' is not used in the Convention of Belém do Pará, in which again domestic abuse is approached simply as a facet of violence against women. Article 1 of this instrument states:

> For the purposes of this Convention, violence against women shall be understood as any act or conduct, based on gender, which causes death or physical, sexual or psychological harm or suffering to women, whether in the public or the private sphere.

Article 2 expands on this definition, stating that 'violence against women' should be understood to include:

> physical, sexual and psychological violence that occurs within the family or domestic unit or within any other interpersonal relationship, whether or not

40 General Assembly Resolution 48/104 (1993).

41 Article 4(c).

42 Report of the Special Rapporteur on violence against women, its causes and consequences – A framework for model legislation on domestic violence, E/CN.4/1996/53/Add.2, 2 February 1996.

43 Beijing Platform for Action, U.N. Doc.A/CONF.177/20 (1995).

> the perpetrator shares or has shared the same residence with the woman, including, among others, rape, battery and sexual abuse.[44]

Likewise, Article 3 asserts: 'Every woman has the right to be free from violence in both the public and private spheres.' Similarly, the term 'domestic violence' is not used in the Maputo Protocol; however, under Article 1(b) of this instrument, 'violence against women' is defined as encompassing 'all acts perpetrated against women which cause or could cause them physical, sexual, psychological, and economic harm, including the threat to take such acts'.

It seems therefore that the Istanbul Convention adopts a more sophisticated approach to the definition of domestic violence than do the earlier instruments that emanated from the UN and regional systems. Understanding of the phenomenon of domestic violence has increased substantially in recent years and there is now a much greater awareness of male victims of domestic abuse. It appears that one of the reasons for the more nuanced approach of the Istanbul Convention to defining domestic violence can be found in the events that led up to the drafting of this instrument. As discussed in Chapter 3, prior to the adoption of the Istanbul Convention, consideration had been given to the adoption of an instrument solely focused on domestic violence. The European Committee on Crime Problems (CDPC) had recommended the adoption of such a convention in a report published on 12 June 2007.[45] Although accepting that domestic violence between adults is gendered,[46] the report nevertheless stated:

> Even though the majority of victims are women, a convention would preferably use gender-neutral terminology. That would not preclude a gender-based analysis of the underlying problem, nor a gender-sensitive implementation of the convention. Furthermore, it would provide the tools to address male victimisation in domestic violence when necessary.[47]

The language of the Istanbul Convention is certainly by no means gender-neutral. Nevertheless, the fact that a gender-neutral convention on domestic violence had been considered may well have constituted a factor in the decision to include male victims of domestic violence within the ambit of the Istanbul Convention, even if only to a very limited extent.

As discussed in Chapter 3, in May 2009 the Ad Hoc Committee on Preventing and Combating Violence against Women and Domestic Violence (known as 'CAHVIO'), which drafted the Istanbul Convention, stated that the focus of such an instrument

44 Article 2(a).

45 European Committee on Crime Problems, 'Feasibility study for a convention against domestic violence', 12 June 2007, Council of Europe, Strasbourg, CDPC (2007)09 rev.

46 At p.4.

47 At p.13.

> should be on the elimination of violence against women. Furthermore, the future convention should deal with domestic violence which affects women disproportionately. The convention should also allow for the application of its provisions to all victims of domestic violence.[48]

This was essentially the approach that was adopted in the final document itself.

It should be noted that although Article 4(3) of the Convention states that the implementation of the Convention's provisions shall be secured without discrimination on any ground such as gender, Article 4(4) nevertheless emphasises that '[s]pecial measures that are necessary to prevent and protect women from gender-based violence shall not be considered discrimination under the terms of this Convention'. Therefore, if a state party to the Convention were to take measures that protected only victims of domestic violence who are women, such an approach would not constitute discrimination. In Article 3(d), 'gender-based violence against women' is defined as 'violence that is directed against a woman because she is a woman or that affects women disproportionately'. Domestic violence is clearly encompassed by this definition as women experience this form of violence to a substantially greater extent than men, as discussed previously in this chapter.

This 'special measures' approach is in line with that of UN human rights treaties such as CEDAW. For example, Article 4(1) of CEDAW states: 'Adoption by States Parties of temporary special measures aimed at accelerating de facto equality for men and women shall not be considered discrimination as defined in the present Convention.' In its General Recommendation No. 25 on Temporary Special Measures, the CEDAW Committee commented that it:

> views the application of these measures not as an exception to the norm of non-discrimination, but rather as an emphasis that temporary special measures are part of a necessary strategy by States parties directed towards the achievement of de facto or substantive equality of women with men in the enjoyment of their human rights and fundamental freedoms.[49]

Likewise, the European Court of Human Rights has held that differential treatment in relation to the enjoyment of rights is not unlawful under Article 14 of the European Convention on Human Rights, if there is an objective and reasonable justification for this difference in treatment. In the *Belgian Linguistic*

48 Interim Report of the Ad Hoc Committee on Preventing and Combating Violence against Women and Domestic Violence, 27 May 2009, at para. IIA(6).

49 General Recommendation No. 25, on article 4, paragraph 1, of the Convention on the Elimination of All Forms of Discrimination against Women, on temporary special measures (2004) at para. 18.

case, the European Court stated that positive action is permissible, and commented that 'certain legal inequalities tend only to correct factual inequalities'.[50]

It is also worthy of note that the definition of domestic violence used in the Istanbul Convention encompasses 'economic violence', as well as physical, sexual and psychological abuse. As Mullender and Morley comment, 'Although we normally think of domestic violence as physical, commonly the physical is but one aspect of a pattern of abuse which also includes sexual, emotional, and material abuses.'[51] Again, the inclusion of 'economic violence' in the Istanbul Convention is evidence of the developments in the comprehension of domestic violence that have taken place in recent times. As Schneider comments, 'practical experience blurs the distinction between physical abuse and other aspects of the battering relationship'.[52] The encompassing of 'economic violence' means that the scope of the Istanbul Convention extends beyond that of instruments such as the Convention of Belém do Pará or General Recommendation No. 19 of the CEDAW Committee. However, it is noteworthy that the Maputo Protocol's definition of violence against women also includes reference to 'economic harm'.[53]

The Istanbul Convention's definition of domestic violence encompasses situations in which the perpetrator and the victim do not share the same residence, or indeed have never shared the same residence. In addition, as with the Home Office's cross-government definition of domestic violence and abuse, the Istanbul Convention's definition includes violence between family members other than former or current spouses or partners.

State responsibility and due diligence

Article 5(1) of the Convention states: 'Parties shall refrain from engaging in any act of violence against women and ensure that state authorities, officials, agents, institutions and other actors acting on behalf of the state act in conformity with this obligation.' Article 5(2) proceeds to place a duty on states parties to 'take the necessary legislative and other measures to exercise due diligence to prevent, investigate, punish and provide reparation for acts of violence covered by the scope of this Convention that are perpetrated by non-state actors'. Interestingly, almost identical wording is found in Article 7(a) of the Convention of Belém do Pará, which places an obligation on states parties to 'refrain from engaging in any act or practice of violence against women and to ensure that their authorities,

50 *Case 'Relating to Certain Aspects of the Laws on the Use of Languages in Education in Belgium' v Belgium* (app. no. 1474/62; 1677/62; 1691/62; 1769/63; 1994/63; 2126/64, 23 July 1968), at para. 10.

51 Mullender A. and Morley R., 'Context and Content of a New Agenda', in A. Mullender and R. Morley (eds), *Children Living with Domestic Violence*, 1994, Whiting & Birch, London, 2–16 at 6.

52 Schneider E., *Battered Women and Feminist Lawmaking*, 2000, Yale University Press, Connecticut, at p.66.

53 Article 1(b).

officials, personnel, agents, and institutions act in conformity with this obligation'. Likewise, under Article 7(b) states must 'apply due diligence to prevent, investigate and impose penalties for violence against women'.

The fact that reference is made in both the Istanbul Convention and the Convention of Belém do Pará to the concept of 'due diligence', explicit mention of which is rare among treaties, is very significant. The principles of state responsibility and positive obligations[54] have played an invaluable role in the recognition of domestic violence as a human rights issue. As discussed in Chapter 2, human rights law was initially developed in such a manner as to create a public/private divide whereby human rights norms were upheld in the public sphere where the state was involved, but were not applied in the private sphere. The rights norms that emerged were generally formulated in a negative manner, whereby the state was required only to refrain from violating the rights in question. There were no duties on the state to adopt positive measures to ensure that the rights of the individual were not violated, and the state was not required to protect the rights of the individual from being breached by another private party. Therefore, domestic violence did not fall within the ambit of traditional human rights principles. Nevertheless, the public/private divide in international human rights law is being gradually eroded. For example, although CEDAW does not make any explicit reference to domestic violence, it has been interpreted in such a manner as to encompass this issue. General Recommendation No. 19 of the CEDAW Committee was immensely important as it officially interpreted CEDAW as prohibiting violence against women in both the public and private spheres. This Recommendation stated:

> [D]iscrimination under the Convention is not restricted to action by or on behalf of Governments . . . Under general international law and specific human rights covenants, States may be responsible for private acts if they fail to act with due diligence to prevent violations of rights or to investigate and punish acts of violence, and for providing compensation.[55]

In a similar manner, Article 4(c) of the UN General Assembly's Declaration on the Elimination of Violence against Women of 1993 asserts that states should 'exercise due diligence to prevent, investigate and, in accordance with national legislation, punish acts of violence against women, whether those acts are perpetrated by the State or by private persons'.[56] This statement was reiterated in the Beijing Platform for Action.[57] The 'due diligence' concept has also been used

54 For a discussion of the positive obligation of states to take measures as regards violations committed by non-state actors, see Clapham A., *Human Rights in the Private Sphere*, 1993, Clarendon, Oxford.

55 U.N. Doc A/47/38 (1992), at para. 9.

56 General Assembly Resolution 48/104 (1993), Article 4(c).

57 U.N. Doc.A/CONF.177/20 (1995), at para. 124(b).

to great effect by the UN Special Rapporteur on violence against women, its causes and consequences. For example, in 2006 the then Special Rapporteur, Yakin Ertürk, issued a report entitled 'The Due Diligence Standard as a Tool for the Elimination of Violence against Women',[58] in which she commented that 'it can be concluded that there is a rule of customary international law that obliges states to prevent and respond to acts of violence against women with due diligence'.[59] Similarly, the concept of due diligence is used in both the Convention of Belém do Pará and the Istanbul Convention to place obligations on states parties in relation to acts of violence perpetrated in the private sphere.

As Chinkin comments, the due diligence standard 'has long been accepted in international law with respect to attributing state responsibility for the wrongful acts of non-state actors'.[60] The concept of due diligence has increasingly influenced case law in relation to domestic violence and violence against women. The judicial branches of both the Inter-American and Council of Europe systems have been extremely instrumental in this process. The Inter-American Court of Human Rights is credited with one of the earliest formulations of the principle of state responsibility in the case of *Velasquez Rodriguez v Honduras*,[61] which concerned the disappearance of Manfredo Velasquez. In this case, the Inter-American Court held that Honduras had failed to fulfil its duties under Article 1(1) of the American Convention on Human Rights. The Court stated:

> An illegal act which violates human rights and which is initially not directly imputable to a State (for example, because it is the act of a private person or because the person responsible has not been identified) can lead to international responsibility of the State, not because of the act itself, but because of the lack of due diligence to prevent the violation or to respond to it as required by the Convention.[62]

The Court went on to assert that the duty of states to prevent violations:

> includes all those means of a legal, political, administrative and cultural nature that promote the protection of human rights and ensure that any violations are considered and treated as illegal acts, which, as such, may lead to the punishment of those responsible and the obligation to indemnify the victims for damages.[63]

58 'The Due Diligence Standard as a Tool for the Elimination of Violence against Women', Report of the Special Rapporteur on violence against women, its causes and consequences, Yakin Ertürk, 20 January 2006, U.N. Doc. E/CN./2006/61.
59 At para. 29.
60 Chinkin (2014), op. cit., at p.479.
61 Judgment of 29 July 1988, Inter-Am. Ct. H.R., (Ser. C) No. 4.
62 At para. 172.
63 At para. 175.

The decision of the Inter-American Commission on Human Rights in the case of *Jessica Lenahan (Gonzales) v United States* provides a seminal example of the use of the due diligence concept in a case involving domestic violence.[64] This case arose from a petition presented to the Commission against the United States by representatives of the American Civil Liberties Union. The petition was presented on behalf of Jessica Lenahan, formerly Jessica Gonzales, and her three daughters who were deceased. The United States is not a party to either the Convention of Belém do Pará or the American Convention on Human Rights. However, the claimants alleged that the US had breached several provisions of the American Declaration of the Rights and Duties of Man, due to a failure to exercise due diligence in protecting Jessica Lenahan and her daughters from domestic violence that had been perpetrated by Ms Lenahan's former husband (Simon Gonzales). The claimants argued that the police had failed to respond in a sufficient manner to Ms Lenahan's repeated telephone calls reporting that her husband had taken their three daughters, who were aged seven, eight and ten, in breach of a domestic violence restraining order. Simon Gonzales had eventually arrived at the police station and opened fire at police. The police returned fire, resulting in his death. The three children were later found shot to death in Simon Gonzales's truck. The petitioners argued that the state had never duly investigated the circumstances of the deaths of the children, and had not provided Ms Lenahan with an adequate remedy for the failures on the part of the police.

The Inter-American Commission held that the US had failed to act with due diligence to protect Ms Lenahan and her daughters from domestic violence, and that this amounted to a breach of several provisions of the American Declaration of the Rights and Duties of Man, namely Article I (the right to life), Article II (the right to equality), Article VII (relating to the special protection of children) and Article XVIII (the right to judicial protection). A wide range of recommendations were made to the state, both with regard to Ms Lenahan's position specifically and also at a more general level. The decision of the Inter-American Commission in this case is certainly of a dynamic nature. The Commission is to be commended for its willingness to use the provisions of the American Declaration of the Rights and Duties of Man and the concept of due diligence to place duties on the state in relation to the issue of domestic violence, even in the absence of state ratification of either the Convention of Belém do Pará or the American Convention on Human Rights.[65]

64 Case 12.626, Report No. 80/11 (2011).

65 For further discussion of this case, see McQuigg R., 'Domestic Violence and the Inter-American Commission on Human Rights: *Jessica Lenahan (Gonzales) v United States*', (2012) 12 *Human Rights Law Review*, 122–34. For further discussion of the concept of state responsibility, see Cook R.J., 'State Responsibility for Violations of Women's Rights', (1994) 7 *Harvard Human Rights Journal*, 125–75; and Romany C., 'State Responsibility Goes Private: A Feminist Critique of the Public/Private Distinction in International Human Rights Law', in R.J. Cook (ed.), *Human Rights of Women: National and International Perspectives*, 1994, University of Pennsylvania Press, Philadelphia, 85–115.

Likewise, the European Court of Human Rights has developed a very substantial body of jurisprudence on the concept of positive obligations, which it has used to great effect in its case law on the issue of domestic violence. This case law was discussed in Chapter 3.[66]

Integration of policies

Chapter II of the Istanbul Convention places obligations on states parties regarding integration of policies and data collection. These obligations relate to all forms of violence encompassed by the Convention, including domestic violence. The need for inter-agency cooperation between all those concerned with domestic violence is well recognised. The issue of domestic violence involves a complex mass of difficulties which necessitates input from a variety of services. It is therefore essential that there is cooperation between these service providers. As Berry comments:

> Ideally, all of the entities and agencies that are involved in domestic violence issues within a given community or region should meet and interact on a regular basis to share ideas, plan strategies, develop protocols, and promote an ongoing dialogue with one another and with the public.[67]

Article 7(1) of the Convention states:

> Parties shall take the necessary legislative and other measures to adopt and implement State-wide effective, comprehensive and co-ordinated policies encompassing all relevant measures to prevent and combat all forms of violence covered by the scope of this Convention and offer a holistic response to violence against women.

Under Article 7(2), 'Parties shall ensure that policies referred to in paragraph 1 place the rights of the victim at the centre of all measures and are implemented by way of effective co-operation among all relevant agencies, institutions and organisations.' Article 7(3) establishes that '[m]easures taken pursuant to this article shall involve, where appropriate, all relevant actors, such as government

66 For further discussion of the due diligence standard in the context of domestic violence, see Hasselbacher L., 'State Obligations Regarding Domestic Violence: The European Court of Human Rights, Due Diligence, and International Legal Minimums of Protection', (2010) 8 *Northwestern Journal of International Human Rights*, 190–215.

67 Berry D.B., *The Domestic Violence Sourcebook*, 1998, Lowell House, Los Angeles, at p.195. See also Robinson A. and Payton J., 'Independent Advocacy and Multi-Agency Responses to Domestic Violence', in S. Hilder and V. Bettinson (eds), *Domestic Violence: Interdisciplinary Perspectives on Protection, Prevention and Intervention*, 2016, Palgrave Macmillan, London, 249–71.

agencies, the national, regional and local parliaments and authorities, national human rights institutions and civil society organisations'. Under Article 8:

> Parties shall allocate appropriate financial and human resources for the adequate implementation of integrated policies, measures and programmes to prevent and combat all forms of violence covered by the scope of this Convention, including those carried out by non-governmental organisations and civil society.

Article 9 states: 'Parties shall recognise, encourage and support, at all levels, the work of relevant non-governmental organisations and of civil society active in combating violence against women and establish effective co-operation with these organisations.' It is noteworthy that the Explanatory Report to the Convention states:

> Although Article 9 refers only to NGOs and civil society active in combating violence against women, this should not prevent Parties from going further and supporting the work that is carried out by NGOs and civil society focusing on domestic violence in its wider scope.[68]

It seems that work that focuses on domestic violence 'in its wider scope' is a reference to domestic abuse against men. The fact, however, that Article 9 places no actual obligation on states parties to support the work of organisations seeking to combat domestic violence against men is strongly reflective of the primary focus of the Istanbul Convention as being on violence against women in all of its forms.

Under Article 10(1) of the Convention, 'Parties shall designate or establish one or more official bodies responsible for the co-ordination, implementation, monitoring and evaluation of policies and measures to prevent and combat all forms of violence covered by this Convention.'[69] Article 18(1) states:

> Parties shall take the necessary legislative or other measures, in accordance with internal law, to ensure that there are appropriate mechanisms to provide

68 Council of Europe, 'Explanatory Report to Council of Europe Convention on preventing and combating violence against women and domestic violence', available at https://rm.coe.int/CoERMPublicCommonSearchServices/DisplayDCTMContent?documentId=09000016800d383a (accessed 18 October 2016), at para. 69.

69 The concept envisaged under Article 10(1) of the Istanbul Convention appears to be similar to that of Article 33 of the UN Convention on the Rights of Persons with Disabilities (CRPD) which provides that states parties should designate one or more focal points within government for matters relating to the implementation of the CRPD, and should afford due consideration to the establishment or designation of a coordination mechanism within government to facilitate action in various sectors and at various levels. (The CRPD (2515 U.N.T.S. 3) was adopted by the UN General Assembly on 13 December 2006 and entered into force on 3 May 2008.)

> for effective co-operation between all relevant state agencies, including the judiciary, public prosecutors, law enforcement agencies, local and regional authorities as well as non-governmental organisations and other relevant organisations and entities, in protecting and supporting victims and witnesses of all forms of violence covered by the scope of this Convention.

It is notable that as regards domestic violence the UN human rights bodies have also recognised that in order for an effective strategy to be implemented, it is necessary for an integrated approach to be adopted. As far back as 1985, in its Resolution 40/36, the UN General Assembly urged member states to ensure coordination of social welfare and criminal justice measures.[70] The General Assembly expanded on this recommendation in 1990 by urging member states:

> to begin or continue to explore, develop and implement multidisciplinary policies, measures and strategies, within and outside of the criminal justice system, with respect to domestic violence in all its facets, including legal, law enforcement, judicial, societal, educational, psychological, economic, health-related and correctional aspects.[71]

Again in 1993 the General Assembly urged states to '[c]onsider the possibility of developing national plans of action to promote the protection of women against any form of violence . . . taking into account . . . such cooperation as can be provided by non-governmental organizations'.[72] Similarly, in 2001 the Commission on Human Rights called upon states 'to establish and/or strengthen, at the national level, collaborative relationships with relevant non-governmental and community-based organizations'.[73] This statement was reiterated by the Commission in 2004.[74] The particular need to work in conjunction with non-governmental organisations has therefore been recognised at the UN level, and this emphasis is also reflected in the Istanbul Convention.

Data collection and research

Article 11(1)(a) of the Convention places an obligation on states parties to 'collect disaggregated relevant statistical data at regular intervals on cases of all forms of violence covered by the scope of this Convention'. Under Article 11(1)(b), states parties should 'support research in the field of all forms of violence covered by the scope of this Convention in order to study its root causes and effects, incidences and conviction rates, as well as the efficacy of measures taken

70 General Assembly Resolution 40/36 (1985), at para. 7(j).
71 General Assembly Resolution 45/114 (1990), at para. 1.
72 General Assembly Resolution 48/104 (1993), Article 4(e).
73 Commission on Human Rights Resolution 2001/49, at para. 10(d).
74 Commission on Human Rights Resolution 2004/46, at para. 15(j).

to implement this Convention'. The Explanatory Report states in relation to this provision: 'Research is a key element of evidence-based policy-making and can thus contribute greatly to improving day-to-day, real-world responses to violence against women and domestic violence by the judiciary, support services and law enforcement agencies.'[75] Article 11(2) asserts: 'Parties shall endeavour to conduct population-based surveys at regular intervals to assess the prevalence of and trends in all forms of violence covered by the scope of this Convention.' Under Article 11(4), 'Parties shall ensure that the information collected pursuant to this article is available to the public.'

It is notable that the need for research to be carried out with regard to violence against women was also recognised by the drafters of the Convention of Belém do Pará. Article 8(h) of this instrument places an obligation on states parties:

> to ensure research and the gathering of statistics and other relevant information relating to the causes, consequences and frequency of violence against women, in order to assess the effectiveness of measures to prevent, punish and eradicate violence against women and to formulate and implement the necessary changes.

Awareness-raising

As Heisecke states:

> Raising awareness of the different forms of violence against women and domestic violence is an important element in the prevention of violence against women, because heightened awareness is a first step in changing attitudes and behaviour that perpetuate or condone the various forms of violence against women.[76]

Domestic violence advocates have long argued that in order to address the issue of domestic violence adequately, it is vital to raise awareness of the problem within society as a whole. For example, Berry comments that there is a view among certain sections of the community that violence against women in the home is acceptable in some circumstances, or at least that it is not as serious as violence between strangers.[77] Connelly and Cavanagh state that if legislative initiatives 'are not paralleled by education programs, which challenge the common myths and misconceptions around domestic abuse, operating and enforcing legislative

75 Council of Europe, 'Explanatory Report to Council of Europe Convention on preventing and combating violence against women and domestic violence', at para. 77.

76 Heisecke K., 'Raising Awareness of Violence against Women: Article 13 of the Istanbul Convention', 2014, Council of Europe, Strasbourg, at p.5.

77 Berry, op. cit., at p.193.

provisions will be difficult'.[78] Hester and Westmarland remark that publicity campaigns 'should use a wide range of media such as radio, television, posters and stickers. They should aim to educate local residents and staff across agencies that domestic violence is a public crime, and indicate local sources of support.'[79] Outreach workers should regularly visit community groups to discuss domestic violence and publicise domestic violence projects.[80]

The need to raise awareness within society as a whole is recognised in the Istanbul Convention, Article 12(1) of which places an obligation on states parties to:

> take the necessary measures to promote changes in the social and cultural patterns of behaviour of women and men with a view to eradicating prejudices, customs, traditions and all other practices which are based on the idea of the inferiority of women or on stereotyped roles for women and men.

The Explanatory Report to the Convention asserts that this provision aims 'to reach the hearts and minds of individuals who, through their behaviour, contribute to perpetuate the forms of violence covered by the scope of this Convention'.[81]

Article 12(4) states: 'Parties shall take the necessary measures to encourage all members of society, especially men and boys, to contribute actively to preventing all forms of violence covered by the scope of this Convention.' The Explanatory Report states:

> Bearing in mind the fact that the majority of men and boys are not perpetrators, the drafters wanted to point out that their contribution can take on many forms in particular as role models, agents of change and advocates for equality between women and men and mutual respect.[82]

Under Article 13(1):

> Parties shall promote or conduct, on a regular basis and at all levels, awareness-campaigns or programmes, including in co-operation with national human rights institutions and equality bodies, civil society and non-governmental organisations, especially women's organisations, where appropriate, to increase awareness and understanding among the general public of the different manifestations of all forms of violence covered by the scope of this

78 Connelly C. and Cavanagh K., 'Domestic Abuse, Civil Protection Orders and the "New Criminologies": Is There Any Value in Engaging with the Law?', (2007) 15 *Feminist Legal Studies*, 259–87 at 283.

79 Hester M. and Westmarland N., 'Tackling Domestic Violence: Effective Interventions and Approaches', 2005, Home Office Research Study 290, at p.xiii.

80 Hester and Westmarland, op. cit., at p.xiii.

81 Council of Europe, 'Explanatory Report to Council of Europe Convention on preventing and combating violence against women and domestic violence', at para. 85.

82 At para. 88.

Convention, their consequences on children and the need to prevent such violence.

The Explanatory Report comments:

> Awareness-raising activities should include the dissemination of information on equality between women and men, non-stereotyped gender roles, and non-violent conflict resolution in interpersonal relationships. Moreover, the drafters considered it important that any campaign highlight the harmful consequences for children which violence against women and domestic violence may have in its direct or indirect form.[83]

Article 13(2) of the Convention states: 'Parties shall ensure the wide dissemination among the general public of information on measures available to prevent acts of violence covered by the scope of this Convention.'

Commentators working in the area of domestic violence have also highlighted the need to ensure that school pupils are educated in relation to the issues involved in domestic violence. For example, Schneider comments that education regarding domestic violence 'must take place in every elementary school and high school, every court, welfare office, hospital, and law school around the country'.[84] Hester and Westmarland state that domestic violence prevention programmes should be implemented in both primary and secondary schools, and that a cross-curricular approach should be adopted.[85] Article 14(1) of the Convention therefore provides:

> Parties shall take, where appropriate, the necessary steps to include teaching material on issues such as equality between women and men, non-stereotyped gender roles, mutual respect, non-violent conflict resolution in interpersonal relationships, gender-based violence against women and the right to personal integrity, adapted to the evolving capacity of learners, in formal curricula and at all levels of education.

Article 14(2) states: 'Parties shall take the necessary steps to promote the principles referred to in paragraph 1 in informal educational facilities, as well as in sports, cultural and leisure facilities and the media.' Under Article 17(1):

> Parties shall encourage the private sector, the information and communication technology sector and the media, with due respect for freedom of expression and their independence, to participate in the elaboration and implementation of policies and to set guidelines and self-regulatory standards to prevent violence against women and to enhance respect for their dignity.

83 At para. 91.
84 Schneider, op. cit., at p.210.
85 Hester and Westmarland, op. cit., at p.viii.

The provisions contained in the Istanbul Convention relating to the obligations of states parties to adopt awareness-raising measures reflect the fact that the relevant UN bodies have also paid substantial attention to the need for states to raise awareness among society as a whole of the issues involved in domestic violence. For example, in its General Recommendation No. 19, the CEDAW Committee asserted that states should provide public education programmes to change attitudes concerning the status of men and women.[86] In 1996 the UN Special Rapporteur on violence against women, its causes and consequences emphasised the need for 'demystifying domestic violence',[87] and in 2003 the Special Rapporteur encouraged 'the adoption of a societal project to delink masculinity from an association with oppressive uses of power'.[88]

The Beijing Platform for Action also highlighted the necessity for measures to be taken to increase societal awareness of the issues involved in domestic violence. This document stated that governments should support initiatives of women's organisations to raise awareness of the issue of violence against women[89] and that they should organise and fund community-based campaigns to raise awareness about violence against women as a human rights violation.[90] Governments should also '[o]rganize and fund information campaigns and educational and training programmes in order to sensitize girls and boys and women and men to the personal and social detrimental effects of violence in the family, community and society'.[91] In addition, the Platform for Action stated that governments should:

> [r]aise awareness of the responsibility of the media in promoting non-stereotyped images of women and men, as well as in eliminating patterns of media presentation that generate violence, and encourage those responsible for media content to establish professional guidelines and codes of conduct; also raise awareness of the important role of the media in informing and educating people about the causes and effects of violence against women and in stimulating public debate on the topic.[92]

86 Committee on the Elimination of Discrimination against Women, U.N. Doc A/47/38 (1992), at para. 24(t)(ii).
87 Report of the Special Rapporteur on violence against women, its causes and consequences, E/CN.4/1996/53, 5 February 1996, at para. 141.
88 Report of the Special Rapporteur on violence against women, its causes and consequences, E/CN.4/2004/66, 26 December 2003, at para. 58.
89 U.N. Doc.A/CONF.177/20 (1995), at para. 125(d).
90 At para. 125(e).
91 At para. 125(g).
92 At para. 125(j). For other UN documents dealing with the need to raise societal awareness of domestic violence, see General Assembly Resolution 45/114 (1990), at para. 1(c); General Assembly Resolution 48/104 (1993), Article 4(j); Commission on Human Rights Resolution 2001/49, at paras 10(e) and (g); Commission on Human Rights Resolution 2004/46, at paras 15(k) and (m); and General Assembly Resolution 61/143 (2007), at para. 8(n).

The necessity for awareness-raising measures to be implemented is also recognised by the Convention of Belém do Pará, Article 8(a) of which places a duty on states parties 'to promote awareness and observance of the right of women to be free from violence, and the right of women to have their human rights respected and protected'. Article 8(b) proceeds to place an obligation on states parties to take measures:

> to modify social and cultural patterns of conduct of men and women, including the development of formal and informal educational programs appropriate to every level of the educational process, to counteract prejudices, customs and all other practices which are based on the idea of the inferiority or superiority of either of the sexes or on the stereotyped roles for men and women which legitimize or exacerbate violence against women.

Under Article 8(e) states parties should 'promote and support governmental and private sector education designed to raise the awareness of the public with respect to the problems of and remedies for violence against women', and under Article 8(g) states parties should 'encourage the communications media to develop appropriate media guidelines in order to contribute to the eradication of violence against women in all its forms, and to enhance respect for the dignity of women'.

Likewise, Article 5 of the Maputo Protocol places an obligation on states parties with respect to the 'creation of public awareness in all sectors of society regarding harmful practices (which negatively affect the human rights of women and which are contrary to recognised international standards) through information, formal and informal education and outreach programmes'. Article 2(2) of the Protocol also asserts:

> States Parties shall commit themselves to modify the social and cultural patterns of conduct of women and men through public education, information, education and communication strategies, with a view to achieving the elimination of harmful cultural and traditional practices and all other practices which are based on the idea of the inferiority or the superiority of either of the sexes, or on stereotyped roles for women and men.

Article 12(1)(b) obliges states parties to 'integrate gender sensitisation and human rights education at all levels of education curricula including teacher training'.

Educating professionals

As Hague and Malos comment, the work of agencies such as social and health care services is extremely important for victims of domestic violence. Essentially, the attitudes displayed by these agencies can greatly affect whether or not victims make use of them.[93] Mullender states that 'helping agencies need to develop sensitivity, consistency and a believing and non-blaming approach to the women who approach them'.[94] Davidson *et al.* remark: 'Educational interventions for health professionals and health service staff need to be designed to address local circumstances, and to be based on research that has explored women's views about the service and staff attitudes and needs.'[95] Attention has also been drawn to the need to educate lawyers about domestic violence. As Burman states, 'Without proper training, lawyers may actually harm, rather than help, their clients who are victims of domestic violence, a clear violation of their ethical and legal obligations to help clients.'[96]

Article 15(1) of the Istanbul Convention reflects these concerns and states:

> Parties shall provide or strengthen appropriate training for the relevant professionals dealing with victims or perpetrators of all acts of violence covered by the scope of this Convention, on the prevention and detection of such violence, equality between women and men, the needs and rights of victims, as well as on how to prevent secondary victimisation.

Article 15(2) proceeds to state: 'Parties shall encourage that the training referred to in paragraph 1 includes training on co-ordinated multi-agency co-operation to allow for a comprehensive and appropriate handling of referrals in cases of violence covered by the scope of this Convention.' The Explanatory Report to the Convention states: 'The relevant professionals may include professionals in the judiciary, in legal practice, in law enforcement agencies and in the fields of health care, social work and education.'[97]

The need to train the relevant professionals regarding issues relating to domestic violence was also previously recognised by the UN human rights bodies. For example, in its General Recommendation No. 19 the CEDAW Committee stated that gender-sensitive training of judicial and law enforcement officers and other public officials was essential for the effective implementation of CEDAW.[98] The 1996 report of the Special Rapporteur on violence against women, which contained a framework for model legislation on domestic violence, commented that one of the aims of the draft legislation was to '[t]rain judges to be aware of

93 Hague G. and Malos E., *Domestic Violence: Action for Change*, 2005, New Clarion Press, Cheltenham, at p.131.

94 Mullender A., *Re-thinking Domestic Violence*, 1996, Routledge, London, at p.61.

95 Davidson L.L., King V., Garcia J. and Marchant S., 'What Role Can the Health Services Play?', in J. Taylor-Browne (ed.), *What Works in Reducing Domestic Violence? A Comprehensive Guide for Professionals,* 2001, Whiting & Birch, London, 95–122 at 117.

96 Burman J.M., 'Lawyers and Domestic Violence: Raising the Standard of Practice', (2003) 9 *Michigan Journal of Gender & Law*, 207–59 at 209.

97 Council of Europe, 'Explanatory Report to Council of Europe Convention on preventing and combating violence against women and domestic violence', at para. 100.

98 U.N. Doc A/47/38 (1992), at para. 24(b).

the issues relating to child custody, economic support and security for the victims in cases of domestic violence by establishing guidelines for protection orders and sentencing guidelines which do not trivialize domestic violence'.[99] Likewise, this report also stated that police officers should receive training as regards '[t]he nature, extent, causes and consequences of domestic violence'[100] and the legal rights, services and facilities available to victims.[101] In addition, police officers should be taught techniques for handling incidents of domestic violence that promote the safety of the victim.[102] Also, in 2002 the Special Rapporteur asserted: 'States should train all public officials in the administration of justice, education and health sectors to be sensitive and energetic with regard to issues relating to violence against women.'[103]

In a similar manner, Article 8(c) of the Convention of Belém do Pará places an obligation on states parties to 'promote the education and training of all those involved in the administration of justice, police and other law enforcement officers as well as other personnel responsible for implementing policies for the prevention, punishment and eradication of violence against women'. Article 8 of the Maputo Protocol obliges states parties to adopt measures to ensure that 'law enforcement organs at all levels are equipped to effectively interpret and enforce gender equality rights'.

Treatment programmes for perpetrators

Article 16(1) of the Istanbul Convention states:

> Parties shall take the necessary legislative or other measures to set up or support programmes aimed at teaching perpetrators of domestic violence to adopt non-violent behaviour in interpersonal relationships with a view to preventing further violence and changing violent behavioural patterns.

Article 16(3) provides that, in taking such measures, 'parties shall ensure that the safety of, support for and the human rights of victims are of primary concern and

99 Report of the Special Rapporteur on violence against women, its causes and consequences – A framework for model legislation on domestic violence, E/CN.4/1996/53/Add.2, 2 February 1996, at para. 2(k).

100 At para. 62(a).

101 At paras 62(b) and (c).

102 At para. 62(e).

103 Report of the Special Rapporteur on violence against women, its causes and consequences, E/CN.4/2002/83, 31 January 2002, at para. 128. For other UN documents dealing with the need to educate professionals in the issues involved in domestic violence, see General Assembly Resolution 40/36 (1985), at para. 7(g); General Assembly Resolution 45/114 (1990), at para. 1(c); General Assembly Resolution 48/104 (1993), Article 4(i); Beijing Platform for Action, U.N. Doc.A/CONF.177/20 (1995), at para. 124(g); Commission on Human Rights Resolution 2001/49, at para. 10(f); and Commission on Human Rights Resolution 2004/46, at para. 15(g).

that, where appropriate, these programmes are set up and implemented in close co-ordination with specialist support services for victims'.

Placing a duty on states parties to provide treatment programmes for perpetrators of domestic violence may be rather controversial. It appears that there is little evidence for the proposition that such programmes are effective.[104] As Burton states, 'The efficacy of these programmes has been subject to much debate and the methodology of some studies has been seriously questioned.'[105] Nevertheless, in certain circumstances it may be more beneficial to develop treatment programmes for perpetrators of domestic violence than to apply classic criminal justice measures. In many cases the victim wishes the relationship to continue and attendance by the perpetrator at a battery treatment programme may help to achieve this goal. Hester and Lilley comment: 'In leading perpetrators to accept responsibility for their violence, perpetrator programmes are crucial to overcoming belief systems that tolerate, justify or outright condone violence against women.'[106]

The UN human rights bodies have also paid some attention to the issue of educating perpetrators of violence against women. For example, General Recommendation No. 19 of the CEDAW Committee asserted that states should provide rehabilitation programmes for perpetrators.[107] The report of the Special Rapporteur outlining a framework for model legislation also recommended that states deliver services to assist in the rehabilitation of abusers,[108] although it commented that '[t]he law shall mandate counselling programmes for perpetrators as a supplement to and not as an alternative to the criminal justice system'.[109] The report stated that funding for perpetrator programmes should not be taken from resources that are assigned to assist victims.[110]

104 Becker M., 'Access to Justice: The Social Responsibility of Lawyers: Access to Justice for Battered Women', (2003) 12 *Washington University Journal of Law & Policy*, 63–98 at 86.

105 Burton, op. cit., at p.131.

106 Hester M. and Lilley S., 'Preventing Violence against Women: Article 12 of the Istanbul Convention', 2014, Council of Europe, Strasbourg, at p.5. For further discussion of perpetrator programmes, see Hilder S. and Freeman C., 'Working with Perpetrators of Domestic Violence and Abuse', in S. Hilder and V. Bettinson (eds), *Domestic Violence: Interdisciplinary Perspectives on Protection, Prevention and Intervention*, 2016, Palgrave Macmillan, London, 273–96.

107 U.N. Doc A/47/38 (1992), at para. 24(r)(iv).

108 Report of the Special Rapporteur on violence against women, its causes and consequences – A framework for model legislation on domestic violence, E/CN.4/1996/53/Add.2, 2 February 1996, at para. 61(b).

109 At para. 70.

110 At para. 72. For other UN documents dealing with the development of rehabilitation programmes for perpetrators of domestic violence, see General Assembly Resolution 40/36 (1985), at para. 7(a); Report of the World Conference to Review and Appraise the Achievements of the United Nations Decade for Women: Equality, Development and Peace, held in Nairobi, July 1985, including Nairobi Forward-Looking Strategies for the Advancement of Women, U.N. Doc A/CONF.116/28/Rev.1 (85.IV.10), at para. 123; General Assembly Resolution 45/114 (1990), at para. 1(d); Beijing Platform for Action, U.N. Doc.A/CONF.177/20 (1995), at para. 125(i); Commission on Human Rights

Support for victims

It is widely accepted by those working in the area of combating domestic violence that legal responses alone are insufficient. As Schneider states, 'Legal intervention may provide women certain protection from battering, but it does not provide women housing, support, child care, employment, community acceptance, or love. It also does not deal with the economic realities of life.'[111] Randall comments that legal responses can only be part of a comprehensive strategy to deal with such a complex problem as domestic violence.[112] Schneider states that far more important than criminalisation:

> is the need for provision of state and state-supported resources to deal with the real problems that battered women face – child care, shelters, welfare, work . . . and thus make it possible for women to have the economic and social independence that is a prerequisite to women's freedom from abuse.[113]

Mullender and Hague assert:

> According to survivors' testimonies and to research evidence, one of the principal needs of women and children escaping violence in the home is for access to safe and secure temporary and permanent housing options – in other words, for somewhere safe to go.[114]

Indeed, Sullivan comments that some women believe that their partners would actually cease being violent if they knew that the women had access to resources and that accommodation was available.[115] Randall states that it is essential that there are economic policies in place that would make leaving a viable option for all women suffering from domestic violence.[116] Recent research carried out by Women against Violence Europe (WAVE) on the role of specialist women's

Resolution 2001/49, at para. 10(g); and Commission on Human Rights Resolution 2004/46, at para. 15(k).

111 Schneider, op. cit., at p.52.

112 Randall M., 'Symposium: Domestic Violence & the Law: Theory, Policy, and Practice: Domestic Violence and the Construction of "Ideal Victims": Assaulted Women's "Image Problems" in Law', (2004) 23 *Saint Louis University Public Law Review*, 107–54 at 144.

113 Schneider, op. cit., at pp.196–7.

114 Mullender A. and Hague G., 'Women Survivors' Views', in J. Taylor-Browne (ed.), *What Works in Reducing Domestic Violence? A Comprehensive Guide for Professionals*, 2001, Whiting & Birch, London, 1–33 at 14. See also Burnet G., 'Housing: More Than Just Bricks and Mortar. Domestic Abuse Interventions within the Housing Sector', in S. Hilder and V. Bettinson (eds.), *Domestic Violence: Interdisciplinary Perspectives on Protection, Prevention and Intervention*, 2016, Palgrave Macmillan, London, 227–48.

115 Sullivan C.M., 'Using the ESID Model to Reduce Intimate Male Violence against Women', (2003) 32 *American Journal of Community Psychology*, 295–303 at 297.

116 Randall, op. cit., at p.151.

support services across Europe found that there was 'an urgent need to expand quantity and accessibility of specialist services based on a gender sensitive analysis of domestic violence and a human rights approach to service delivery'.[117]

The vital necessity for the provision of support to victims is recognised within the Istanbul Convention, which sets out the obligations placed upon states parties in this respect in an impressive amount of detail. Article 18(1) of the Convention states: 'Parties shall take the necessary legislative or other measures to protect all victims from any further acts of violence.' Under Article 18(3), states parties should ensure that measures adopted with the aim of protecting and supporting victims are 'based on a gendered understanding of violence against women and domestic violence and . . . focus on the human rights and safety of the victim'; and are 'based on an integrated approach which takes into account the relationship between victims, perpetrators, children and their wider social environment'. Such measures should aim to avoid secondary victimisation and promote the empowerment and economic independence of women victims of violence. Where appropriate, a range of protection and support services should be located on the same premises. Article 18(4) states: 'The provision of services shall not depend on the victim's willingness to press charges or testify against any perpetrator.'

Under Article 19, 'Parties shall take the necessary legislative or other measures to ensure that victims receive adequate and timely information on available support services and legal measures in a language they understand.' Article 20(1) states:

> Parties shall take the necessary legislative or other measures to ensure that victims have access to services facilitating their recovery from violence. These measures should include, when necessary, services such as legal and psychological counselling, financial assistance, housing, education, training and assistance in finding employment.

Under Article 20(2):

> Parties shall take the necessary legislative or other measures to ensure that victims have access to health care and social services and that services are adequately resourced and professionals are trained to assist victims and refer them to the appropriate services.

Article 21 states: 'Parties shall ensure that victims have information on and access to applicable regional and international individual/collective complaints mechanisms. Parties shall promote the provision of sensitive and knowledgeable

117 Violence against Women Europe (WAVE), 'WAVE Report 2015 on the Role of Specialist Women's Support Services in Europe', January 2016, WAVE, Vienna, at p.8.

assistance to victims in presenting any such complaints.' Such mechanisms could include, for example, taking a case to the European Court of Human Rights or making a complaint to the CEDAW Committee under the Optional Protocol mechanism. It seems that there is certainly a need for states to take steps to increase awareness of such mechanisms. As Murdoch comments in relation to the individual complaints mechanism under CEDAW, 'The minimal utilisation of the right of communication . . . suggests(s) a widespread lack of awareness or understanding of the Optional Protocol on the part of individuals'.[118] The communications that have been made to the CEDAW Committee regarding the issue of domestic violence will be discussed in detail in Chapter 5.

Under Article 22(1) of the Istanbul Convention:

> Parties shall take the necessary legislative or other measures to provide or arrange for, in an adequate geographical distribution, immediate, short- and long-term specialist support services to any victim subjected to any of the acts of violence covered by the scope of this Convention.

Article 22(2) states: 'Parties shall provide or arrange for specialist women's support services to all women victims of violence and their children.' Under Article 23, states parties must adopt 'the necessary legislative or other measures to provide for the setting-up of appropriate, easily accessible shelters in sufficient numbers to provide safe accommodation for and to reach out pro-actively to victims, especially women and their children'.

Under Article 24, states parties should adopt:

> the necessary legislative or other measures to set up state-wide round-the-clock (24/7) telephone helplines free of charge to provide advice to callers, confidentially or with due regard for their anonymity, in relation to all forms of violence covered by the scope of this Convention.

The Explanatory Report to the Convention states in relation to this provision:

> Helplines are one of the most important ways of enabling victims to find help and support. A helpline with a widely advertised public number that provides support and crisis counselling and refers to face-to-face services, such as shelters, counselling centres or the police, forms the cornerstone of any support and advice service in relation to all the forms of violence covered by the scope of this Convention.[119]

118 Murdoch J., 'Unfulfilled Expectations: The Optional Protocol to the Convention on the Elimination of All Forms of Discrimination against Women', (2010) *European Human Rights Law Review*, 26–46 at 45.

119 Council of Europe, 'Explanatory Report to Council of Europe Convention on preventing and combating violence against women and domestic violence', at para. 136.

Article 26(1) provides:

> Parties shall take the necessary legislative or other measures to ensure that in the provision of protection and support services to victims, due account is taken of the rights and needs of child witnesses of all forms of violence covered by the scope of this Convention.

Under Article 26(2), such measures should include age-appropriate psychosocial counselling and must give due regard to the best interests of the child. As stated in the Explanatory Report, 'Exposure to physical, sexual or psychological violence and abuse between parents or other family members has a severe impact on children. It breeds fear, causes trauma and adversely affects their development.'[120]

The need to provide sufficient social support measures to victims of domestic violence has also been recognised by the UN human rights bodies. For example, in its General Recommendation No. 19, the CEDAW Committee asserted that states should provide '[p]rotective measures, including refuges, counselling, rehabilitation and support services for women who are the victims of violence or who are at risk of violence'.[121] The 1996 report of the Special Rapporteur on violence against women, which contained the framework for model legislation on domestic violence, detailed the precise services that states should provide. For example, the state must provide emergency services including immediate transport from the victim's home to a medical centre, shelter or other place of safety, emergency legal counselling and crisis counselling.[122] States should also provide services to assist in the rehabilitation of victims through counselling and job training,[123] and programmes for domestic violence to be administered independently of welfare assistance programmes.[124] Another report issued by the Special Rapporteur in 1996 asserted that '[r]ecognizing the nexus between domestic violence and homelessness, priority should be given to victim-survivors of domestic violence in State-sponsored housing'.[125]

120 At para. 143.
121 U.N. Doc A/47/38 (1992), at para. 24(t)(iii).
122 Report of the Special Rapporteur on violence against women, its causes and consequences – A framework for model legislation on domestic violence, E/CN.4/1996/53/Add.2, 2 February 1996, at para. 60.
123 At para. 61(a).
124 At para. 61(c).
125 Report of the Special Rapporteur on violence against women, its causes and consequences, E/CN.4/1996/53, 5 February 1996, at para. 142(m). For other UN documents dealing with the need for social support measures for victims of domestic violence, see General Assembly Resolution 40/36 (1985), at paras 7(e) and 7(f); Report of the World Conference to Review and Appraise the Achievements of the United Nations Decade for Women: Equality, Development and Peace, held in Nairobi, July 1985, including Nairobi Forward-Looking Strategies for the Advancement of Women, U.N. Doc A/CONF.116/28/Rev.1 (85.IV.10), at para. 231; General Assembly Resolution 48/104 (1993), Article 4(g); Beijing Platform for Action, U.N. Doc.A/CONF.177/20 (1995), at para. 125(a); Commission on

Similarly, under Article 8(d) of the Convention of Belém do Pará, states parties have a duty to adopt measures with the aim of providing 'appropriate specialized services for women who have been subjected to violence, through public and private sector agencies, including shelters, counseling services for all family members where appropriate, and care and custody of the affected children'. Under Article 8(f), measures should be taken to 'provide women who are subjected to violence access to effective readjustment and training programs to enable them to fully participate in public, private and social life'.

Likewise, under Article 4(2)(e) of the Maputo Protocol, states have a duty to 'implement programmes for the rehabilitation of women victims'. Article 4(2)(f) places an obligation on states parties to 'establish mechanisms and accessible services for effective information, rehabilitation and reparation for victims of violence against women'. Under Article 5, states parties must provide the 'necessary support to victims of harmful practices through basic services such as health services, legal and judicial support, emotional and psychological counselling as well as vocational training to make them self-supporting'. Article 12 places a duty on states parties to 'provide access to counselling and rehabilitation services to women who suffer abuses'.

Civil law measures

As Connelly and Cavanagh comment, 'Engaging with the civil law enables women to actively respond to current abuse and seek to stop future abuse without reliance on the criminal law and its agents.'[126] The importance of civil law measures is recognised by the Istanbul Convention. Under Article 29, states parties must take measures to provide victims with adequate civil remedies, both against perpetrators and against state authorities that have failed to take appropriate preventive or protective measures. Article 53(1) states: 'Parties shall take the necessary legislative or other measures to ensure that appropriate restraining or protection orders are available to victims of all forms of violence covered by the scope of this Convention.' Under Article 53(2), such orders must be available for immediate protection and without undue financial or administrative burdens being placed on the victim; issued for a specified period or until modified or discharged; where necessary, issued on an *ex parte* basis which has immediate effect; available irrespective of, or in addition to, other legal proceedings; and allowed to be introduced in subsequent legal proceedings. Article 53(3) places an obligation on states parties to take measures to ensure that breaches of restraining or protection orders are subject to 'effective, proportionate and dissuasive criminal or other legal sanctions'.

The need for adequate civil law measures has also been recognised by the UN human rights bodies. For example, in its General Recommendation No. 19, the

Human Rights Resolution 2001/49, at para. 2; and Commission on Human Rights Resolution 2004/46, at para. 15(g).

126 Connelly and Cavanagh, op. cit., at p.261.

CEDAW Committee stated that '[e]ffective legal measures, including . . . civil remedies'[127] were necessary to protect women from violence occurring in the private sphere. Likewise, the report of the Special Rapporteur on violence against women containing the framework for model legislation on domestic violence, went into a substantial amount of detail regarding the restraining orders and protection orders that states should make available.[128] According to this report, such orders should have the capacity *inter alia* to compel the offender to vacate the family home, regulate the offender's access to dependent children, restrain the offender from contacting the victim and compel the offender to pay the victim's medical bills.[129] Likewise, Article 7(c) of the Convention of Belém do Pará encompasses the placing of an obligation on states parties to 'include in their domestic legislation . . . civil . . . provisions that may be needed to prevent, punish and eradicate violence against women'.

Article 31 of the Istanbul Convention addresses the area of custody and visitation rights, an issue that is of particular relevance to domestic violence. This provision states: 'Parties shall take the necessary legislative or other measures to ensure that, in the determination of custody and visitation rights of children, incidents of violence covered by the scope of this Convention are taken into account.'[130] In addition: 'Parties shall take the necessary legislative or other measures to ensure that the exercise of any visitation or custody rights does not jeopardize the rights and safety of the victim or children.'[131] Article 45(2) allows for the 'withdrawal of parental rights, if the best interests of the child, which may include the safety of the victim, cannot be guaranteed in any other way'. The Explanatory Report to the Convention states in relation to this provision:

> Ensuring contact with the abusive parent may not only have a negative impact on the child, but may also pose a serious risk to the safety of the abuser's victim, because it often gives the perpetrator a reason to contact or see the victim and may not be in line with a restraining or barring order in place. It is important to ensure that all legal measures taken to protect victims are consistent and are not thwarted by legal measures taken in other contexts.[132]

127 U.N. Doc A/47/38 (1992), at para. 24(t)(i).

128 Report of the Special Rapporteur on violence against women, its causes and consequences – A framework for model legislation on domestic violence, E/CN.4/1996/53/Add.2, 2 February 1996, at paras. 26–43.

129 For other UN documents dealing with the necessity for adequate civil law measures in relation to domestic violence, see General Assembly Resolution 40/36 (1985), at para. 7; General Assembly Resolution 48/104 (1993), Article 4(d); and Commission on Human Rights Resolution 2004/46, at para. 15(h).

130 Istanbul Convention, Article 31(1).

131 Article 31(2).

132 Council of Europe, 'Explanatory Report to Council of Europe Convention on preventing and combating violence against women and domestic violence', at para. 233.

It is worth noting that the UN Special Rapporteur on violence against women has also given consideration to the issue of child contact in cases of domestic violence. A report issued by the Special Rapporteur in 1996 stated:

> In cases of domestic violence, women should be granted full custody of the children. In cases of woman-battering, the batterer should not be granted visitation . . . In cases in which visitation rights are granted, visitation should be supervised and arranged in a way so as not to cause the woman any contact with the batterer. Details such as transportation, the site of the visitations, financial support for the visits and the persons authorized to supervise the visits should all be included in the court decree.[133]

Criminal law measures

The Istanbul Convention contains detailed consideration of how the criminal justice systems of states parties should respond to the issue of violence against women. It is notable that the Convention does not require that states enact a specific offence of 'domestic violence'; however, states parties have a duty to ensure that conduct that constitutes domestic violence is criminalised. Under Articles 35 and 36 of the Convention, physical and sexual violence must be criminalised through legislative or other measures. The criminalisation of physical and sexual violence within the family is uncontroversial and unlikely to be problematic for states parties (although it is noteworthy that it was not until the landmark case of *R v R*[134] in 1991 that the House of Lords in the UK overturned the common law rule that a man could not be held guilty of raping his wife). However, Article 33 states: 'Parties shall take the necessary legislative or other measures to ensure that the intentional conduct of seriously impairing a person's psychological integrity through coercion or threats is criminalised.' The criminalisation of 'psychological violence' may be more problematic for states parties. For example, as discussed earlier in this chapter, the extent to which psychological abuse in intimate relationships is criminalised in England and Wales has only recently been expanded, with the enactment of section 76 of the Serious Crime Act 2015. It seems that the drafters of the Istanbul Convention were aware of this potential difficulty, as seen in the fact that under Article 78(3), when signing or ratifying the Convention, a state party may declare that it reserves the right to provide for non-criminal sanctions, instead of criminal sanctions, for the behaviours referred to in Article 33. At the time of writing, however, only one of the current states parties to the Convention has entered such a reservation.[135]

133 Report of the Special Rapporteur on violence against women, its causes and consequences, E/CN.4/1996/53, 5 February 1996, at para. 142(k).

134 [1991] 4 All ER 481.

135 Romania deposited such a reservation on 23 May 2016. The issue of reservations will be discussed in detail in Chapter 6. For a full list of the reservations and declarations made by

It is also noteworthy that although, as discussed earlier in the chapter, the definition of domestic violence under the Convention includes acts of 'economic violence', there is no express obligation to criminalise such conduct. However, this is unsurprising as defining such behaviour for the purposes of criminal law would be problematic. It seems that the Convention reflects the fact that it can be very difficult to ensure that all aspects of domestic violence are criminalised.

As noted above, the Istanbul Convention does not require states parties to enact a specific offence of domestic violence. However, there has been some debate about whether it would be beneficial for such an approach to be adopted by states. As Burton remarks, 'The issue of whether the criminal law should seek to distinguish between different forms of violence according to the context is a thorny one.'[136] However, commentators such as Tadros argue that there should be a specific offence of domestic violence in order to identify the distinctive type of wrong that is involved.[137] As Youngs states, 'A compelling principle in favour of a specific offence is that of fair labelling.'[138] It may also encourage victims to seek help 'if the law communicates that what they have suffered is criminal'.[139]

Conversely, the primary argument against the creation of such an offence is that this may serve to give the misleading impression that domestic violence is essentially a family matter, and is to be distinguished from other forms of violence as being less serious. Burton comments:

> Symbolically the marking out of domestic violence as a distinctive wrong is defensible, but the educative value of the criminal law may be overstated if it is assumed that the separation of the offence can effectively communicate a message that domestic violence is a serious form of misconduct which the state will not tolerate.[140]

Article 46 of the Istanbul Convention sets out a list of factors that should be taken into consideration as aggravating circumstances in the determination of the sentence in relation to the offences established in accordance with the Convention. These include a number of factors that may have particular relevance to offences relating to domestic violence – for example, if the offence was committed against a former or current spouse or partner, by a member of the family, a person cohabiting with the victim or a person having abused her or his

states parties to the Istanbul Convention, see www.coe.int/en/web/conventions/full-list/-/conventions/treaty/210/declarations?p_auth=VHYoKh1z (accessed 14 October 2016), Council of Europe.

136 Burton, op. cit., at p.66.

137 Tadros V., 'The Distinctiveness of Domestic Abuse: A Freedom Based Account' in A. Duff and S. Green (eds), *Defining Crimes*, 2005, Oxford University Press, Oxford, 119–42.

138 Youngs J., 'Domestic Violence and the Criminal Law: Reconceptualising Reform', (2015) 79 *Journal of Criminal Law*, 55–70 at 65.

139 Youngs, op. cit., at p.66.

140 Burton, op. cit., at p.68.

authority;[141] if the offence, or related offences, were committed repeatedly;[142] if the offence was committed against a person made vulnerable by particular circumstances;[143] if the offence was committed against or in the presence of a child;[144] if the offence was preceded or accompanied by extreme levels of violence;[145] if the offence was committed with the use or threat of a weapon;[146] if the offence resulted in severe physical or psychological harm for the victim;[147] and if the perpetrator had previously been convicted of offences of a similar nature.[148]

Article 49(1) of the Convention states:

> Parties shall take the necessary legislative or other measures to ensure that investigations and judicial proceedings in relation to all forms of violence covered by the scope of this Convention are carried out without undue delay while taking into consideration the rights of the victim during all stages of the criminal proceedings.

Under Article 49(2), states parties must adopt 'the necessary legislative or other measures, in conformity with the fundamental principles of human rights and having regard to the gendered understanding of violence, to ensure the effective investigation and prosecution of offences established in accordance with this Convention'. According to the Explanatory Report to the Convention, 'This means, for example, establishing the relevant facts, interviewing all available witnesses, and conducting forensic examinations, based on a multi-disciplinary approach and using state-of-the-art criminal investigative methodology to ensure a comprehensive analysis of the case.'[149] Under Article 50, states parties must ensure that law enforcement agencies respond promptly and appropriately to instances of violence against women by offering adequate and immediate protection to victims. Article 51 provides that in such cases, assessments must be carried out as regards the seriousness of the situation and the risk of repeated violence. As stated in the Explanatory Report, 'Concerns for the victim's safety must lie at the heart of any intervention in cases of all forms of violence covered by the scope of this Convention.'[150] Under Article 52:

> Parties shall take the necessary legislative or other measures to ensure that the competent authorities are granted the power to order, in situations of

141 Istanbul Convention, Article 46(a).
142 Article 46(b).
143 Article 46(c).
144 Article 46(d).
145 Article 46(f).
146 Article 46(g).
147 Article 46(h).
148 Article 46(i).
149 Council of Europe, 'Explanatory Report to Council of Europe Convention on preventing and combating violence against women and domestic violence', at para. 256.
150 At para. 260.

> immediate danger, a perpetrator of domestic violence to vacate the residence of the victim or person at risk for a sufficient period of time and to prohibit the perpetrator from entering the residence of or contacting the victim or person at risk.

Under Article 55(1), states parties must ensure that prosecutions of offences involving violence against women are not wholly dependent upon complaints being filed by victims, and that the proceedings may continue even if the victim withdraws her complaint. Again this is an issue of particular relevance to domestic violence. In many cases, women who have suffered domestic violence do not want to have their assailants prosecuted for a variety of reasons, such as a belief that a prosecution will simply lead to an escalation of violence. The question of whether a prosecution should proceed even without the consent of the victim is an extremely difficult issue. Should the wishes of the victim be respected in all cases or are there some instances in which the violence is simply so horrific that intervention is essential regardless of the victim's views? In such cases, is a prosecution necessary in the interests of society? The Convention does not attempt to lay down guidelines with regard to the circumstances in which prosecutions should proceed without the victim's consent; it simply states that it must be possible for this to happen. Nevertheless, it has to be remembered that the question of how to balance punishing offenders with protecting victims in cases of domestic violence is extremely controversial. There does not appear to be any real consensus among those working in the field of domestic violence as to how to proceed in a case in which a victim of severe domestic violence does not wish her assailant to be prosecuted. It is perhaps too much to expect a human rights treaty to arrive at a definitive conclusion on this issue, as it is certainly arguable that it is not the function of human rights bodies to make decisions regarding such controversial details of policy.[151]

Nevertheless, the obligations placed on states parties as regards the responses of their criminal justice systems to instances of violence against women are described in an impressive amount of detail. Article 55(2) states:

> Parties shall take the necessary legislative or other measures to ensure, in accordance with the conditions provided for by their internal law, the possibility for governmental and non-governmental organisations and domestic violence counsellors to assist and/or support victims, at their request, during investigations and judicial proceedings concerning the offences established in accordance with this Convention.

151 See further McQuigg R., *International Human Rights Law and Domestic Violence*, 2011, Routledge, Abingdon, at pp.25 and 98.

The Explanatory Report notes:

> Good practice examples have shown that victims who are supported or assisted by a specialist support service during investigations and proceedings are more likely to file a complaint and testify and are better equipped to take on the emotionally challenging task of actively contributing to the outcome of proceedings.[152]

Under Article 56(1), victims must be informed, at least in cases where they may be in danger, if the perpetrator escapes from detention or is released.[153] Victims must also be informed of their rights and the services at their disposal, and of the progress of the investigation or proceedings.[154] They must be enabled to supply evidence and have their views and concerns presented and considered.[155] Contact between victims and perpetrators at court and law enforcement agency premises should be avoided where possible.[156] Measures should also be adopted to enable victims to testify in court without being present or without the presence of the alleged perpetrator, through the use of appropriate communication technologies, where available.[157]

The UN human rights bodies have also paid a substantial amount of attention to the measures that states should adopt in the criminal law sphere in relation to domestic violence. For example, in its General Recommendation No. 19, the CEDAW Committee stated that measures needed to overcome family violence included 'criminal penalties where necessary'[158] and that 'states parties should ensure that laws against family violence and abuse . . . give adequate protection to all women, and respect their integrity and dignity'.[159] The framework for model legislation on domestic violence produced by the Special Rapporteur on violence against women dealt in a relatively detailed manner with how a state's criminal justice system should respond to cases of domestic violence. For example, in relation to complaint mechanisms this document stated:

> The law shall provide for victims, witnesses of domestic violence, family members and close associates of victims, State and private medical service providers and domestic violence assistance centres to complain of incidents of domestic violence to the police or file action in court.[160]

152 Council of Europe, 'Explanatory Report to Council of Europe Convention on preventing and combating violence against women and domestic violence', at para. 282.
153 Istanbul Convention, Article 56(1)(b).
154 Article 56(1)(c).
155 Article 56(1)(d).
156 Article 56(1)(g).
157 Article 56(1)(i).
158 U.N. Doc A/47/38 (1992), at para. 24(r)(i).
159 At para. 24(b).
160 Report of the Special Rapporteur on violence against women, its causes and consequences – A framework for model legislation on domestic violence, E/CN.4/1996/53/Add.2, 2 February 1996, at para. 12.

The duties of police officers in domestic violence cases were laid down in detail by the Special Rapporteur. For example, the law should provide that police officers should respond to every request for assistance in cases of alleged domestic violence.[161] Also, police officers should not regard calls concerning alleged domestic abuse as being of lower priority than calls alleging violence by strangers.[162] The police must respond promptly even where the person reporting the incident was not the victim, but a witness of the violence, a friend of the victim or a professional working at a domestic violence assistance centre.[163] Police officers should interview the parties in separate rooms,[164] record the details of the complaint,[165] advise the victim of her rights[166] and arrange transport for the victim to a medical facility if necessary.[167] The police should also arrange transport for the victim and her children to a shelter, if needed.[168] The offender must be removed from the home or, if this is not possible and the victim remains in danger, the offender should be arrested.[169] The police officer should also provide the victim with a written statement outlining all the legal procedures available to her.[170] Overall, the police should take all reasonable measures to ensure that the victim is safe.[171] In addition, the Special Rapporteur set out the particulars that should be included in a report of an incident involving domestic violence.[172] The police commissioner should compile annually the data collected from the domestic violence reports and submit a summary report to Parliament.[173]

The Special Rapporteur also laid down proper practice for prosecutors and courts in cases involving violence against women in the home. For example, if a court dismisses criminal charges, the specific reasons for dismissal should be recorded.[174] During the course of the trial, the defendant should have no unsupervised contact with the plaintiff.[175] Clear sentencing guidelines should be established[176] and an order for counselling should not be made in place of a sentence in cases involving aggravated assault.[177]

161 At para. 13.
162 At para. 14.
163 At para. 16.
164 At para. 17(a).
165 At para. 17(b).
166 At para. 17(c).
167 At para. 17(e).
168 At para. 17(f).
169 At para. 17(h).
170 At para. 21(e).
171 At para. 21(d).
172 At para. 23.
173 At para. 24.
174 At para. 45.
175 At para. 49.
176 At para. 55.
177 At para. 54. For other UN documents dealing with the question of how the criminal justice system should respond to cases of domestic violence, see Report of the World Conference

The need for adequate criminal law measures to be adopted is also recognised in the Convention of Belém do Pará, of which Article 8(b) places a duty on states parties to 'apply due diligence to prevent, investigate and impose penalties for violence against women'. Under Article 8(c), states parties must 'include in their domestic legislation penal . . . provisions . . . to prevent, punish and eradicate violence against women'. Likewise, under Article 4(2) of the Maputo Protocol, states parties must take appropriate and effective measures to 'enact and enforce laws to prohibit all forms of violence against women . . . whether the violence takes place in private or public';[178] 'adopt such other legislative . . . measures as may be necessary to ensure the prevention, punishment and eradication of all forms of violence against women';[179] and 'punish the perpetrators of violence against women'.[180]

Migration and asylum

Article 59 of the Istanbul Convention relates to residence status. Under Article 59(1):

> Parties shall take the necessary legislative or other measures to ensure that victims whose residence status depends on that of the spouse or partner as recognised by internal law, in the event of the dissolution of the marriage or the relationship, are granted in the event of particularly difficult circumstances, upon application, an autonomous residence permit irrespective of the duration of the marriage or the relationship.

Article 59(2) places a duty on states parties to adopt the necessary measures to ensure that victims may obtain the suspension of expulsion proceedings in relation to a residence status dependent on that of their spouse or partner in order to allow them to apply for an autonomous residence permit. Under Article 59(3), states parties should issue a renewable residence permit to victims where the competent

of the United Nations Decade for Women: Equality, Development and Peace, Copenhagen, July 1980, U.N. Doc A/CONF. 94/35 (80.IV.3), at para. 65; General Assembly Resolution 40/36 (1985), at paras 3 and 7; Report of the World Conference to Review and Appraise the Achievements of the United Nations Decade for Women: Equality, Development and Peace, held in Nairobi, July 1985, including Nairobi Forward-Looking Strategies for the Advancement of Women, U.N. Doc A/CONF.116/28/Rev.1 (85.IV.10), at para. 76; General Assembly Resolution 45/114 (1990), at para. 2; General Assembly Resolution 48/104 (1993), Articles 4(d) and (f); Beijing Platform for Action, U.N. Doc.A/CONF.177/20 (1995), at paras 112, 113 and 124; Commission on Human Rights Resolution 2001/49, at para. 10(c); Commission on Human Rights Resolution 2004/46, at para. 15; and General Assembly Resolution 60/143 (2007), at paras 7 and 8(i).

178 Maputo Protocol, Article 4(2)(a).

179 Article 4(2)(b).

180 Article 4(2)(e).

authority considers that their stay is necessary owing to their personal situation; or where the competent authority considers that their stay is necessary for the purpose of their cooperation with the competent authorities in investigation or criminal proceedings.

As the Explanatory Report to the Convention states:

> Asylum law has long failed to address the difference between women and men in terms of why and how they experience persecution. This gender blindness in the establishment of refugee status and of international protection has resulted in situations where claims of women fleeing from gender-based violence have gone unrecognised.[181]

Article 60(1) states:

> Parties shall take the necessary legislative or other measures to ensure that gender-based violence against women may be recognised as a form of persecution within the meaning of Article 1, A (2), of the 1951 Convention relating to the Status of Refugees[182] and as a form of serious harm giving rise to complementary/subsidiary protection.

Under Article 61(2), states parties should adopt measures to ensure that victims of violence against women who are in need of protection are not returned to any country where their life would be at risk or where they might be subjected to torture or inhuman or degrading treatment or punishment.

Conclusion

One of the most striking features of the Istanbul Convention is the very detailed nature of its provisions. As Hester and Lilley comment, these provisions 'are based on state-of-the-art knowledge of what works to prevent violence against women'.[183] The focus of this book is on the particular issue of domestic violence, and the level of detail in which the obligations of states parties as regards this issue are described is unprecedented in an instrument of this nature. The measures contained in the Istanbul Convention are in general not new. As has been seen throughout the discussion in this chapter, the majority of the measures encompassed by the Convention had already been recommended by entities such as the CEDAW Committee and the UN Special Rapporteur on violence against women, its causes and consequences prior to the adoption of the Convention by the

181 Council of Europe, 'Explanatory Report to Council of Europe Convention on preventing and combating violence against women and domestic violence', at para. 310.

182 The Convention relating to the Status of Refugees (189 U.N.T.S. 137) was adopted by the UN General Assembly on 28 July 1951 and entered into force on 22 April 1954.

183 Hester and Lilley, op. cit., at p.41.

Council of Europe. However, the crucial difference between the recommendations of the UN human rights bodies in the area of domestic violence and the obligations found in the Istanbul Convention is that the latter are legally binding duties.

The provisions found in the Convention of Belém do Pará and the Maputo Protocol are of course legally binding on their respective states parties; however, neither of these instruments contain obligations described in anywhere near the degree of precision found in the Istanbul Convention. The Maputo Protocol is an instrument on the rights of women more generally, as opposed to being an instrument specifically on gender-based violence, and therefore a more general approach is to be expected. However, it is noteworthy that the provisions of the Istanbul Convention on domestic violence are so much more detailed than those contained in the Convention of Belém do Pará, a fact that may be explained by recent developments in understandings of domestic violence and of the measures necessary to address this issue. Indeed, the provisions of the Convention of Belém do Pará that relate to domestic violence are simply subsumed in the more general provisions on violence against women, due to the integrated approach adopted by this instrument.

The detailed nature of the provisions of the Istanbul Convention certainly appears to constitute a very positive feature of this instrument. It is, however, arguable that there may be a potential difficulty with this approach. It is possible that the level of precision with which the obligations of states parties are delineated could in practice discourage states from becoming parties to the Convention, particularly as under Article 78 of this instrument no reservations are permitted, apart from a number of very narrow exceptions. This issue will be discussed further in Chapter 6. Chapter 5 will examine another crucial aspect of the Convention: the monitoring procedures contained therein.

5 Monitoring mechanisms

The aim of this chapter is to examine the monitoring procedures of the Istanbul Convention. The monitoring mechanisms are a crucial part of any human rights treaty. As Keller and Ulfstein remark, 'treaty ratifications do not suffice to ensure the protection of human rights', and treaty monitoring bodies therefore have an essential role to play as regards the supervision of compliance by states with their treaty obligations.[1] Under Article 66(1) of the Istanbul Convention, implementation is monitored by a Group of Experts on Action against Violence against Women and Domestic Violence, known as 'GREVIO'. The members of GREVIO are to be elected by a body known as 'the Committee of the Parties' which is comprised of representatives of the states that are parties to the Convention. The main monitoring mechanism is a reporting procedure, with an inquiry procedure also being established. The Committee of the Parties met for the first time on 4 May 2015, and the first meeting of GREVIO took place on 21–23 September 2015.

In examining the monitoring mechanisms of the Istanbul Convention, this chapter will again engage in comparative analysis. For example, the Optional Protocol to the Convention on the Elimination of All Forms of Discrimination against Women (CEDAW)[2] encompasses a communications mechanism, under which individuals may submit complaints concerning violations to the UN Committee on the Elimination of Discrimination against Women (CEDAW Committee). Likewise, an individual complaints mechanism whereby petitions may be lodged with the Inter-American Commission on Human Rights is encompassed by the Inter-American Convention on the Prevention, Punishment, and Eradication of Violence against Women (the Convention of Belém do Pará).

1 Keller H. and Ulfstein G., 'Conclusions', in H. Keller and G. Ulfstein (eds), *UN Human Rights Treaty Bodies: Law and Legitimacy*, 2012, Cambridge University Press, Cambridge, 414–25 at 414–5.

2 CEDAW (1249 U.N.T.S. 13) was adopted by the UN General Assembly on 18 December 1979 and entered into force on 3 September 1981. The Optional Protocol to CEDAW was adopted by the General Assembly on 6 October 1999 and entered into force on 22 December 2000.

Such a mechanism is not included in the Istanbul Convention, and the question of whether the omission of a communications mechanism will lessen the effectiveness of this instrument will be discussed. In analysing this issue, reference will be made to the communications concerning domestic violence that have been examined by the CEDAW Committee under the Optional Protocol procedure,[3] and to the relevant jurisprudence of the Inter-American Commission, such as the seminal case of *Maria da Penha Maia Fernandes v Brazil*.[4]

The Group of Experts on Action against Violence against Women and Domestic Violence (GREVIO) and the Committee of the Parties

The Istanbul Convention's monitoring mechanisms are set out in Articles 66–70. Article 66(1) establishes that implementation of the provisions of the Convention by states parties is to be monitored by a Group of Experts on Action against Violence against Women and Domestic Violence (known as 'GREVIO'). Under Article 66(2), GREVIO is to be composed of between ten and 15 members, taking into account a gender and geographical balance, in addition to multidisciplinary expertise. The members of GREVIO are to be elected by a body known as the 'Committee of the Parties' (see below) from among candidates nominated by the states parties for a term of office of four years, renewable once. The candidates nominated should be nationals of the states parties. Under Article 66(3), an initial election of ten members must be held within a period of one year following the entry into force of the Convention. Five additional members should be elected after 25 states have ratified or acceded to the treaty.

Under Article 67(1) of the Convention, the Committee of the Parties (as referred to above) is to be comprised of the representatives of the states parties to the Convention. Article 67(2) states that the Committee of the Parties is to be convened by the Secretary General of the Council of Europe. Its first meeting had to be held within a period of one year following the entry into force of the Convention in order to elect the members of GREVIO,[5] and it will subsequently meet whenever one-third of the states parties to the Convention, the President of the Committee of the Parties or the Secretary General so requests. Under Article 67(3), the Committee of the Parties shall

3 *AT v Hungary* (Communication No. 2/2003, 26 January 2005, CEDAW/C/32/D/2/2003); *Goekce v Austria* (Communication No. 5/2005, 6 August 2007, CEDAW/C/39/D/5/2005); *Yildirim v Austria* (Communication No. 6/2005, 1 October 2007, CEDAW/C/39/D/6/2005); *VK v Bulgaria* (Communication No. 20/2008, 17 August 2011, CEDAW/C/49/D/20/2008); *Jallow v Bulgaria* (Communication No. 32/2011, 28 August 2012, CEDAW/C/52/D/32/2011).

4 Case 12.051, Report No. 54/01 (2001).

5 This meeting took place on 4 May 2015.

adopt its own rules of procedure.[6] The Explanatory Report to the Convention states:

> The setting up of this body will ensure equal participation of all the Parties alike in the decision-making process and in the monitoring procedure of the Convention and will also strengthen co-operation between the Parties and between them and GREVIO to ensure the proper and effective implementation of the Convention.[7]

The establishment of a body comprising representatives of the states parties may well prove to be beneficial as regards contributing to implementation of the Istanbul Convention. It is noteworthy that a similar body has now been set up in relation to the Convention of Belém do Pará. Although no such body was established by the terms of the Convention of Belém do Pará itself, in 2004 a follow-up mechanism to this Convention, known as MESECVI, was created.[8] One of the organs set up under this mechanism is the Conference of States Parties, which is comprised of representatives of all of the states parties to the Convention, and which holds a regular meeting every two years and special meetings as often as is deemed to be necessary.[9] Likewise, Article 10(1) of the UN Convention on the Rights of Persons with Disabilities (CRPD) provides for states parties to meet regularly in a Conference of States Parties in order to consider matters relating to the implementation of this treaty.[10]

Article 66(4) of the Istanbul Convention sets out the principles on which the election of the members of GREVIO should be based. Members should be chosen according to a transparent procedure from among persons of high moral character, known for their recognised competence in the fields of human rights, gender equality, violence against women and domestic violence, or for their assistance to and protection of victims, or for having demonstrated professional experience in the areas covered by the Convention.[11] No two members of GREVIO may be

6 The rules of procedure of the Committee of the Parties were adopted during its first meeting on 4 May 2015.
7 Council of Europe, 'Explanatory Report to Council of Europe Convention on preventing and combating violence against women and domestic violence', available at https://rm.coe.int/CoERMPublicCommonSearchServices/DisplayDCTMContent?documentId=09000016800d383a (accessed 14 October 2016), at para. 347.
8 For further information on MESECVI, see www.oas.org/en/mesecvi/about.asp, Organization of American States (accessed 14 October 2016).
9 Statute of the Mechanism to follow up on the Implementation of the Inter-American Convention on the Prevention, Punishment, and Eradication of Violence against Women, Convention of Belém do Pará, Article 5(2).
10 The CRPD (2515 U.N.T.S. 3) was adopted by the UN General Assembly on 13 December 2006 and entered into force on 3 May 2008.
11 Istanbul Convention, Article 66(4)(a).

nationals of the same State;[12] they should represent the main legal systems;[13] and they should represent relevant actors and agencies in the field of violence against women and domestic violence.[14] Members of GREVIO sit in their individual capacity, should be independent and impartial in the exercise of their functions, and should be available to carry out their duties in an effective manner.[15] Article 66(6) states that GREVIO should adopt its own rules of procedure.[16]

Article 66(5) of the Convention states that the election procedure of the members of GREVIO should be determined by the Committee of Ministers of the Council of Europe, after consulting with and obtaining the unanimous consent of the states parties, within six months of the entry into force of the Convention. This election procedure was indeed subsequently set out by the Committee of Ministers in a Resolution adopted on 19 November 2014.[17] Under Rule 9 of this Resolution, the government of each state party to the Istanbul Convention could submit to the Secretary General of the Council of Europe the names and the curricula vitae of up to three candidates to serve on GREVIO. Under Rule 10 of the Resolution, each state party should ensure that the national selection procedure leading to the nomination of candidates for GREVIO is transparent and open to competition in order to lead to the nomination of the most qualified candidates. The Secretary General should then transmit the nominations received to the Committee of the Parties. Under Rule 11, the members of GREVIO are elected by the Committee of the Parties. Rule 12 states that in filling vacant seats in GREVIO the Committee of the Parties should give priority to electing experts who possess competences and/or professional experience not sufficiently represented among the members of GREVIO; experts from geographical areas not represented in GREVIO; those representing a main legal system not represented in GREVIO; and those of the sex under-represented in GREVIO. Under Rule 13 the Committee of the Parties should elect members of GREVIO by secret ballot. Rule 14 states that a member elected to fill a seat that has become vacant before the end of the four-year term of office of the previous member shall hold the seat for the remainder of the predecessor's term. Under Rule 15, if more than five members of GREVIO are re-elected for a second term of office in the same elections, the Committee of the Parties may decide to shorten the term of office of three members by two years. These members should be identified by the drawing of lots by the Committee of the Parties.

12 Article 66(4)(b).
13 Article 66(4)(c).
14 Article 66(4)(d).
15 Article 66(4)(e).
16 The rules of procedure of GREVIO were adopted during its first meeting on 21–23 September 2015.
17 Resolution CM/Res (2014)43 on rules on the election procedure of the members of the Group of Experts on Action against Violence against Women and Domestic Violence (GREVIO).

The Committee of Ministers invited the states parties to submit to the Secretary General of the Council of Europe nominations for GREVIO candidates by 2 March 2015. Of the 12 states that submitted nominations, only Austria, Italy and Serbia chose to submit the maximum three nominations each. Albania, Montenegro and Sweden each nominated two candidates, with Denmark, France, Malta, Portugal, Spain and Turkey each nominating one candidate. Interestingly but perhaps unsurprisingly, 20 of the 21 candidates nominated by the states parties were women.[18] The Committee of the Parties to the Istanbul Convention met for the first time on 4 May 2015 in Strasbourg. At this meeting it adopted its own rules of procedure, and it also elected ten GREVIO members. The first ten members of GREVIO are Feride Acar of Turkey,[19] Biljana Brankovic of Serbia, Françoise Brié of France, Helena Maria Carvallho Martins Leitão of Portugal, Gemma Gallego of Spain, Simona Lanzoni of Italy, Rosa Logar of Austria, Iris Luarasi of Albania, Marceline Naudi of Malta and Vesna Ratkovic of Montenegro.[20] The first meeting of GREVIO was held on 21–23 September 2015 in Strasbourg, at which Professor Acar was elected as the first President of GREVIO, with Ms Logar and Dr Naudi being elected as Vice Presidents.[21]

Reporting procedure

Article 68 of the Istanbul Convention sets out the details of the monitoring procedures to be carried out by GREVIO. The main monitoring mechanism is a reporting procedure, similar to those of the UN human rights treaties, such as CEDAW. For example, every four years, states parties to CEDAW must present a report to the CEDAW Committee. Under General Recommendation No. 19, these reports should contain information on the prevalence of violence against women,[22] and the legal, protective and preventive measures that the state in question is taking to protect women from violence. Information should also be provided on the effectiveness of such measures.[23] In 1999 non-governmental organisations were invited to submit their own reports on the issues in question. These reports tend to adopt a more critical approach, and often present a more

18 The only male nominee was Dr Ugljesa Jankovic, an academic from the University of Montenegro, Podgorica.

19 It is notable that Professor Acar is also a member and former Chairperson of the CEDAW Committee.

20 Professor Acar, Ms Logar and Dr Naudi were members of the Ad Hoc Committee on Preventing and Combating Violence against Women and Domestic Violence (CAHVIO). Professor Acar and Ms Logar were also members of the Task Force to Combat Violence against Women, including Domestic Violence. Both of these bodies were discussed in Chapter 3. Ms Logar is the President of WAVE (Women against Violence Europe).

21 The President and Vice Presidents of GREVIO each have a two-year term of office.

22 Committee on the Elimination of Discrimination against Women, U.N. Doc A/47/38 (1992), Article 24(u).

23 Article 24(v).

informative assessment of the situation of women living in the state in question. Byrnes remarks:

> The examination of a state's report under a treaty can provide an occasion for exerting international pressure on the state. If members of a supervisory body are strongly critical of a state or express the view that the state has not carried out its obligations under the treaty, this can serve to put some pressure on a government, particularly if the proceedings receive publicity internationally or nationally.[24]

Article 68(1) of the Istanbul Convention states: 'Parties shall submit to the Secretary General of the Council of Europe, based on a questionnaire prepared by GREVIO, a report on legislative and other measures giving effect to the provisions of this Convention.' This report will then be considered by GREVIO in conjunction with representatives of the state party in question.[25] GREVIO adopted its baseline questionnaire at its fifth meeting which took place on 11 March 2016.[26] Completion of this questionnaire requires states parties to provide detailed information on their compliance with all aspects of the Istanbul Convention. Non-governmental organisations and civil society groups working in the area of combating violence against women are also invited to submit information on the implementation of the Convention on the basis of this questionnaire. The timetable that has been adopted by GREVIO with regard to the monitoring of states parties aims at diversity in terms of geographical location and of legal systems, and takes into account the order in which states ratified the Convention.[27] Under the timetable for 2016 and 2017, Austria and Monaco were sent the questionnaire in March 2016 and submitted their reports on 1 September 2016. These reports will be considered by GREVIO at a meeting in November 2016.[28] Denmark and Albania are due to receive the questionnaire in September 2016, with their reports to be submitted by January 2017. Montenegro and Turkey will be sent the questionnaire in February 2017 and should submit their reports by June 2017. Sweden and Portugal are then due to receive the questionnaire in July 2017, and must submit their reports by November 2017. In adopting the approach of asking just two states at any one time to submit reports, it seems that GREVIO is determined

24 Byrnes A., 'Enforcement Through International Law and Procedures', in R.J. Cook (ed.), *Human Rights of Women: National and International Perspectives*, 1994, University of Pennsylvania Press, Philadelphia, 189–227 at 207.

25 Article 68(2).

26 The questionnaire can be found at https://rm.coe.int/CoERMPublicCommonSearchServices/DisplayDCTMContent?documentId=09000016805c95b0, Council of Europe (accessed 14 October 2016).

27 The timetable is available at www.coe.int/en/web/istanbul-convention/evaluation, Council of Europe (accessed 14 October 2016).

28 See www.coe.int/en/web/istanbul-convention/-/grevio-receives-first-state-reports-from-austria-and-monaco, Council of Europe (accessed 14 October 2016).

to avoid the problems of backlogs and delays in the consideration of states' reports that have arisen as regards the UN human rights treaty monitoring bodies, such as the CEDAW Committee. These difficulties will be discussed in detail in Chapter 6. Conversely however, it could be argued that the approach being adopted by GREVIO in respect of monitoring state compliance is rather too gradual. For example, there are six states parties in which the Convention entered into force in 2014, but which have not been included in the provisional reporting timetable for 2016 and 2017. This means that these states parties will not be required to submit initial reports on their compliance with the Convention until at least 2018, around four years after the Convention entered into force in their jurisdictions.[29]

Under Article 68(3) of the Convention, subsequent evaluation procedures will then be divided into rounds, the length of which is to be determined by GREVIO. At the commencement of each round, GREVIO will choose the specific provisions of the Convention on which the evaluation procedure will be based and will send out a questionnaire accordingly. It can be seen therefore that monitoring by GREVIO will focus on specific facets of the compliance of states parties, instead of always examining the compliance of the state party with the whole of the Convention. There could well be distinct advantages with the approach to be taken by GREVIO in this respect. First, it will allow the aspect of state compliance chosen for monitoring to be analysed in greater detail than would otherwise be the case. Second, it may enable GREVIO to carry out its work in a more efficient manner and help to avoid the considerable backlogs in the examination of reports that have caused substantial problems for the UN human rights treaty bodies. It is also worth noting that although states do include information on violence against women in their reports to the CEDAW Committee, states will be required to include much more detailed information on their responses to this issue in their reports under the Istanbul Convention. In addition, GREVIO will be able to analyse this information in far more depth than it is currently possible for the CEDAW Committee to do. As Gormley comments, 'As CEDAW is a complex treaty with many substantive issues to cover, it is simply not possible to have enough time to deal with the complexity of violence against women in detail.'[30]

Article 68(5) of the Istanbul Convention states that GREVIO may receive information on the implementation of the Convention from non-governmental organisations and civil society, as well as from national institutions for the protection of human rights. This approach is in line with the practice of the UN bodies

29 The Istanbul Convention entered into force in Bosnia and Herzegovina, Italy, Serbia and Spain on 1 August 2014; and in France and Malta on 1 November 2014. None of these six states have been included in the provisional monitoring timetable for 2016 and 2017.

30 Gormley L., 'The Council of Europe Convention on Preventing and Combating Violence against Women and Domestic Violence: A Consolidation of Existing International Law, or a Significant Progression?', (2014) *European Human Rights Law Review*, 606–17 at 609.

of accepting 'shadow reports' from civil society groups, in addition to the main state report. Under Article 68(6), GREVIO will take due consideration of the existing information available from other regional and international instruments and bodies in areas falling within the scope of this Convention. Article 68(8) states that GREVIO may also receive information on the implementation of the Convention from the Council of Europe Commissioner for Human Rights, the Parliamentary Assembly and relevant specialised bodies of the Council of Europe, as well as those established under other international instruments. Complaints presented to these bodies and the outcomes of these complaints will be made available to GREVIO.

Article 68(9) of the Convention provides for the organisation by GREVIO of country visits, in cooperation with the national authorities and with the assistance of independent national experts, if the information obtained is insufficient. During these visits, GREVIO may be assisted by specialists in specific fields.

Under Article 68(10), following its examination of the response of the state party in question, GREVIO will prepare a draft report containing its analysis concerning the implementation of the provisions on which the evaluation is based, as well as its suggestions and proposals regarding the way in which the state party in question may deal with any difficulties that have been identified. This draft report will then be transmitted for comment to the state party concerned. These comments will be taken into account by GREVIO when adopting its report. Under Article 68(11), on the basis of all the information received and the comments by the state party, GREVIO will adopt its report and conclusions concerning the measures taken by the state party to implement the provisions of the Convention. This report and the conclusions will be sent to the state party in question and to the Committee of the Parties. The report and conclusions of GREVIO will be made public as from their adoption, along with eventual comments by the state party concerned. This procedure is broadly similar to that of the practice of the UN human rights treaty bodies of issuing Concluding Observations on the measures that states parties should adopt to comply with the provisions of the instruments in question. Under Article 68(12) of the Istanbul Convention, the Committee of the Parties may adopt, on the basis of the report and conclusions of GREVIO, recommendations addressed to the state party concerning the measures to be taken to implement the conclusions of GREVIO, if necessary setting a date for submitting information on their implementation, and aiming at promoting cooperation with that state party as regards the proper implementation of the Convention.

It is noteworthy that the reporting mechanism contained in the Istanbul Convention is much more formalised and detailed than that which originally pertained to the Convention of Belém do Pará. Under Article 10 of the latter, states parties must include in their more general reports to the Inter-American Commission of Women information on measures that they have adopted in relation to the issue of violence against women, and on factors that contribute to the occurrence of violence against women in their particular jurisdictions. This duty is, however, expressed in rather vague terms. By contrast, the Istanbul

Convention encompasses detailed information on what will be expected of states parties in relation to the reporting procedure. It should, however, be noted that under MESECVI, the follow-up mechanism to the Convention of Belém do Pará created in 2004, a Committee of Experts was established. The responsibilities of this body include preparing and circulating questionnaires on the implementation of the Convention by states parties, evaluating the responses of states parties, making recommendations to strengthen the implementation of the Convention, and producing reports.[31] The Committee of Experts is comprised of experts on the issue of violence against women. Unlike the Conference of States Parties, the members of the Committee of Experts perform their functions in their personal capacities.[32]

The reporting mechanism encompassed by the Istanbul Convention is much more detailed than that found in the Protocol to the African Charter on Human and Peoples' Rights on the Rights of Women in Africa (the Maputo Protocol). Under Article 26(1) of this Protocol, states parties should indicate the legislative and other measures that they have undertaken to achieve the realisation of the Protocol's provisions in the periodic reports which they must submit every two years to the African Commission on Human and Peoples' Rights in accordance with Article 62 of the African Charter. As with Article 10 of the Convention of Belém do Pará, again this is a somewhat vague provision which stands in stark contrast to the level of detail on reporting that is found in the Istanbul Convention. Also, as the Maputo Protocol is simply a Protocol as opposed to being a stand-alone treaty, it does not have its own monitoring body, but instead falls within the ambit of the African Commission on Human and Peoples' Rights.

Inquiry procedure

Article 68(13) of the Istanbul Convention provides that if GREVIO receives reliable information indicating a situation where problems require immediate attention to prevent or limit the scale or number of serious violations of the Convention, it may request the urgent submission of a special report concerning measures taken to prevent a serious, massive or persistent pattern of violence against women. Under Article 68(14), taking into consideration the information submitted by the state party concerned, as well as any other reliable information available to it, GREVIO may designate one or more of its members to conduct an inquiry and to report back urgently to GREVIO. Where warranted and with the consent of the state party, the inquiry may include a visit to its territory. Article 68(15) states that after examining the findings of such an inquiry, GREVIO

31 For further information, see www.oas.org/en/mesecvi/about.asp, Organization of American States (accessed 14 October 2016).

32 Statute of the Mechanism to follow up on the Implementation of the Inter-American Convention on the Prevention, Punishment, and Eradication of Violence against Women, Convention of Belém do Pará, Article 5(3).

will transmit these findings to the state party in question and, where appropriate, to the Committee of the Parties and the Committee of Ministers of the Council of Europe, along with any comments or recommendations.

The approach adopted under the Istanbul Convention in this regard may be compared with the approach under CEDAW. The main CEDAW provisions do not incorporate an inquiry procedure; however, the Optional Protocol to CEDAW, which entered into force in December 2000, does establish such a procedure in respect of states that are party to the Protocol.[33] Under this procedure, if the CEDAW Committee receives reliable information indicating grave or systematic breaches by a state party, the Committee may invite the state in question to cooperate in the examination of that information by submitting observations. The Committee may then conduct an inquiry. If the state party consents, the inquiry may incorporate a visit to the state. The Committee transmits the findings of the inquiry to the state party concerned, and the state then has six months to submit its observations to the Committee.[34] The inquiry procedure under the Istanbul Convention is broadly similar to the inquiry procedure under the Optional Protocol to CEDAW; however, importantly the inquiry procedure has been incorporated into the main provisions of the Istanbul Convention and no reservations can be entered in respect of this aspect of the Convention. Therefore, unlike the position under CEDAW, all states parties to the Istanbul Convention are subject to the inquiry mechanism. There are no inquiry procedures under either the Convention of Belém do Pará or the Maputo Protocol.

Under Article 66(7) of the Istanbul Convention, members of GREVIO, and other members of delegations carrying out the country visits referred to in Article 68, enjoy the privileges and immunities established in the appendix to the Convention. These include 'immunity from personal arrest or detention and from seizure of their personal baggage, and immunity from legal process of every kind in respect of words spoken or written and all acts performed by them in their official capacity';[35] and exemption from restrictions on their freedom of movement on exit from and return to their country of residence, and entry into and exit from the country in which they exercise their functions, as well as from alien registration in the country that they are visiting or through which they are passing in the exercise of their functions.[36] In addition, the members of GREVIO and the other members of the country visit delegations will, as regards customs and exchange control, be accorded the same facilities as those accorded to representatives of

33 For discussion of the Optional Protocol to CEDAW, see Egan S., *The UN Human Rights Treaty System: Law and Procedure*, 2011, Bloomsbury Professional, Dublin, pp.371–89; and Isa F.G., 'The Optional Protocol for the Convention on the Elimination of All Forms of Discrimination against Women: Strengthening the Protection of Women's Human Rights', (2003) 20 *Arizona Journal of International and Comparative Law*, 291–322.

34 Article 8 of the Optional Protocol to the Convention on the Elimination of All Forms of Discrimination against Women.

35 At para. 2(a) of the appendix to the Istanbul Convention.

36 At para. 2(b) of appendix.

foreign governments on temporary official duty.[37] The documents relating to the evaluation of the implementation of the Convention carried by members of GREVIO and other members of the country visit delegations are to be inviolable insofar as they concern the activity of GREVIO. No stoppage or censorship may be applied to the official correspondence of GREVIO or to official communications of members of GREVIO and other members of the country visit delegations.[38] It is also provided that the immunity from legal process in respect of words spoken or written and all acts done by members of GREVIO and the other members of the country visit delegations in discharging their duties shall continue to be accorded, notwithstanding that the persons concerned are no longer engaged in the discharge of such duties, in order to secure for such persons complete freedom of speech and complete independence in the discharge of their duties.[39] It is, however, emphasised that such privileges and immunities are granted in order to safeguard the independent exercise of the functions of the individuals concerned in the interests of GREVIO and are not for their personal benefit. Such immunities may be waived by the Secretary General of the Council of Europe in any instance where, in his or her opinion, the immunity would impede the course of justice and where it can be waived without prejudice to the interests of GREVIO.[40]

General recommendations

Under Article 69 of the Istanbul Convention, GREVIO may adopt, where appropriate, general recommendations on the implementation of this instrument. The Explanatory Report to the Convention states:

> Although these general recommendations are not legally-binding, they serve as an important reference for Parties by developing a greater understanding of the different themes in the Convention and offering clear guidance that can contribute to an effective implementation of the provisions contained in the Convention.[41]

Again, this is similar to the practice of issuing General Recommendations that is utilised by the UN human rights treaty bodies. Indeed, the Explanatory Report states that the inspiration for Article 69 was drawn from Article 21(1) of CEDAW, which provides for the making of General Recommendations by the CEDAW Committee.

37 At para. 3 of appendix.
38 At para. 4 of appendix.
39 At para. 5 of appendix.
40 At para. 6 of appendix.
41 Council of Europe, 'Explanatory Report to Council of Europe Convention on preventing and combating violence against women and domestic violence', at para. 359.

Parliamentary involvement in monitoring

Article 70(1) of the Istanbul Convention provides that national parliaments shall be invited to participate in the monitoring of the measures taken for the implementation of the Convention, and, under Article 70(2), states parties shall submit the reports of GREVIO to their national parliaments. The Explanatory Report to the Convention states:

> The drafters emphasised the important role which national parliaments take on in implementing the Convention, which, in many cases, requires legislative changes. As a result, they considered it essential to involve national parliaments in assessing the implementation of the Convention.[42]

Article 70(3) states that the Parliamentary Assembly of the Council of Europe shall be invited to take stock regularly regarding the implementation of the Convention. This is the first time that a provision of this nature has been included in a Council of Europe Convention. The Explanatory Report states: 'With this provision, the drafters wished to recognise the important role which the Parliamentary Assembly played in placing the issue of violence against women on the political agenda both of the Council of Europe and of its member states.'[43]

The role of civil society in monitoring

The role to be played by civil society in the reporting procedure is expressly stated in the Convention. As noted above, Article 68(5) provides that GREVIO may receive information on the implementation of the Convention from non-governmental organisations and civil society. However, the potential for NGOs and civil society groups to play a part in the effectiveness of the monitoring procedures, and thus the effective implementation of the Convention, stretches beyond what is expressly set out in the text of the Convention itself. The European Women's Lobby has put together a 'Lobbying Kit' which gives advice to NGOs seeking to play a part in ensuring that the monitoring procedures are effective.[44] This document states that in order to ensure effective monitoring mechanisms, civil society and in particular women's NGOs play an important role in a number of ways. These include advocacy within the states parties regarding the nomination of strong candidates to GREVIO. In this respect, the Lobbying Kit advises that NGOs find out which ministry is in charge of nominations, and that they

42 At para. 360.
43 At para. 361.
44 European Women's Lobby, 'A European Women's Lobby Lobbying Kit for a transparent monitoring process of the Council of Europe Convention on Preventing and Combating Violence against Women and Domestic Violence', 2014, available at www.womenlobby.org/EWL-Observatory-on-Violence-against-Women-publishes-Lobbying-Kit-on-the (accessed 14 October 2016).

approach this ministry through letter or personal contacts to inquire about the national selection procedure. NGOs should ask whether the selection procedure is an open call, and, if not, how it is ensured that the process is transparent and open to competition. They should also inquire as to how the call for applications is disseminated to ensure that all potential candidates are reached, and which criteria are applied. In addition, NGOs have a role to play in encouraging suitably qualified candidates to apply.

Beyond the appointment process of members of GREVIO, the Lobbying Kit emphasises that civil society also has an important part to play as regards making active contributions to the monitoring process, such as through the making of shadow reports to GREVIO. In addition, NGOs should advocate for a meaningful application of the mechanism regarding the involvement of national parliaments in the evaluation and monitoring process, which is found in Article 70 of the Convention, as referred to above.

Lack of a communications mechanism

It is of particular note that, despite the detailed provisions on the reporting mechanism and on the inquiry procedure, the one very obvious omission from the enforcement mechanisms of the Istanbul Convention is the lack of an individual complaints mechanism. The omission of such a mechanism is somewhat surprising, given that individual complaints can be taken under CEDAW, the Convention of Belém do Pará and the Maputo Protocol.[45]

For example, Article 2 of the Optional Protocol to CEDAW allows individuals or groups of individuals who are victims of any breaches of CEDAW to submit complaints to the CEDAW Committee. Crucially, communications may also be submitted on behalf of individuals with their consent, unless acting on their behalf without their consent may be justified. This is a much wider test of standing than that contained, for example, in Article 34 of the European Convention on Human Rights. Under this provision the person bringing the case must be the actual victim;[46] however, under the Optional Protocol a communication may be made on behalf of an individual or a group of individuals. For example, a domestic violence group could make a communication alleging that the state has failed to fulfil its duties under CEDAW. Under Article 4 of the Optional Protocol, the CEDAW Committee may only consider a communication if all domestic remedies have been exhausted, or if the application of such remedies would be unnecessarily

45 For discussion of individual complaints mechanisms as regards the UN human rights treaties, see Ulfstein G., 'Individual Complaints', in H. Keller and G. Ulfstein (eds), *UN Human Rights Treaty Bodies: Law and Legitimacy*, 2012, Cambridge University Press, Cambridge, 73–115.

46 See further McQuigg R., 'The Victim Test under the Human Rights Act 1998 and its Implications for Domestic Violence Cases', (2011) *European Human Rights Law Review*, 294–303.

prolonged or unlikely to bring relief to the complainant. A communication is inadmissible if the same matter has already been examined by the CEDAW Committee or has been considered by another international procedure. A communication is also inadmissible if it is incompatible with CEDAW, manifestly ill-founded, an abuse of the right to petition, or if the subject of the communication occurred prior to the entry into force of the Optional Protocol for the state in question. Under Article 5, the CEDAW Committee may recommend interim measures to the state party at any time between the receipt of a communication and its decision. Under Article 7, when a communication is submitted, the Committee should bring it to the attention of the state in question. The state then has six months to submit an explanation to the Committee. Communications are considered by the Committee in closed meetings. The views of the Committee are then transmitted to the parties. The state is required to respond in writing within six months, including a description of any action that it has taken on the matter. The Preamble to the Optional Protocol asserts that it is a reaffirmation of the determination of states parties 'to ensure the full and equal enjoyment by women of all human rights and fundamental freedoms and to take effective action to prevent violations of these rights and freedoms'.

However, it must be remembered that the Optional Protocol is optional. States that have ratified CEDAW are under no obligation to ratify the Protocol. Also, although the communications procedure allows the CEDAW Committee to make recommendations as to the measures that should be adopted to remedy a breach of CEDAW, it has no means of forcing the state concerned to comply with these recommendations. As Byrnes remarks:

> In general, it is true to say that where decisions are rendered against a state under [a complaints procedure], the state will take steps to bring its domestic law and practice into conformity with the international law position as determined or opined by the relevant supervisory body. However, this is not to say that there are not exceptions or that the steps taken by a state party to rectify inconsistencies will adopt a generous approach to remedying the defects identified by the international body.[47]

As Ritz comments, 'The Optional Protocol lacks compelling sanctions and penalties for non-compliance.'[48] Essentially, similar enforcement difficulties arise in relation to the Optional Protocol as arise concerning the main CEDAW provisions. These difficulties will be discussed further in Chapter 6.

47 Byrnes, op. cit., at p.203.

48 Ritz K.L., 'Soft Enforcement: Inadequacies of Optional Protocol as a Remedy for the Convention on the Elimination of All Forms of Discrimination against Women', (2001) 25 *Suffolk Transnational Law Review*, 191–216 at 211.

AT v Hungary[49] was the first decision of the CEDAW Committee on the merits of a communication under the Optional Protocol. The views of the Committee were adopted on 26 January 2005. In this case the complainant alleged that for the past four years she had been subjected to severe domestic abuse and serious threats by her partner. The couple had two children, one of whom suffered from severe brain damage. The perpetrator was in possession of a firearm and had threatened to kill the complainant; however, the latter had been unable to go to a shelter, as there were no shelters that were equipped to take in the disabled child, together with his mother and sister. There were also no protection orders or restraining orders available under Hungarian law. The perpetrator eventually moved out of the family apartment, but his subsequent visits involved more incidents of violence, which were aggravated by him being in a drunken state. When he left the family home, he took most of the furniture and household items with him, and he did not pay child support for three years. The complainant alleged that the state had violated her rights under Article 2 of CEDAW, under which states parties agree to 'pursue by all appropriate means and without delay a policy of eliminating discrimination against women' and, to this end, undertake 'to embody the principle of the equality of men and women in their national constitutions or other appropriate legislation if not yet incorporated therein and to ensure, through law and other appropriate means, the practical realization of this principle';[50] 'to adopt appropriate legislative and other measures, including sanctions where appropriate, prohibiting all discrimination against women';[51] and 'to take all appropriate measures to eliminate discrimination against women by any person, organization or enterprise'.[52] In addition, the complainant alleged that the state had violated Article 5(a) of CEDAW, under which:

> States Parties shall take all appropriate measures to modify the social and cultural patterns of conduct of men and women, with a view to achieving the elimination of prejudices and customary and all other practices which are based on the idea of the inferiority or the superiority of either of the sexes or on stereotyped roles for men and women.

The complainant also alleged that there had been a breach of Article 16 under which 'States Parties shall take all appropriate measures to eliminate discrimination against women in all matters relating to marriage and family relations'.

In examining the complaint, the CEDAW Committee stated that the obligations contained in Article 2(a), (b) and (e) of the Convention 'extend to the prevention of and protection from violence against women, which obligations in the present

49 Communication No. 2/2003, views adopted 26 January 2005, CEDAW/C/32/D/2/2003.
50 Convention on the Elimination of All Forms of Discrimination against Women, Article 2(a).
51 Article 2(b).
52 Article 2(e).

case, remain unfulfilled and constitute a violation of the [complainant's] human rights and fundamental freedoms, particularly her right to security of person'.[53] In relation to Articles 5(a) and 16 of the Convention, the Committee noted that 'traditional attitudes by which women are regarded as subordinate to men contribute to violence against them'.[54] In applying this principle to the situation in question, the Committee stated:

> For four years and continuing to the present day, the [complainant] has felt threatened by her former common law husband, the father of her two children. The [complainant] has been battered by this same man, her former common law husband. She has been unsuccessful, either through civil or criminal proceedings, to temporarily or permanently bar [him] from the apartment where she and her children have continued to reside. The [complainant] could not have asked for a restraining or protection order since neither option currently exists in the State party. She has been unable to flee to a shelter because none are equipped to accept her together with her children, one of whom is fully disabled.[55]

The Committee therefore proceeded to find the state party to be in violation of Articles 2(a), (b) and (e), 5(a) and 16 of CEDAW.

In relation to the complainant herself, the Committee recommended that the state adopt immediate measures to guarantee her physical and mental integrity and that of her family. She should also be given a safe home in which to live with her children, appropriate child support and legal assistance, and reparation proportionate to the physical and mental harm that she had suffered and to the seriousness of the breach of her rights. At a more general level, the Committee recommended *inter alia* that the state '[r]espect, protect, promote and fulfil women's human rights, including their right to be free from all forms of domestic violence, including intimidation and threats of torture', and that the state should '[a]ssure victims of domestic violence the maximum protection of the law by acting with due diligence to prevent and respond to such violence against women'.[56] The Committee also recommended that the state adopt all necessary measures to provide regular training on CEDAW and the Optional Protocol thereto to judges, lawyers and law enforcement officials. The state should introduce a specific law prohibiting domestic violence against women and providing for protection and exclusion orders as well as support services, including shelters, and should '[i]nvestigate promptly, thoroughly, impartially and seriously all allegations of domestic violence and bring the offenders to justice in accordance with international standards'.[57] In addition,

53 At para. 9.3.
54 At para. 9.4.
55 At para. 9.4.
56 At para. 9.6.
57 At para. 9.6.

victims of domestic violence should be provided with 'safe and prompt access to justice, including free legal aid where necessary, in order to ensure them available, effective and sufficient remedies and rehabilitation'.[58] The Committee also recommended that the state provide offenders with rehabilitation programmes and programmes on non-violent conflict resolution methods.

It is worth noting that the decision in *AT v Hungary* demonstrates the fact that the CEDAW Committee has adopted a flexible approach to the admissibility requirements under the Optional Protocol. As stated above, under Article 4 of the Protocol, the CEDAW Committee may only consider a communication if all domestic remedies have been exhausted, or if the application of such remedies would be unnecessarily prolonged or unlikely to bring relief to the complainant. In this instance, there were domestic civil proceedings pending as regards the perpetrator's access to the apartment; however, the Committee recognised that these proceedings were unlikely to result in effective relief. Criminal proceedings had also been initiated, but these proceedings had been delayed for more than three years and in the opinion of the Committee this constituted an 'unreasonable prolonged delay' for the purposes of Article 4 of the Optional Protocol. Also, even though the majority of the violence in this case had in fact taken place prior to the entry into force of the Optional Protocol in Hungary, the Committee nevertheless was of the view that in examining the complaint the inaction of the state as regards all of the violence should be considered.[59] Egan remarks that the Committee 'did so, quite correctly, on the basis that the incidents cited formed an uninterrupted series of attacks . . . the nature of which was central to the allegation of culpable inaction on the part of the State party'.[60]

In August 2007 the CEDAW Committee examined two more communications surrounding the issue of domestic violence. *Goekce v Austria*[61] concerned a victim of domestic violence who had eventually been killed by her husband. The communication was brought by the Vienna Intervention Centre against Domestic Violence and the Association for Women's Access to Justice, on behalf of the family members of the deceased. In examining the complaint the Committee noted that the state had established a comprehensive model to address domestic violence which encompassed legislation, criminal and civil law remedies, awareness-raising measures, education and training, the provision of shelters, counselling for victims and work with perpetrators. However, the Committee then stated:

58 At para. 9.6.

59 Chinkin C., 'Violence against Women' in M.A. Freeman, C. Chinkin and B. Rudolf (eds), *The UN Convention on the Elimination of All Forms of Discrimination against Women: A Commentary*, 2012, Oxford University Press, Oxford, 443–74 at 456.

60 Egan, op. cit., at p.380. For further discussion of *AT v Hungary*, see Rudolf B. and Eriksson A., 'Women's Rights under International Human Rights Treaties: Issues of Rape, Domestic Slavery, Abortion and Domestic Violence', (2007) 5 *International Journal of Constitutional Law*, 507–25 at 519–22.

61 Communication No. 5/2005, views adopted 6 August 2007, CEDAW/C/39/D/5/2005.

> [I]n order for the individual woman victim of domestic violence to enjoy the practical realization of the principle of equality of men and women and of her human rights and fundamental freedoms, the political will that is expressed in the aforementioned comprehensive system of Austria must be supported by State actors, who adhere to the State party's due diligence obligations.[62]

The Committee noted that the police had been called frequently during the three-year period prior to the shooting of the victim, in relation to disturbances, disputes and incidents of battering. The police had issued prohibition to return orders to the perpetrator on three occasions, and had twice requested, without success, that the Public Prosecutor order that the perpetrator be detained. Indeed, a three-month interim injunction had been in effect at the time of the victim's death which prohibited the perpetrator from returning to the family apartment and its immediate environs and from contacting the victim or their children. The Committee also noted that the victim had called the emergency call service a few hours before she had been killed, but no police patrol car had been sent to the scene of the crime. In the view of the Committee, due to this combination of factors, the police either knew or should have known that the victim was in serious danger, and should therefore have treated the last call from her as an emergency. The police were thus accountable for failing to exercise due diligence in protecting the victim. In addition, the Committee stated that the Public Prosecutor should not have denied the requests that had been made by the police to arrest and detain the perpetrator.

The Committee therefore held that the state had violated its obligations under Article 2(a) of CEDAW. The state had also breached its duties under Article 2(c), (d), (e) and (f), namely that it should 'establish legal protection of the rights of women on an equal basis with men and . . . ensure through competent national tribunals and other public institutions the effective protection of women against any act of discrimination';[63] 'refrain from engaging in any act or practice of discrimination against women and . . . ensure that public authorities and institutions shall act in conformity with this obligation';[64] 'take all appropriate measures to eliminate discrimination against women by any person, organization or enterprise';[65] and 'take all appropriate measures, including legislation, to modify or abolish existing laws, regulations, customs and practices which constitute discrimination against women'.[66] In addition, the state had violated its obligations under Article 3 of the Convention, under which states must take all appropriate measures 'to ensure the full development and advancement of women, for the

62 At para. 12.1.2.
63 CEDAW, Article 2(c).
64 Article 2(d).
65 Article 2(e).
66 Article 2(f).

purpose of guaranteeing them the exercise and enjoyment of human rights and fundamental freedoms on a basis of equality with men', when taken in conjunction with the definition of 'discrimination against women' found in Article 1 and with General Recommendation No. 19.

The Committee therefore recommended that the state act with due diligence to prevent and respond to violence against women and provide for adequate sanctions for the failure to do so. The state should also:

> [v]igilantly and in a speedy manner prosecute perpetrators of domestic violence in order to convey to the offenders and to the public that society condemns domestic violence as well as ensure that criminal and civil measures are utilized in cases where the perpetrator in a domestic violence situation poses a dangerous threat to the victim; and also ensure that in all action taken to protect women from violence, due consideration is given to the safety of women, emphasizing that the perpetrator's rights cannot supersede women's human rights to life and to physical and mental integrity.[67]

In addition, the state should ensure enhanced coordination among law enforcement and judicial officers, and strengthen training programmes on domestic violence for judges, lawyers and law enforcement officials, including on CEDAW, the Optional Protocol thereto and General Recommendation No. 19. It was also recommended that the state ensure that 'all levels of the criminal justice system (police, public prosecutors, judges) routinely cooperate with non-governmental organizations that work to protect and support women victims of gender-based violence'.[68]

Yildirim v Austria[69] also concerned a victim of domestic violence who had eventually been killed by her husband. Again the communication was brought by the Vienna Intervention Centre against Domestic Violence and the Association for Women's Access to Justice, on behalf of the family members of the deceased. In this instance, the victim had been in ongoing contact with the police and had authorised the prosecution of her husband. The police had made requests to the Public Prosecutor for the arrest and detention of the perpetrator, but these requests had been denied. The perpetrator had made continuous efforts to contact the victim and had threatened by phone and in person to kill her, despite the existence of an interim injunction that prohibited him from returning to the couple's apartment, the immediate surroundings and the victim's workplace, as well as from contacting the victim. The CEDAW Committee stated that the facts disclosed a situation that was extremely dangerous to the victim of which the state

67 *Goekce v Austria* (Communication No. 5/2005, views adopted 6 August 2007, CEDAW/C/39/D/5/2005), at para. 12.3(b).

68 At para. 12.3(c).

69 Communication No. 6/2005, views adopted 6 August 2007, CEDAW/C/39/D/6/2005.

authorities knew or ought to have known, and as such the Public Prosecutor should not have denied the requests of the police to arrest the perpetrator and place him in detention. Indeed, the Public Prosecutor's denial of these requests constituted a violation of the state's due diligence obligation to protect the victim. Again the Committee emphasised that 'the perpetrator's rights cannot supersede women's human rights to life and to physical and mental integrity'.[70] As in *Goekce v Austria*, the Committee found violations of Articles 2(a), 2(c) through (f) and 3 of CEDAW, read in conjunction with Article 1 and General Recommendation No. 19. The recommendations that had been made to the state in *Goekce v Austria* were then reiterated.

The approaches adopted by the CEDAW Committee in examining the complaints in *Goekce v Austria* and *Yildirim v Austria* were certainly very positive. Nevertheless, it has been commented that the Committee could actually have taken an even stronger approach. For instance, Chinkin notes that in examining these cases the Committee did not state that even the extreme forms of domestic abuse that had occurred in these instances, and which had indeed resulted in the deaths of the victims, amounted to torture.[71]

Another communication relating to domestic violence was considered by the CEDAW Committee on 27 September 2011. In *VK v Bulgaria*[72] the complainant alleged that the state had failed to provide her with effective protection against domestic violence on the part of her husband. The complainant had been subjected to psychological, emotional and economic abuse, and later also to physical violence. Her husband had not permitted her to work, despite her education and qualifications. The complainant was entirely dependent economically on her husband, who alone decided on the spending of the family's income and who provided the complainant with money only for the basic needs of the family. In addition, the complainant was not permitted to communicate freely with friends and family members. The complainant's attempts to discuss the situation with her husband resulted in conflicts and in physical violence. In considering the complaint, the Committee noted that the state had adopted legislation against domestic violence, which encompassed a fast-track procedure for issuing immediate protection orders. However, a permanent protection order had not been issued against the complainant's husband, and in addition no shelter provision had been available. The Committee stated that in order for the complainant:

70 At para. 12.1.5.

71 Chinkin (2012), op. cit., at p.473. Various academic commentators have likened domestic violence to torture – for example, Copelon R., 'Intimate Terror: Understanding Domestic Violence as Torture', in R.J. Cook (ed.), *Human Rights of Women: National and International Perspectives*, 1994, University of Pennsylvania Press, Philadelphia, 116–52; and Grdinic E., 'Application of the Elements of Torture and Other Forms of Ill-Treatment, as Defined by the European Court and Commission of Human Rights, to the Incidents of Domestic Violence', (2000) 23 *Hastings International and Comparative Law Review*, 217–60.

72 Communication No. 20/2008, views adopted 27 September 2011, CEDAW/C/49/D/20/2008.

> to enjoy the practical realization of the principle of equality between women and men and of her human rights and fundamental freedoms, the political will that is expressed in such specific legislation must be supported by all State actors, including the courts, which are bound by the obligations of the State party.[73]

The Committee was of the view that in refusing to issue a permanent protection order, the national courts had applied 'an overly restrictive definition of domestic violence'[74] which was not warranted by the domestic legislation. The courts had 'focused exclusively on the issue of direct and immediate threat to the life or health of the [complainant] and on her physical integrity, while neglecting her emotional and psychological suffering'.[75] According to the Committee, such an approach reflected 'a stereotyped and overly narrow concept of what constitutes domestic violence',[76] and the refusal of the domestic courts to issue a permanent protection order against the complainant's husband was therefore based on 'preconceived and thus discriminatory notions of what constitutes domestic violence'.[77] The comments of the Committee serve to emphasise the importance of recognising psychological and economic aspects of domestic abuse, as does the definition of domestic violence found in Article 3(b) of the Istanbul Convention, as discussed in Chapter 4 of this book. The CEDAW Committee was also of the view that the unavailability of shelters constituted a breach of the state's obligations under Article 2(c) and (e) of the Convention to provide for the immediate protection of women from violence, including from domestic abuse. Overall, the Committee found that the state had failed to fulfil its obligations under Article 2(c), (d), (e) and (f), in conjunction with Article 1, and Article 5(a), in conjunction with Article 16, as well as with General Recommendation No. 19.

The Committee proceeded to recommend that the state provide adequate financial compensation to the complainant commensurate with the gravity of the violation of her rights. At a more general level, the Committee recommended *inter alia* that the state amend the national legislation on domestic violence to ensure that protection orders are available without placing undue administrative and legal burdens on applicants. The state should also ensure that a sufficient number of state-funded shelters are available to victims of domestic violence and their children, and provide support to non-governmental organisations that offer shelter and other means of support to victims of domestic violence. In addition, the state should provide mandatory training for judges, lawyers and law enforcement personnel on the application of the national domestic violence legislation, including on the definition of domestic violence and on gender stereotypes, as

73 At para. 9.4.
74 At para. 9.9.
75 At para. 9.9.
76 At para. 9.12.
77 At para. 9.12.

well as appropriate training on CEDAW, the Optional Protocol thereto, and the Committee's general recommendations, in particular General Recommendation No. 19.

Another communication concerning Bulgaria's response to the issue of domestic violence was considered by the CEDAW Committee on 23 July 2012. *Jallow v Bulgaria*[78] involved a situation wherein both parties to a relationship had made allegations of domestic violence; however, the complainant argued that the state had not provided her with the same protection as had been afforded to her husband. The complainant was a Gambian national who was illiterate and spoke only her native language and English at an average level. The Committee commented:

> In contrast with her husband's application under the [national domestic violence legislation] that was duly heard, the State party's authorities failed to act with due diligence, to provide her with effective protection and to take into account her vulnerable position, as an illiterate migrant woman with a small daughter without a command of Bulgarian or relatives in the State party.[79]

In considering the complaint, the Committee stated that 'traditional attitudes by which women are regarded as subordinate to men contribute to violence against them'.[80] The Committee noted that in the case in question the state authorities had relied on the husband's statement and actions, despite being aware of the complainant's vulnerable position and her dependency on him. The Committee commented that 'the authorities based their activities on a stereotyped notion that the husband was superior and that his opinions should be taken seriously, disregarding the fact that domestic violence proportionately affects women considerably more than men'.[81] Due to an emergency protection order that had been issued in favour of the complainant's husband, the complainant had been separated from her daughter for almost eight months, during which time she had received no information regarding the care that her daughter was receiving, and had been granted no visitation rights. The Committee considered therefore that both the complainant and her daughter were victims of gender-based discrimination due to the fact that the state had failed to protect the complainant's equal rights in marriage and as a parent, and had failed to regard her daughter's interests as being paramount. The emergency protection order had been issued without due consideration having been taken of the complainant's claim that she and her

78 Communication No. 32/2011, views adopted 23 July 2012, CEDAW/C/52/D/32/2011.
79 At para. 8.2.
80 At para. 8.6.
81 At para. 8.6.

daughter were in fact the ones who were in need of protection from domestic violence.

The Committee was thus of the view that the state had failed to fulfil its obligations under Article 2(b), (c), (d), (e) and (f) and Article 5(a) of CEDAW. In addition, the state had failed to fulfil its duties under Article 16(c), (d) and (f), namely to ensure, on a basis of equality of men and women, '[t]he same rights and responsibilities during marriage and at its dissolution';[82] '[t]he same rights and responsibilities as parents, irrespective of their marital status, in matters relating to their children';[83] and '[t]he same rights and responsibilities with regard to guardianship, wardship, trusteeship and adoption of children, or similar institutions where these concepts exist in national legislation'.[84] Article 16(d) and (f) also state that 'in all cases the interests of the children shall be paramount'.

The Committee therefore recommended that the state provide the complainant and her daughter with appropriate compensation commensurate with the gravity of the violation of their rights. At a more general level, the Committee asserted that the state should:

> take measures to ensure that women victims of domestic violence, in particular migrant women, have effective access to services related to protection against domestic violence and to justice, including interpretation or translation of documents, and that the manner in which domestic courts apply the law is consistent with the State party's obligations under the Convention.[85]

The state should also:

> take the legislative or other measures necessary to ensure that, in the determination of custody and visitation rights of children, incidents of violence are taken into account and that the rights and safety of the victim or children are not jeopardized.[86]

In addition, the state should:

> [p]rovide for appropriate and regular training on the Convention, its Optional Protocol and its general recommendations for judges, prosecutors . . . and law enforcement personnel in a gender-sensitive manner, having particular regard to multiple discrimination, so as to ensure that complaints regarding gender-based violence are received and considered adequately.[87]

82 CEDAW, Article 16(c).
83 Article 16(d).
84 Article 16(f).
85 *Jallow v Bulgaria* (Communication No. 32/2011, views adopted 23 July 2012, CEDAW/C/52/D/32/2011), at para. 8.8.
86 At para. 8.8.
87 At para. 8.8.

As Byrnes and Bath remark, 'The major substantive contribution thus far of the Committee under the individual complaints procedure is with regard to the due diligence standard in relation to violence, particularly in the family context.'[88] In its consideration of the complaints surrounding the issue of domestic violence, the Committee has clearly emphasised that not only must an adequate legal framework be in place, but that this framework must be implemented in a substantive and meaningful way by the relevant officials, such as police and prosecutors. Egan states that in responding to the communications relating to domestic violence, the CEDAW Committee has made 'powerful use of the text of the (Optional Protocol) in making detailed policy recommendations to States parties on how to eliminate systematic practices that lie at the heart of the individual complaints in these cases'.[89] However, it seems that there remains a general lack of awareness of the Optional Protocol and its potential. As Murdoch comments, 'The minimal utilisation of the right of communication . . . suggests[s] a widespread lack of awareness or understanding of the Optional Protocol on the part of individuals'.[90] Egan remarks of the Optional Protocol that 'the dearth of views rendered by the CEDAW Committee under it is striking'.[91] In referring to individual complaints mechanisms under the UN human rights treaties in general, Smith states: 'The principal criticism which may be levied against the present individual petition system is underutilization.'[92] It could therefore be argued that the omission of a communications procedure from the Istanbul Convention may not lessen the effectiveness of this instrument to any great extent.

The Convention of Belém do Pará also incorporates an individual complaints mechanism. Under Article 12 of this instrument, any person or group of persons, or any non-governmental entity, may lodge petitions with the Inter-American Commission on Human Rights concerning complaints of violations of Article 7 of the Convention. It is noteworthy that it is only breaches of the obligations contained in Article 7 regarding which complaints may be made. These duties are somewhat limited in nature. Under Article 7, states parties must include in their domestic legislation provisions to prevent, punish and eradicate violence against

88 Byrnes A. and Bath E., 'Violence against Women, the Obligation of Due Diligence, and the Optional Protocol to the Convention on the Elimination of All Forms of Discrimination against Women – Recent Developments', (2008) 8 *Human Rights Law Review*, 517–33 at 533.

89 Egan, op. cit., at pp.388–9.

90 Murdoch J., 'Unfulfilled Expectations: The Optional Protocol to the Convention on the Elimination of All Forms of Discrimination against Women', (2010) *European Human Rights Law Review*, 26–46 at 45.

91 Egan, op. cit., at p.385.

92 Smith R.K.M., *Textbook on International Human Rights*, 6th edn, 2014, Oxford University Press, Oxford, at p.173. For discussion of the responses of states to decisions made by treaty bodies under individual complaints mechanisms, see Van Alebeek R. and Nollkaemper A., 'The Legal Status of Decisions by Human Rights Treaty Bodies in National Law', in H. Keller and G. Ulfstein (eds), *UN Human Rights Treaty Bodies: Law and Legitimacy*, 2012, Cambridge University Press, Cambridge, 356–411.

women;[93] adopt legal measures to require the perpetrator to refrain from harassing, intimidating or threatening the woman;[94] and take all appropriate measures to amend or repeal existing laws and regulations or to modify legal or customary practices that sustain violence against women.[95] States parties must also establish fair and effective legal procedures for women who have been subjected to violence;[96] establish the necessary legal and administrative mechanisms to ensure that women subjected to violence have access to just and effective remedies;[97] and adopt such legislative or other measures as may be necessary to give effect to the Convention.[98]

However, Article 7 does not include obligations on states parties to provide social support measures for victims, or to take measures to increase awareness among society of the issues involved in violence against women. These categories of duties are found in Article 8 of the Convention. The measures encompassed by Article 8 include the adoption of programmes aimed at promoting awareness of the right of women to be free from violence,[99] and at modifying social and cultural patterns of conduct of men and women to counteract prejudices based on the idea of the inferiority or superiority of either of the sexes that legitimise violence against women.[100] Under Article 8, states parties should promote the education and training of all those involved in the administration of justice, police and other law enforcement officers responsible for implementing policies for the prevention, punishment and eradication of violence against women.[101] They should 'provide appropriate specialized services for women who have been subjected to violence, through public and private sector agencies, including shelters, counseling services for all family members where appropriate, and care and custody of the affected children'.[102] In addition, states parties should provide women who have been subjected to violence with access to effective readjustment and training programmes to enable them to participate fully in public, private and social life.[103] Complaints to the Inter-American Commission cannot, however, be made on the basis of alleged violations of Article 8.

As regards domestic violence, the seminal petition on this issue which was lodged with the Inter-American Commission on Human Rights using the Convention of Belém do Pará is that of *Maria da Penha Maia Fernandes v*

93 Convention of Belém do Pará, Article 7(c).
94 Article 7(d).
95 Article 7(e).
96 Article 7(f).
97 Article 7(g).
98 Article 7(h).
99 Article 8(a).
100 Article 8(b).
101 Article 8(c).
102 Article 8(d).
103 Article 8(f).

Brazil.[104] This petition alleged that the state had condoned domestic violence that had been perpetrated against Mrs Fernandes by her husband. This violence had culminated in her attempted murder. In finding violations of the American Convention on Human Rights and of the Convention of Belém do Pará, the Commission held that the failure to prosecute and convict the perpetrator indicated that the state had condoned the violence in question. The Commission commented: 'The condoning of this situation by the entire system only serves to perpetuate the psychological, social, and historical roots and factors that sustain and encourage violence against women.'[105] It stated: '[I]n this case, which represents the tip of the iceberg, ineffective judicial action, impunity, and the inability of victims to obtain compensation provide an example of the lack of commitment to take appropriate action to address domestic violence.'[106] In its decision, the Commission made a wide range of recommendations to the state. These included completing criminal proceedings against the perpetrator in a rapid and effective manner; conducting an investigation to determine responsibility for the irregularities that prevented effective prosecution of the perpetrator; and adopting the measures necessary for the state to grant compensation to Mrs Fernandes. At a broader level, the Commission recommended *inter alia* that the state adopt measures to simplify criminal judicial proceedings so that the time taken for proceedings could be reduced. In addition, the state should increase the number of special police stations to address the rights of women and ensure the provision of sufficient resources to process and investigate effectively all complaints relating to domestic violence.[107]

The approach that was adopted by the drafters of the Maputo Protocol to an individual complaints mechanism under this instrument is rather unclear. The Protocol does not expressly state that individuals may lodge petitions with a particular body concerning violations of the Protocol by states parties. However, Article 27 states: 'The African Court on Human and Peoples' Rights shall be seized with matters of interpretation arising from the application or implementation of this Protocol.' Also, Article 32 states: 'Pending the establishment of the African Court on Human and Peoples' Rights, the African Commission on Human and Peoples' Rights shall be seized with matters of interpretation arising from the application and implementation of this Protocol.' It seems that these provisions, taken in conjunction with the complaints procedure provided for under the African Charter, allow individuals to bring complaints of violations of the Maputo Protocol by states parties to the African Commission or to the African Court. No individual complaints regarding the issue of domestic violence have, however, been made as yet.

104 Case 12.051, Report No. 54/01 (2001).
105 At para. 55.
106 At para. 57.
107 At para. 61.

Conclusion

It can be seen that the drafters of the Istanbul Convention chose to incorporate very similar monitoring mechanisms in the new treaty to those that exist under the main UN human rights treaties, such as CEDAW. As with the UN treaties, the primary monitoring procedure is constituted by a reporting mechanism. There are, however, certain innovative divergences from the CEDAW reporting model, such as the selection by GREVIO at the commencement of each round of reporting of specific provisions of the Convention on which the evaluation procedure will be based, and the subsequent preparation by GREVIO of a questionnaire. There could well be distinct advantages with the adoption of such an approach as it will allow the aspect of state compliance chosen for monitoring to be analysed in greater detail than would otherwise be the case. Such an approach may also enable GREVIO to carry out its work in a more time-efficient manner.

Unlike the Convention of Belém do Pará or the Maputo Protocol, the monitoring mechanisms of the Istanbul Convention also encompass an inquiry procedure, broadly similar to that found in the Optional Protocol to CEDAW. However, unlike the position under CEDAW, all states parties to the Istanbul Convention are subject to the inquiry mechanism. As with the UN human rights bodies, GREVIO may also adopt general recommendations regarding the implementation of the Convention. However, the lack of an individual complaints mechanism under the Istanbul Convention appears to constitute a rather surprising omission, given that individual complaints can be taken under CEDAW, the Convention of Belém do Pará and the Maputo Protocol. Nevertheless, given the seeming general lack of awareness of CEDAW's Optional Protocol, it is arguable that the omission of a communications procedure from the Istanbul Convention may not lessen the effectiveness of this instrument to any great extent.

Chapter 6 will proceed to analyse a number of advantages relating to the adoption of the Istanbul Convention. The chapter will also examine potential difficulties that may arise concerning the Convention's operation.

6 Advantages of the Istanbul Convention and potential challenges

This chapter will highlight a number of the advantages brought about by the adoption of the Istanbul Convention by the Council of Europe as regards combating domestic violence. The fact that domestic violence has now been expressly included in a human rights treaty in the European context constitutes an immensely important development in itself, and one showing the impetus that has been built up over a relatively short period of time in relation to the movement to combat domestic abuse. This development gives further support to the proposition that domestic violence constitutes a breach of human rights standards, as opposed to, for example, simply a violation of criminal law. This too is important, as use of the language of rights carries significant symbolic weight in and of itself. In addition, the inclusion of the principle of due diligence in the Istanbul Convention, as discussed in Chapter 4, serves to emphasise the fact that the public/private dichotomy, which has historically created such immense difficulties with regard to the effectiveness of human rights law and in particular the rights of women, has now been surmounted to a substantial extent.

The importance of the Istanbul Convention, however, reaches beyond a purely symbolic role. The Convention places detailed legally binding duties on states parties in relation to the measures that they must adopt as regards violence against women, including domestic violence. Although the measures themselves are not new, the fact that these have now been included in a legally binding treaty in the European context is highly significant. In particular, the legally binding nature of these obligations is a factor that can be used by non-governmental organisations working in the area of gender-based violence to place further pressure on governments in states that have ratified this instrument to adopt measures to combat domestic abuse, as well as other forms of gender-based violence.

In addition, the provisions of the Istanbul Convention relating to domestic violence build substantially on the obligations that have been placed upon states by the European Court of Human Rights as regards this issue. In particular, although the European Court has placed positive obligations on states to ensure that their criminal justice systems are of a certain standard in responding to domestic violence, the Court has not placed duties upon states in relation to other aspects of their responses to domestic abuse, such as the provision of social support measures to victims or the implementation of public awareness campaigns.

The provisions found in the Istanbul Convention are, however, much more comprehensive in scope. There are also other benefits entailed in having a Convention monitored by a reporting mechanism, as opposed to placing the onus on victims to bring cases to court, as is the situation under the European Convention on Human Rights, particularly when addressing an 'unseen crime' such as domestic violence. Another benefit of utilising a strategy other than that of litigation is that a substantially more detailed approach can be adopted. Judges must confine themselves to dealing with the precise issues in the cases that come before them, whereas a monitoring body such as the Group of Experts on Action against Violence against Women and Domestic Violence (GREVIO), as established by Article 66 of the Istanbul Convention, is free to adopt a much broader approach.[1] Essentially, there are limits to the extent to which a litigation strategy can be used effectively to promote change.

It is argued that the Istanbul Convention constitutes an immensely positive development, and one that is certainly very much to be welcomed. However, there are a number of challenges that may be faced by the Convention, and the chapter will also provide an analysis of these potential difficulties. The first challenge is that of ensuring that all or most of the states within the Council of Europe ratify the Convention, in order to ensure that the optimal level of effectiveness of this instrument is secured. It is possible that a number of states may be reluctant to ratify the Convention, due to the very detailed nature of the obligations that it places upon states parties. Nevertheless, the signs are encouraging, in that a large majority of the states within the Council of Europe have either ratified the Convention or indicated their intention to do so by signing this instrument.[2] It is also possible that some difficulties may be encountered which relate to the issue of reservations – a matter that has proven to be immensely problematic for the Convention on the Elimination of All Forms of Discrimination against Women (CEDAW).[3] However, perhaps most hazardous for the potential effectiveness of the Istanbul Convention are the difficulties surrounding implementation and enforcement that are endemic to human rights law. Although these problems are not specific to the Istanbul Convention itself, it is nevertheless difficult to see how they will be avoided, given that they affect all of the UN human rights treaties.

Advantages

Symbolic importance

The Istanbul Convention certainly constitutes an extremely significant development as regards the movement to combat domestic violence, not least because of

1 Detailed discussion of GREVIO can be found in Chapter 5.

2 At the time of writing, the Istanbul Convention has been ratified by 22 states, and has been signed but not yet ratified by another 20 states.

3 CEDAW (1249 U.N.T.S. 13) was adopted by the UN General Assembly on 18 December 1979 and entered into force on 3 September 1981.

its symbolic importance. The adoption of this instrument clearly shows recognition on the part of the Council of Europe of the extent of the problem of violence against women in its various forms and of the vital need for action to be taken to address this issue. For example, the Preamble to the Convention asserts clearly that the member states of the Council of Europe recognise 'with grave concern, that women and girls are often exposed to serious forms of violence such as domestic violence'. As discussed in Chapter 2, it is only relatively recently that domestic violence has been recognised as an issue meriting the attention of any form of law, let alone human rights law. The fact that, for the first time, domestic violence has been expressly included in a human rights treaty in the European context constitutes an immensely important development in itself, and one demonstrating the momentum that has been built up in a relatively rapid manner in relation to the movement to combat domestic abuse.

In addition, the fact that there is now a human rights treaty in the European context that expressly states that domestic violence constitutes a human rights violation serves to emphasise further that domestic violence does amount to a breach of human rights standards. Although this fact has been recognised by the European Court of Human Rights since 2007, as was discussed in Chapter 3, the codification of this principle in treaty form gives added weight to this proposition. The couching of domestic violence as a violation not only of criminal law standards but also of human rights is important as the use of rights language in itself can be empowering. As Smart remarks, 'To couch a claim in terms of rights is a major step towards a recognition of a social wrong.'[4] The use of rights language carries substantial symbolic weight in that it gives status to the individual who is making the claim, who is regarded as a person with dignity demanding fairness. Edwards comments: 'The language of human rights can . . . be a powerful force for change, representing as it does a (relatively) universal language in which to frame grievances.'[5] As Smart states, 'It is almost as hard to be against rights as it is to be against virtue.'[6]

As discussed in Chapter 4, Article 5 of the Istanbul Convention contains the concept of due diligence. The fact that this concept has now been codified in a Council of Europe treaty in the context of violence against women is also very significant.[7] As discussed in Chapter 2, the public/private divide has historically caused substantial problems for the effectiveness of human rights law. As Rehman states:

> [O]ne legitimate criticism has been that international law has failed to focus directly on violations conducted by non-State actors . . . It is noticeable that

4 Smart C., *Feminism and the Power of Law*, 1989, Routledge, London, at p.143.

5 Edwards A., *Violence against Women under International Human Rights Law*, 2013, Cambridge University Press, Cambridge, at p.6.

6 Smart, op. cit., at p.143.

7 As discussed in Chapter 4, this concept has also been codified in the Inter-American context. Article 7(b) of the Inter-American Convention on the Prevention, Punishment, and Eradication of Violence against Women (Convention of Belém do Pará) places an obligation on states parties to 'apply due diligence to prevent, investigate and impose penalties for violence against women'.

> many of the violations of individual and group rights are conducted by private individuals themselves against vulnerable groups such as refugees, minorities, women and children.[8]

This public/private divide has caused immense difficulties as regards the application of human rights law to violence against women, and indeed to many issues relating to the rights of women. As Charlesworth comments, the primary effect of the public/private dichotomy was 'to muffle, and often completely silence, the voices of women'.[9] Rehman remarks: 'A major problem which has led to a negative impact on the position of women is the reluctance of international human rights law to intervene in what is perceived as private (as opposed to the public) matters.'[10]

As discussed in Chapter 3, the European Court of Human Rights has used the concept of positive obligations to great effect to transcend the public/private divide in relation to domestic violence and also as regards many other issues which would historically have been viewed as falling within the private sphere, and therefore beyond the scope of human rights law, as traditionally interpreted. Likewise, as was explained in Chapter 2, the UN human rights bodies have used the concept of state responsibility in an effective manner to transcend the public/private divide. For example, in its General Recommendation No. 19 the UN Committee on the Elimination of Discrimination against Women (CEDAW Committee) stated:

> [D]iscrimination under the Convention is not restricted to action by or on behalf of Governments . . . Under general international law and specific human rights covenants, States may be responsible for private acts if they fail to act with due diligence to prevent violations of rights or to investigate and punish acts of violence, and for providing compensation.[11]

The inclusion of the principle of due diligence in the Istanbul Convention serves again to emphasise the fact that the public/private divide in human rights law has now been surmounted to a substantial extent.

Legally binding obligations

The fundamental importance of the Istanbul Convention, however, reaches beyond a purely symbolic role. Essentially, the Convention places detailed legally

8 Rehman J., *International Human Rights Law*, 2nd edn, 2010, Pearson Education, Harlow, at p.12.

9 Charlesworth H., 'What are "Women's International Human Rights"?', in R.J. Cook (ed.), *Human Rights of Women: National and International Perspectives*, 1994, University of Pennsylvania Press, Philadelphia, 58–84 at 68.

10 Rehman, op. cit., at p.513.

11 Committee on the Elimination of Discrimination against Women, U.N. Doc A/47/38 (1992), at para. 9.

binding obligations on states parties as regards the measures that they must adopt in relation to violence against women, including domestic violence. The actual measures themselves are not new. As was discussed in Chapter 4, most of the measures have in fact been previously articulated by UN bodies such as the CEDAW Committee and the UN Special Rapporteur on violence against women, its causes and consequences. However, the key point is that, in technical terms, such documents are not legally binding on states. Although CEDAW itself is, of course, a legally binding instrument, CEDAW contains no explicit mention of domestic violence, as explained in Chapter 2. It could thus be argued that the statements of the CEDAW Committee and of the other UN bodies in this area are based on a rather insecure foundation. The adoption by the Council of Europe of a Convention that essentially puts the recommendations issued by the UN human rights bodies on a secure and legally binding footing is certainly very much to be welcomed.

The fact that these duties are now legally binding on states that have ratified the Istanbul Convention is of great importance. For example, in calling for a global treaty on violence against women, Rashida Manjoo, the then UN Special Rapporteur on violence against women, its causes and consequences, commented in November 2012, 'How do I hold States accountable if there is no specific legally binding instrument on violence against women? . . . It is time to adopt a comprehensive international convention on violence against women at the UN level.' She also referred to the good practices of the Council of Europe and the Inter-American regional systems with regard to their adoption of the Istanbul Convention and the Inter-American Convention on the Prevention, Punishment, and Eradication of Violence against Women (the Convention of Belém do Pará) respectively.[12] Similarly, in 2014 the Special Rapporteur stated that 'even though soft laws may be influential in developing norms, their non-binding nature effectively means that States cannot be held responsible for violations'.[13]

The legally binding nature of the duties contained in the Istanbul Convention is a factor that can be used by non-governmental organisations working in the area of gender-based violence to place further pressure on governments in states that have ratified this instrument. Indeed, as discussed in Chapter 5, the European Women's Lobby has put together a 'Lobbying Kit' which advises non-governmental organisations on how to play a role in ensuring that the monitoring procedures of the Convention are effective.[14] This Lobbying Kit emphasises that civil society

12 UN Women, 'Needed: specific international legally binding instrument on violence against women', 1 November 2012, available at www.unwomen.org/en/news/stories/2012/11/needed-specific-international-legally-binding-instrument-on-violence-against-women (accessed 18 October 2016). The concept of a global treaty on violence against women will be discussed briefly in Chapter 7.

13 Report of the Special Rapporteur on Violence against Women, its causes and consequences to the UN General Assembly, U.N.Doc.A/69/368, 1 September 2014, at para. 59.

14 European Women's Lobby, 'A European Women's Lobby Lobbying Kit for a transparent monitoring process of the Council of Europe Convention on Preventing and Combating

has an important part to play in this process – for example, through the making of shadow reports to GREVIO.[15] However, non-governmental organisations in states that have ratified the Istanbul Convention can also place pressure directly upon governments by publicising the existence of the obligations contained in this instrument, and the legally binding nature of these duties. It is submitted therefore that the Convention represents an effective tool that can be used by groups working to combat domestic violence, and also gender-based violence more broadly. Merry remarks in relation to CEDAW that the impact of this treaty 'depends on its cultural legitimacy and its embodiment in local cultures and legal consciousness'.[16] The same comment could be made concerning the Istanbul Convention. Non-governmental organisations can play an important role in ensuring that the Convention is firmly embedded in local cultures. In relation to CEDAW, Chinkin and Freeman state: 'NGOs have made a considerable contribution to the articulation of rights under the Convention and more generally to the gendered analysis of human rights principles.'[17] Non-governmental organisations will have an equally important contribution to make in ensuring the effectiveness of the Istanbul Convention.

Comprehensive obligations

As discussed in Chapter 2, the European Court of Human Rights has addressed the issue of domestic violence in a series of recent cases. Beginning in 2007, the Court has now built up a substantial body of jurisprudence on this issue and has placed clear positive obligations on states as regards measures that they must adopt in responding to domestic violence.[18] It has been recognised by the Court that

Violence against Women and Domestic Violence', 2014, available at www.womenlobby.org/EWL-Observatory-on-Violence-against-Women-publishes-Lobbying-Kit-on-the (accessed 18 October 2016).

15 Article 68(5) of the Istanbul Convention provides that GREVIO may receive information on the implementation of the Convention from non-governmental organisations and civil society.

16 Merry S.E., 'Constructing a Global Law – Violence against Women and the Human Rights System', (2003) 28 *Law and Social Inquiry*, 941–74 at 941.

17 Chinkin C. and Freeman M.A., 'Introduction', in M.A. Freeman, C. Chinkin and B. Rudolf (eds), *The UN Convention on the Elimination of All Forms of Discrimination against Women: A Commentary*, 2012, Oxford University Press, Oxford, 2–33 at 24. For a discussion of the important contribution that non-governmental organisations make as regards the implementation of international human rights law, see Wiseberg L.S., 'The Role of Non-Governmental Organizations (NGOs) in the Protection and Enforcement of Human Rights', in J. Symonides (ed.), *Human Rights: International Protection, Monitoring, Enforcement*, 2003, Ashgate, Aldershot, 347–72.

18 *Kontrova v Slovakia* (app. no. 7510/04, 31 May 2007); *Bevacqua and S. v Bulgaria* (app. no. 71127/01, 12 June 2008); *Branko Tomasic and Others v Croatia* (app. no. 46598/06, 15 January 2009); *Opuz v Turkey* (app. no. 33401/02, 9 June 2009); *E.S. and Others v Slovakia* (app. no. 8227/04, 15 September 2009); *A v Croatia* (app. no. 55164/08, 14 October 2010); *Hajduova v Slovakia* (app. no. 2660/03, 30 November 2010); *Kalucza v*

domestic violence constitutes a clear violation of Articles 2, 3, 8 and 14 of the European Convention on Human Rights. This body of case law is of immense significance and the duties that the European Court has placed on states are of course legally binding obligations. However, these duties are by no means comprehensive in nature in terms of providing an adequate response to domestic violence. Although the Court has placed positive obligations on states to ensure that their criminal justice systems are of a sufficient standard in responding to the issue of domestic violence, duties have not been placed upon states in relation to other aspects of their responses to domestic abuse. For example, and arguably most crucially, the Court has not addressed the necessity for states to provide social support measures to victims of domestic violence, despite the fact that it is frequently measures such as refuge accommodation and financial support that are of most importance to victims.[19] Similarly, the European Court has not addressed the need for public awareness campaigns to be implemented in order to raise levels of understanding of the issues involved in domestic violence and the prevalence of its occurrence.

It is of course not inconceivable that the Court may in the future place duties on states in respect of these matters. Indeed, the Court has repeatedly stated that the European Convention on Human Rights is a 'living instrument which . . . must be interpreted in the light of present-day conditions'.[20] Nevertheless, it is perhaps unsurprising that such issues have not been addressed by the Court, as it is usually substantially more difficult for a court to order that affirmative programmes be put in place than it is for it to hold that a particular practice be

Hungary (app. no. 57693/10, 24 April 2012); *E.M. v Romania* (app. no. 43994/05, 30 October 2012); *Valiuliene v Lithuania* (app. no. 33234/07, 26 March 2013); *Eremia and Others v the Republic of Moldova* (app. no. 3564/11, 28 May 2013); *B. v the Republic of Moldova* (app. no. 61382/09, 16 July 2013); *Mudric v the Republic of Moldova* (app. no. 74839/10, 16 July 2013); *N.A. v the Republic of Moldova* (app. no. 13424/06, 24 September 2013); *T.M. and C.M. v the Republic of Moldova* (app. no. 26608/11, 28 January 2014); *Rumor v Italy* (app. no. 72964/10, 27 May 2014); *Civek v Turkey* (app. no. 55354/11, 23 February 2016); *M.G. v Turkey* (app. no. 646/10, 22 March 2016); and *Halime Kılıç v Turkey* (app. no. 63034/11, 28 June 2016).

19 In a small number of cases the European Court of Human Rights has held that in particular circumstances the state has a duty to provide resources to individuals to prevent violations of their rights. The main case in this regard is *Airey v Ireland* (app. no. 6289/73, 9 October 1979), in which the applicant alleged that her husband had subjected her to physical violence, and the issue revolved around the fact that legal aid was unavailable in Ireland for the purpose of seeking a judicial separation. The European Court found that there had been breaches of Articles 6 and 8. However, although the Court did hold that ensuring effective access to particular means of protection may in certain circumstances entail the expenditure of monetary resources, the Court did not state that civil legal aid must actually be granted in situations such as that which arose in this case. The Court simply held that there must be effective access to the protective measure of a decree of judicial separation. This duty could have been fulfilled by other means – for example, by simplifying the procedures.

20 This principle was first stated by the Court in *Tyrer v United Kingdom* (app. no. 5856/72, 25 April 1978) at para. 31.

stopped. However, by contrast, as discussed in Chapter 4, the Istanbul Convention places very detailed duties on states parties concerning a wide range of aspects of their responses to domestic violence, including both the provision of social support measures to victims and the implementation of public awareness campaigns.

Advantages of the monitoring mechanisms of the Istanbul Convention

There are also other benefits entailed in having a Convention monitored by a reporting mechanism, as opposed to placing the onus on victims to bring cases to court, as is the situation under the European Convention on Human Rights. Article 34 of the latter states: 'The Court may receive applications from any person, non-governmental organisation or group of individuals claiming to be the victim of a violation by one of the High Contracting Parties of the rights set forth in the Convention or the protocols thereto.' Under the European Convention on Human Rights, therefore, the test of standing is very limited. Essentially, a party wishing to bring a case under this instrument must be a 'victim'. This is problematic when applied to the issue of domestic violence, as domestic abuse constitutes an 'unseen' crime which victims are frequently reluctant to report, due to fear or shame.[21] Many incidents of domestic violence never come to the attention of the police. A high percentage of victims simply may not wish to take a case to a national court, let alone to the European Court of Human Rights. This constitutes a major difficulty for the effectiveness of the European Convention on Human Rights in relation to domestic violence. As Epp comments, 'judges . . . cannot make rights-supportive law unless they have rights cases to decide'.[22]

Another benefit of utilising a strategy other than that of litigation is that a substantially more detailed approach can be adopted. Judges must confine themselves to dealing with the precise issues in the cases that come before them. As Gormley states, 'By its very nature, a judgment in an individual case follows a narrative of one person's experience.'[23] This obviously places limitations on the role that litigation can play in promoting change. However, in making recommendations to states, a body such as GREVIO is at liberty to adopt a much broader approach than could a judge in addressing a specific case. As Van Schaack comments, 'An overreliance on adversarial litigation . . . raises . . . concerns . . . about the efficacy of resorting to law and the judicial process to promote durable

21 See, further, McQuigg R., 'The Victim Test under the Human Rights Act 1998 and its Implications for Domestic Violence Cases', (2011) *European Human Rights Law Review*, 294–303.

22 Epp C.R., *The Rights Revolution*, 1998, University of Chicago Press, Chicago and London, at p.15.

23 Gormley L., 'The Council of Europe Convention on Preventing and Combating Violence against Women and Domestic Violence: A Consolidation of Existing International Law, or a Significant Progression?', (2014) *European Human Rights Law Review*, 606–17 at 608.

social change and the ability of the judicial process to address major social . . . problems.'[24] Likewise, Scheingold remarks that the adoption of such an approach 'grossly exaggerates the role that lawyers and litigation can play in a strategy for change'.[25] Epp states that 'the judicial process is costly and slow and produces changes in the law only in small increments'.[26]

There are other limits to the use of a litigation strategy to promote change. For example, if a court were to hold that financial resources should be accorded to victims of domestic violence, it could be argued that the judge may be entering into an area in which it is inappropriate for him or her to adjudicate. Resources are finite, and if a government accords resources to victims of domestic violence, it is likely that as a result fewer resources will be allocated to other issues of concern. Chayes comments that 'the court has little basis for evaluating competing claims on the public purse'.[27] On this basis, it could be argued that judges do not have the specialist knowledge that is necessary to adjudicate on matters that entail the allocation of public finances. As Rosenberg remarks, 'litigation steer[s] activists to an institution that is constrained from helping them'.[28] In addition, the provision of social support measures for victims of domestic violence gives rise to issues relating to socio-economic rights, the implementation of which has always given rise to controversy. Fredman comments that 'socio-economic rights are often considered to be merely aspirational, and their status as human rights doubted'.[29] Oloka-Onyango states: 'Civil and political rights are considered to belong to a first category, or "generation" of rights, while economic, social, and cultural rights have been relegated to a lower less important sphere.'[30] It has been asserted by a number of commentators that states should not be obliged to adopt expensive measures to ensure the rights of an individual. For example, it has been argued that, although states may be reasonably required to refrain from torturing their citizens, it is not clear that they can equally be required to guarantee them a livelihood.[31] Such concerns

24 Van Schaack B., 'With All Deliberate Speed: Civil Human Rights Litigation as a Tool for Social Change', (2004) 57 *Vanderbilt Law Review*, 2305–48 at 2307.

25 Scheingold S., *The Politics of Rights: Lawyers, Public Policy, and Political Change*, 2004, University of Michigan Press, Ann Arbor, at p.5.

26 Epp, op. cit., at p.3.

27 Chayes A., 'The Role of the Judge in Public Law Litigation', (1976) 89 *Harvard Law Review*, 1281–316 at 1309.

28 Rosenberg G.N., *The Hollow Hope: Can Courts Bring About Social Change?*, 1991, University of Chicago Press, Chicago, at p.339.

29 Fredman S., *Human Rights Transformed: Positive Rights and Positive Duties*, 2009, Oxford University Press, Oxford, at p.1.

30 Oloka-Onyango J., 'Reinforcing Marginalized Rights in an Age of Globalization: International Mechanisms, Non-State Actors, and the Struggle for Peoples' Rights in Africa', (2003) 18 *American University International Law Review*, 851–913 at 852.

31 For discussion of such arguments, see Beetham D., 'What Future for Economic and Social Rights?', (1995) 43 *Political Studies*, 41–60. For further discussion of socio-economic rights, see Khaliq U. and Churchill R., 'The Protection of Economic and Social Rights: A Particular

therefore may also contribute to a reluctance on the part of courts to enter into the arena of resource allocation.[32]

Nevertheless, even given the difficulties relating to addressing domestic violence through a litigation approach and despite the adoption of the Istanbul Convention, the case law of the European Court of Human Rights on domestic violence will remain of substantial importance. This is due largely to the fact that the duties established by this case law apply to all 47 member states of the Council of Europe, whereas the obligations found in the Istanbul Convention apply only to the states that have ratified this instrument. At the time of writing, 22 states have ratified the Istanbul Convention, which is substantially fewer states than those that make up the Council of Europe as a whole. As discussed later in this chapter, it is possible that a number of states may be reluctant to ratify the Istanbul Convention due to the very detailed obligations that it places upon states parties. However, even if a state does not choose to ratify the Istanbul Convention, it will still be subject to the positive obligations placed upon states by the European Court of Human Rights as regards domestic violence. It is therefore immensely important that this body of jurisprudence continues to expand and develop.[33]

Potential challenges for the Istanbul Convention

Ensuring that all states within the Council of Europe ratify the Istanbul Convention

As has been discussed so far in this chapter, and indeed throughout this book, the adoption of the Istanbul Convention constitutes a very positive development as regards efforts to combat domestic violence, and also gender-based violence more broadly. However, there are a number of potential difficulties that may serve to hinder the effectiveness of this instrument. The first relates to the question of whether all or most of the member states of the Council of Europe will actually ratify the Istanbul Convention. The Council of Europe currently comprises 47 states. Under Article 75(1) of the Istanbul Convention, this instrument is open for signature by these member states, any non-member states that have participated in the elaboration of the Convention, and the European Union. Instruments

Challenge?', in H. Keller and G. Ulfstein (eds), *UN Human Rights Treaty Bodies: Law and Legitimacy*, 2012, Cambridge University Press, Cambridge, 199–260; and Dennis M.J. and Stewart D.P., 'Justiciability of Economic, Social, and Cultural Rights: Should There Be an International Complaints Mechanism to Adjudicate the Rights to Food, Water, Housing, and Health?', (2004) 98 *American Journal of International Law*, 462–515.

32 For further discussion of the limitations of a litigation approach in the context of domestic violence, see McQuigg R., *International Human Rights Law and Domestic Violence*, 2011, Routledge, Abingdon, at pp.13–18.

33 For discussion of advantages of the Istanbul Convention, see also McQuigg R., 'What Potential Does the Council of Europe Convention on Violence against Women Hold as Regards Domestic Violence?', (2012) 16 *International Journal of Human Rights*, 947–62.

of ratification should be deposited with the Secretary General of the Council of Europe.[34] The Convention opened for signature in Istanbul on 11 May 2011 and was signed initially by 13 states. Under Article 75(3), the Convention had to be ratified by ten parties, including eight member states of the Council of Europe, in order to enter into force. The Convention subsequently entered into force on 1 August 2014. At the time of writing, this instrument has been ratified by 22 states,[35] and has been signed but not yet ratified by another 21 states.[36] Six states have to date neither signed nor ratified the Convention.[37] In order to ensure the optimal level of effectiveness, it is clearly important for the Convention to be ratified by the majority, if not all, of the member states of the Council of Europe. It remains to be seen precisely how many states will ratify the Convention. Nevertheless, progress to date is encouraging, given that 43 of the 47 states – a substantial majority – have either ratified the Convention or indicated by signing this instrument that they intend to do so.

It is possible that a number of states may be reluctant to ratify the Istanbul Convention due to the substantial duties that are placed on states parties to this instrument. In particular, the obligations contained therein which relate to the provision of social support measures for victims necessitate significant levels of expenditure by governments. Also, it is noteworthy that the Istanbul Convention does not use a concept of 'progressive realisation' such as that found in the International Covenant on Economic, Social and Cultural Rights (ICESCR),[38] Article 2(1) of which places a duty on each state party 'to take steps . . . to the maximum of its available resources, with a view to achieving progressively the full realization of the rights recognized in the present Covenant'.

Interestingly, the concept of progressive realisation is also found in the Convention of Belém do Pará. The obligations contained in Article 7 of this instrument are not, however, subject to the progressive realisation approach. Under this provision, states parties should include in their domestic legislation provisions to prevent, punish and eradicate violence against women;[39] adopt legal measures to require the perpetrator to refrain from harassing, intimidating or threatening the woman;[40] and take all appropriate measures to amend or repeal existing laws and regulations or to modify legal or customary practices that sustain

34 Istanbul Convention, Article 75(2).

35 Albania, Andorra, Austria, Belgium, Bosnia and Herzegovina, Denmark, Finland, France, Italy, Malta, Monaco, Montenegro, Netherlands, Poland, Portugal, Romania, San Marino, Serbia, Slovenia, Spain, Sweden and Turkey.

36 Bulgaria, Croatia, Cyprus, Czech Republic, Estonia, Georgia, Germany, Greece, Hungary, Iceland, Ireland, Latvia, Liechtenstein, Lithuania, Luxembourg, Norway, Slovakia, Switzerland, the former Yugoslav Republic of Macedonia, Ukraine and United Kingdom.

37 Armenia, Azerbaijan, Moldova and Russia.

38 The ICESCR (993 U.N.T.S. 3) was adopted by the UN General Assembly on 16 December 1966 and entered into force on 3 January 1976.

39 Convention of Belém do Pará, Article 7(c).

40 Article 7(d).

violence against women.[41] In addition, states parties should establish fair and effective legal procedures for women who have been subjected to violence;[42] establish the necessary legal and administrative mechanisms to ensure that women subjected to violence have effective access to just and effective remedies;[43] and adopt such legislative or other measures as may be necessary to give effect to the Convention.[44] These obligations are absolute and must be complied with by the state party immediately upon ratification of the Convention of Belém do Pará. Article 8 of this Convention contains a number of additional measures that states parties should adopt. However, states parties agree to undertake these measures 'progressively'. The measures encompassed by Article 8 include the adoption of programmes aimed at promoting awareness of the right of women to be free from violence,[45] and at modifying social and cultural patterns of conduct of men and women to counteract prejudices based on the idea of the inferiority or superiority of either of the sexes which legitimise violence against women.[46] States should promote the education and training of all those involved in the administration of justice, police and other law enforcement officers responsible for implementing policies for the prevention, punishment and eradication of violence against women.[47] They should 'provide appropriate specialized services for women who have been subjected to violence, through public and private sector agencies, including shelters, counseling services for all family members where appropriate, and care and custody of the affected children'.[48] States should also provide women who have been subjected to violence with access to effective readjustment and training programmes to enable them to participate fully in public, private and social life.[49]

By contrast, the Istanbul Convention does not encompass the concept of progressive realisation. States parties are instead under immediate obligations upon ratification to comply with all of the provisions of this instrument. The decision to adopt such an approach may reflect the fact that many of the states within the Council of Europe are relatively wealthy; however, the obligations placed upon states parties by this instrument are extensive, and are much more detailed than those found, for example, in the Convention of Belém do Pará. It is thus possible that a number of states may be reluctant to ratify the Istanbul Convention due to the substantial duties that it places on states parties.

41 Article 7(e).
42 Article 7(f).
43 Article 7(g).
44 Article 7(h).
45 Article 8(a).
46 Article 8(b).
47 Article 8(c).
48 Article 8(d).
49 Article 8(f).

Reservations

Potential difficulties may also arise relating to the issue of reservations. It is noteworthy that the Istanbul Convention adopts a strict approach to this issue. Under Article 78(1) of the Convention, no reservations are permitted, apart from a number of very narrow exceptions, as provided for by Article 78(2) and (3). Under Article 78(2), reservations can be entered in respect of Article 30(2), which places an obligation upon states parties to provide adequate state compensation to victims who have sustained serious bodily injury or impairment of health, in instances in which the damage is not covered by other sources such as the perpetrator, insurance or state-funded health and social provisions. Reservations can also be entered in respect of certain aspects of Article 44 as regards extra-territorial application,[50] and in relation to the aspect of Article 55(1) which requires states parties to ensure that investigations into or prosecutions of offences involving intentional acts of physical violence shall not be wholly dependent upon a report or complaint filed by a victim, and that the proceedings may continue even if the victim withdraws the statement or complaint. Any reservation entered in respect of Article 55(1) can, however, relate only to investigations into or prosecutions of 'minor offences', although the Convention does not provide a definition of what constitutes a 'minor offence'. In addition, reservations can be entered in respect of certain aspects of Article 58, which relates to statutes of limitation, and in respect of Article 59, which places a duty on states to ensure that victims whose residence status depends on that of their spouse or partner are granted, in certain circumstances, an autonomous residence permit, in the event of the dissolution of the marriage or the relationship. Under Article 78(3), states parties may also declare that they reserve the right to provide for non-criminal sanctions, as opposed to criminal sanctions, for the behaviours referred to in Articles 33 and 34 of the Convention, namely psychological violence and stalking.[51]

The approach that should be adopted towards reservations by any new Convention is a difficult issue. Essentially, a balance must be struck between, on the one hand, the desire to ensure that as many states as possible ratify the Convention, and thus permitting some leeway in order to encourage them to do so, and, on the other hand, ensuring that states are not allowed to enter reservations that are so extensive that they impact on the very heart of the Convention itself. It is not easy to strike this balance in the correct manner. For example, it is arguable that the approach that has been adopted towards reservations under CEDAW has been of too lenient a nature. Article 28 of CEDAW permits ratification subject to reservations, provided the reservations are not incompatible with

50 Reservations can be entered in respect of Article 44(1)(e), (3) and (4).

51 The criminalisation of psychological violence was also referred to in Chapter 2.

the object and purpose of CEDAW.[52] However, it appears that a broad approach is adopted towards compatibility. Rehman remarks:

> Out of all the human rights treaties, the Women's Convention has attracted the highest number of reservations, some of them so sweeping and overriding in nature that the issue of good faith and principle of integrity of the instrument inevitably comes into question.[53]

Likewise, Cook comments that 'the legal issue of the propriety of reservations to this Convention goes to the heart of both values of universality and integrity'.[54] Although states can of course enter reservations when ratifying other UN human rights treaties, CEDAW nevertheless remains the treaty with the most reservations. As Rehman comments, 'the significant number of reservations do pose a serious challenge'.[55] Isa states that the high number of reservations to CEDAW constitutes '[a] serious problem that has had a profound impact on the effectiveness of CEDAW'.[56] Likewise, Smith remarks that CEDAW is 'beset by problems due to the extraordinarily high number of reservations thereto'.[57] This difficulty has certainly been avoided by the drafters of the Istanbul Convention, given the strict approach to reservations that has been taken. The adoption of such a narrow approach could well serve to increase the effectiveness of the Convention. However, it could also have the effect of deterring some states from ratifying this instrument.

To date, the limited right to enter reservations has been invoked fairly frequently by states parties to the Istanbul Convention.[58] It is also of note that several states – Poland, Lithuania and Latvia – have entered declarations upon signature of the Convention stating that they will apply this instrument in conformity with the principles and provisions of their respective constitutions. Poland's confirmation of this declaration in its instrument of ratification deposited on 27 April 2015 has met with opposition from four other states parties – Austria, Finland, the Netherlands and Sweden. Each of these states has entered objections asserting

52 Article 28(2) states: 'A reservation incompatible with the object and purpose of the present Convention shall not be permitted.'

53 Rehman, op. cit., at p.554.

54 Cook R.J., 'Reservations to the Convention on the Elimination of All Forms of Discrimination against Women', (1989–1990) 30 *Virginia Journal of International Law*, 643–716 at 644.

55 Rehman, op. cit., at p.536.

56 Isa F.G., 'The Optional Protocol for the Convention on the Elimination of All Forms of Discrimination against Women: Strengthening the Protection of Women's Human Rights', (2003) 20 *Arizona Journal of International and Comparative Law*, 291–322 at 302.

57 Smith R.K.M., *Textbook on International Human Rights*, 6th edn, 2014, Oxford University Press, Oxford, at p.164.

58 For a full list of the reservations and declarations made by states parties to the Istanbul Convention, see www.coe.int/en/web/conventions/full-list/-/conventions/treaty/210/declarations?p_auth=VHYoKh1z, Council of Europe (accessed 18 October 2016).

that they view this declaration as a reservation, and that as such it is impermissible as it does not fall within the scope of Article 78 of the Convention. According to the objection submitted by Austria, 'Poland has made a reservation of a general and indeterminate scope which does not clearly define for the other States Parties to the Convention the extent to which the reserving State has accepted the obligations of the Convention.'[59] The objection submitted by Finland expressed the view that such a reservation 'may raise doubts as to the commitment of the Republic of Poland to fulfil its obligations under the Convention'.[60] In addition, Finland referred to the general principle of treaty interpretation that a party may not invoke provisions of domestic law in order to justify a failure to perform its obligations under a treaty. The Netherlands was also of the opinion that such a reservation served to raise doubts in relation to Poland's commitment to 'the object and purpose of the Convention'.[61] The objection submitted by Sweden stated:

> Reservations by which a State Party limits its responsibilities under the Convention by not considering itself bound by certain articles and by invoking general references to national or religious law may cast doubts on the commitments of the reserving state to the object and purpose of the Convention and, moreover, contribute to undermining the basis of international treaty law. It is in the common interest of states that treaties to which they have chosen to become parties also are respected, as to object and purpose, by all parties.[62]

In addition, both Austria and Finland stated that the declaration by Poland constituted a reservation that was incompatible with the object and purposes of the Convention, with Finland referring specifically in this regard to Article 19 of the Vienna Convention on the Law of Treaties.[63]

59 Objection contained in a Note Verbale from the Permanent Representation of Austria, dated 11 April 2016, registered at the Secretariat General on 13 April 2016, available at www.coe.int/en/web/conventions/full-list/-/conventions/treaty/210/declarations?p_auth=VHYoKh1z, Council of Europe (accessed 18 October 2016).

60 Objection contained in a Note Verbale from the Permanent Representation of Finland, dated 26 April 2016, registered at the Secretariat General on 29 April 2016, available at www.coe.int/en/web/conventions/full-list/-/conventions/treaty/210/declarations?p_auth=VHYoKh1z, Council of Europe (accessed 18 October 2016).

61 Objection contained in a Note Verbale from the Permanent Representation of the Netherlands, dated 28 April 2016, registered at the Secretariat General on 29 April 2016, available at www.coe.int/en/web/conventions/full-list/-/conventions/treaty/210/declarations?p_auth=VHYoKh1z, Council of Europe (accessed 18 October 2016).

62 Objection contained in a Note Verbale from the Ministry for Foreign Affairs of Sweden, dated 15 February 2016, registered at the Secretariat General on 3 March 2016, available at www.coe.int/en/web/conventions/full-list/-/conventions/treaty/210/declarations?p_auth=VHYoKh1z, Council of Europe (accessed 18 October 2016).

63 The Vienna Convention on the Law of Treaties (1155 U.N.T.S. 331) was adopted on 22 May 1969 and entered into force on 27 January 1980. Article 19 of this Convention provides: 'A State may, when signing, ratifying, accepting, approving or acceding to a treaty, formulate

Whether or not the entering of a declaration that a state party will apply the Istanbul Convention in conformity with the principles and provisions of its constitution will actually make any practical difference to how the Convention is applied in that particular state remains to be seen. As regards the reporting procedure, which is the primary method for the monitoring of compliance with the Convention, Poland has not been included in the provisional reporting timetable for 2016 and 2017, and will therefore not be required to submit a report to GREVIO until at least 2018.[64] It also remains to be seen whether, during its consideration of Poland's initial report, GREVIO will ask that the state consider withdrawing this declaration. It is noteworthy that under Article 79(3), if a state party makes a reservation in conformity with Article 78(2) or (3), it must provide an explanation to GREVIO of the grounds for justifying the continuance of the reservation, upon request or prior to renewing such a reservation.[65] However, as the declaration in question does not constitute a reservation falling within the ambit of Article 78(2) or (3), the obligation to provide an explanation under Article 79(3) would not apply.

However, on a more general level, the fact that the precedent has now been set for the acceptance of what appears to be a rather sweeping declaration of this nature is somewhat concerning. Those who drafted the Istanbul Convention chose to adopt a narrow approach to the question of the reservations that would be permissible. Although it is possible that such an approach may discourage some states from ratifying the Convention, it is also very likely that this restrictive approach to reservations may ultimately result in more effective implementation of this instrument among states parties. In any event, it seems that there is little to be gained by allowing states parties to submit sweeping declarations upon ratification that have the effect of reservations, albeit without being termed as being such. All this would serve to do would be to circumvent the limited approach to reservations that the drafters of the Convention chose to adopt. The allowing of declarations that in effect amount to reservations not listed in Article 78, and which should therefore be impermissible, would be problematic in and of itself. However, these difficulties are heightened considerably if such declarations amount to reservations that are actually incompatible with the objects and purposes of the Convention, and therefore violate Article 19 of the Vienna

a reservation unless: (a) the reservation is prohibited by the treaty; (b) the treaty provides that only specified reservations, which do not include the reservation in question, may be made; or (c) in cases not falling under sub-paragraphs (a) and (b), the reservation is incompatible with the object and purpose of the treaty.'

64 The reporting procedure is found in Article 68 of the Istanbul Convention and was discussed in detail in Chapter 5. The provisional reporting timetable for 2016 and 2017 is available at www.coe.int/en/web/istanbul-convention/evaluation, Council of Europe (accessed 18 October 2016).

65 Under Article 79(1), reservations are valid for a renewable period of five years from the date of entry into force of the Convention in the state party in question. The procedure for renewing a reservation is found in Article 79(2).

Convention on the Law of Treaties. Extreme care must be taken as regards this issue, particularly given the problems that have been encountered by CEDAW in this respect.

In addition, as noted previously, two other states – Latvia and Lithuania – entered very similar declarations to that of Poland upon signature of the Convention in that they stated that they too would apply this instrument in conformity with the principles and provisions of their respective constitutions. Poland entered its initial declaration upon signing the Convention on 18 December 2012, with Lithuania following suit on 7 June 2013. Latvia entered its declaration upon signature on 18 May 2016. The fact that the declaration by Poland was still accepted at the ratification stage means that should Lithuania or Latvia decide to confirm their declarations upon ratification of the Convention, there would be no option but to accept these declarations. This would be the case despite the probable entering of objections by other states parties, similar to those entered by Austria, Finland, the Netherlands and Sweden in respect of the declaration by Poland. Likewise, should any other state decide to make such a declaration in the future, either upon signature or upon ratification of the Convention, again there would be no choice but to accept such a declaration.

It may of course prove to be the case that Poland's declaration that it will apply the Istanbul Convention in conformity with its constitution will make little or no difference at the practical level as regards its implementation of the Convention. However, it does seem that the allowing of such a declaration is problematic from the perspective of principle, in that it entails in effect an acceptance of the concept that the provisions of the Convention can be subordinated to provisions of the domestic law of a state party. It is difficult to disagree with the comment made by Sweden in its objection that such an approach contributes to 'undermining the basis of international treaty law'. It is also true that a declaration that a state party will apply the Istanbul Convention in conformity with the principles and provisions of its constitution could potentially be very far-reaching. Overall, regardless of the extent to which Poland's declaration impacts on its implementation of the Convention at a practical level, it seems that the allowing of such a declaration upon ratification has set a somewhat dangerous precedent for the future.

Implementation and enforcement

Another potential problem for the Istanbul Convention relates to implementation and enforcement. Of course, this is by no means a difficulty that would be unique to this instrument. Extensive problems with implementation and enforcement affect all of the UN human rights treaties. The implementation of international human rights law has been inconsistent, to say the least.[66] Although human rights

66 Wallace R., *International Human Rights*, 2001, Sweet & Maxwell, London, at p.589.

instruments contain detailed lists of the rights that should be afforded to individuals, in many situations these rights are nevertheless still being violated. As Hafner-Burton and Tsutsui remark, 'government violation of human rights is epidemic'.[67] For human rights standards to be implemented within states, there must be a political will among governments to do so,[68] and often such a will is lacking. Copelon comments that 'the international human rights system still operates more in rhetoric than in reality'.[69] It remains the case that human rights are indeed regarded by many as rhetoric as opposed to constituting legal duties that must be observed.[70] It is extremely difficult to compel states to comply with their duties if they are reluctant to do so. As Byrnes remarks, 'The limitations of international law generally when it comes to enforcement of binding standards are well known, and international human rights law is no exception in that regard.'[71] Indeed, Bayefsky comments that the large numbers of ratifications of the UN human rights treaties 'reflect the widely-held view by states parties that there are not serious consequences associated with ratification'.[72]

It appears that this failure may be due at least partly to the 'lack of an international policing force that demands compliance with international edicts'.[73] The UN has no real method of forcing states to alter their policies. It must instead attempt to persuade nations to comply with their international duties.[74] Risse and Sikkink remark: 'Countries most sensitive to pressure are not those that are economically weakest, but those that care about their international image.'[75] However, if a government is powerful on an international scale, it may be impervious to international human rights law.[76] Merry comments:

67 Hafner-Burton E.M. and Tsutsui K., 'Human Rights in a Globalizing World: The Paradox of Empty Promises', (2005) 110 *American Journal of Sociology*, 1373–411 at 1374.

68 Wallace, op. cit., at p.590.

69 Copelon R., 'International Human Rights Dimensions of Intimate Violence: Another Strand in the Dialectic of Feminist Lawmaking', (2003) 11 *American University Journal of Gender, Social Policy and the Law*, 865–76 at 875.

70 Robinson M., 'Making Human Rights Matter: Eleanor Roosevelt's Time Has Come', (2003) 16 *Harvard Human Rights Journal*, 1–11 at 1.

71 Byrnes A., 'Enforcement Through International Law and Procedures', in R.J. Cook (ed.), *Human Rights of Women: National and International Perspectives*, 1994, University of Pennsylvania Press, Philadelphia, 189–227 at 191–2.

72 Bayefsky A.F., *The UN Human Rights Treaty System: Universality at the Crossroads*, 2001, Transnational Publishers, Ardsley, at p.7.

73 Ulrich J., 'Confronting Gender-Based Violence with International Instruments: Is a Solution to the Pandemic Within Reach?', (2000) 7 *Indiana Journal of Global Legal Studies*, 629–54 at 637.

74 Ulrich, op. cit., at pp.638–9.

75 Risse T. and Sikkink K., 'The Socialization of International Human Rights Norms into Domestic Practices: Introduction', in T. Risse, S.C. Ropp and K. Sikkink (eds), *The Power of Human Rights: International Norms and Domestic Change*, 1999, Cambridge University Press, Cambridge, 1–38 at 37–8.

76 Cassel D., 'Does International Human Rights Law Make a Difference?', (2001) 2 *Chicago Journal of International Law*, 121–35 at 135.

> Countries are concerned about their reputations in the international community, but they clearly differ in their vulnerability to international pressure depending on their size, wealth, form of government, and dependence on the international community for trade, aid, and other symbolic and material forms of exchange.[77]

The effectiveness of human rights treaties therefore depends greatly on the level of commitment held by states to give effect to their duties. As Crawford remarks, 'There are no doubt inherent problems with a system for human rights protection based essentially on self-criticism and good faith.'[78] Egan comments that the UN treaty bodies, national human rights institutions and non-governmental organisations 'face a task of Sisyphean proportions in coaxing States to implement the treaty body recommendations'.[79]

Ulrich remarks that the difficulties relating to implementation and enforcement are magnified as regards treaties that address women's rights.[80] For example, in relation to CEDAW, Schopp-Schilling asserts:

> [M]any States Parties have often not addressed issues of legal reform or programmes to improve the material situation of women to enable and empower them to claim, exercise and enjoy their human rights, even if they ratified the CEDAW 15 or 20 years ago.[81]

Merry comments that 'CEDAW is law without sanctions'.[82] Ritz asserts that 'CEDAW . . . has proven ineffective in ending gender discrimination'.[83] Afsharipour remarks that 'due to a lack of effective enforcement mechanisms, the Convention's success in improving the lives of women has been limited'.[84]

77 Merry, op. cit., at p.959.

78 Crawford J., 'The UN Human Rights Treaty System: A System in Crisis?', in P. Alston and J. Crawford (eds), *The Future of UN Human Rights Treaty Monitoring*, 2000, Cambridge University Press, Cambridge, 1–12 at 7.

79 Egan S., *The UN Human Rights Treaty System: Law and Procedure*, 2011, Bloomsbury Professional, Dublin, at p.477. For discussion of the effectiveness of human rights treaties, see Hathaway O., 'Do Human Rights Treaties Make a Difference?', (2002) 111 *Yale Law Journal*, 1935–2042; Goodman R. and Jinks D., 'Measuring the Effects of Human Rights', (2003) 14 *European Journal of International Law*, 171–83; and Hathaway O., 'Testing Conventional Wisdom', (2003) 14 *European Journal of International Law*, 185–200.

80 Ulrich, op. cit., at p.638.

81 Schopp-Schilling H.B., 'Treaty Body Reform: The Case of the Committee on the Elimination of Discrimination against Women', (2007) 7 *Human Rights Law Review*, 201–24 at 204.

82 Merry, op. cit., at p.943.

83 Ritz K.L., 'Soft Enforcement: Inadequacies of Optional Protocol as a Remedy for the Convention on the Elimination of All Forms of Discrimination against Women', (2001) 25 *Suffolk Transnational Law Review*, 191–216 at 193.

84 Afsharipour A., 'Empowering Ourselves: The Role of Women's NGOs in the Enforcement of the Women's Convention', (1999) 99 *Columbia Law Review*, 129–72 at 129.

Essentially, it is clear that, despite the fact that CEDAW has been ratified by a very large number of states,[85] gender inequality still persists. In 2007, research was carried out that addressed the issue of how states have responded to the comments of the CEDAW Committee on the issue of domestic violence, in which 11 Western European states were examined.[86] It was found that the majority of the states surveyed, including Denmark, Germany, Ireland, Italy, Norway and Spain, were complying with only some of the recommendations of the Committee as regards this issue. Certain states, including Luxembourg, the Netherlands and Sweden, did seem to be complying with most of the Committee's recommendations. However, as was noted in the study, it is difficult to ascertain whether the measures adopted by such states were as a result of the comments made by the CEDAW Committee or whether they were due to other factors, such as pressure being exerted by non-governmental organisations or by academic commentators.

Another study carried out in 2011 examined the implementation in the United Kingdom of the recommendations made by the international human rights bodies on domestic violence.[87] Again it was found that these recommendations suffer from great difficulties as regards their effectiveness. The recommendations had not been uniformly implemented in the UK, and it appeared that the primary reason for this was a lack of will on the part of the state, combined with an absence of enforcement mechanisms. Notably, the most problematic area in relation to the government's response to domestic violence was found to be the provision of social support measures to victims, which is the category of recommendations that necessitates the greatest amount of money to be spent. The study found that even in areas in which the UK did appear to be fulfilling the recommendations of the international human rights bodies, at least to some extent, such as in relation to improving the criminal justice system, it seemed that changes in government policy were more likely to have been due to other factors, such as pressure from domestic violence groups and academic commentators.

The implementation problems suffered by the UN human rights treaties have been exacerbated by difficulties surrounding the reporting procedures, which constitute the primary monitoring mechanisms of these instruments.[88] Egan comments:

> Many States appear to ignore totally the guidelines which the treaty bodies have produced to assist them in preparing their reports. The quality of the

85 At the time of writing, 189 states have ratified CEDAW.

86 McQuigg R., 'The Responses of States to the Comments of the CEDAW Committee on Domestic Violence', (2007) 11 *International Journal of Human Rights*, 461–79.

87 McQuigg R., *International Human Rights Law and Domestic Violence*, 2011, Routledge, Abingdon, at pp.99–124.

88 For discussion generally of the reporting procedures of the UN human rights treaties, see Kalin W., 'Examination of State Reports', in H. Keller and G. Ulfstein (eds), *UN Human Rights Treaty Bodies: Law and Legitimacy*, 2012, Cambridge University Press, Cambridge, 16–72.

> reports can range from being inadequate to blatantly derisory. Formal presentation of the report in the public sessions can often serve to reinforce the impression that the process is not taken seriously by many governments, or is at best regarded as an obligatory, but essentially shallow, diplomatic exercise.[89]

Fortin remarks:

> [T]he reporting mechanism relies on governments to subject their implementation programme to an objective and critical analysis before compiling their reports. The absence of any supervision or coercion over this can lead to reports painting an over-optimistic and complacent picture of governmental achievements.[90]

Smith comments: 'The reports system is often regarded as weak because it is dependent upon the will of States to comply . . . Self-appraisal may be entering mainstream management practice in the developed world but it has yet to reach mainstream international law.'[91] In relation to CEDAW, Merry sets out seven methods by which states may escape proper scrutiny by the CEDAW Committee.[92] First, the state may fail to write a report or do so only after a long delay. Second, the state may write only a superficial report. Third, the state may send only low-level government representatives to present the report. Fourth, the state may avoid answering questions directly. Fifth, the state may promise to make changes but fail to act on such promises. Sixth, the state may enter extensive reservations. Finally, the state may refuse to present its report even after submission. Often states submit their reports only after long delays, and there is also a backlog in relation to the consideration of reports by the CEDAW Committee, which further adds to the delays.[93] As Rehman comments:

> The present reporting procedure as provided in the (CEDAW) Convention, in common with other reporting procedures, has proved less than satisfactory.

89 Egan, op. cit., at pp.172–3.

90 Fortin J., *Children's Rights and the Developing Law*, 2003, Butterworths, London, at p.46. Although this comment was made in the context of a discussion of the UN Convention on the Rights of the Child (1577 U.N.T.S. 3, adopted by the UN General Assembly on 20 November 1989 and entered into force on 2 September 1990), the statement applies equally to the reporting mechanisms under the other UN human rights treaties.

91 Smith, op. cit., at p.165.

92 Merry, op. cit., at p.958.

93 For discussion of reporting compliance under the UN human rights treaties, see 'Status of the UN human rights treaty body system', Report of the Secretary General to the UN General Assembly, UN Doc. A/71/118, 18 July 2016, at paras 5–8. For discussion of backlogs in consideration of states' reports, see paras 29–38 of the Secretary General's Report.

> Reports are often delayed, out-dated and inadequate, with most State parties placing emphasis upon the legislative mechanisms relating to gender equality.[94]

Essentially, '[t]he realisation of the purposes and principles set forth in the Convention through a system of periodic reporting has not been satisfactory'.[95] As Lacey states, 'The critical dialogue potentially set up by CEDAW is, inevitably, distorted at every turn by the realities of political, cultural, and economic power.'[96]

As discussed in Chapter 5, the reporting procedure established under the Istanbul Convention differs in certain respects from the procedures used by the UN treaty bodies. Under Article 68(3) of the Convention, after the initial round of monitoring has taken place, at the commencement of each subsequent round of monitoring GREVIO will choose the specific provisions of the Convention on which the evaluation procedure will be based and will send out a questionnaire accordingly. It therefore seems that monitoring by GREVIO will focus on specific aspects of the compliance of states parties, instead of always examining the compliance of the state party with the whole of the Convention. It appears that such an approach was adopted in an attempt to avoid as much as possible the difficulties that have proven so problematic for the UN human rights treaty bodies in relation to the reporting procedures. In addition, as discussed in Chapter 5, GREVIO is currently asking only two states parties at a time to submit initial reports on compliance. This approach may well enable GREVIO to carry out its work in a more efficient manner and help to avoid the considerable backlogs in the examination of reports that have caused substantial difficulties for the UN human rights treaty bodies. As Egan comments, 'most of the treaty bodies are hopelessly behind schedule in the consideration of reports already submitted by States'.[97] In addition, having to report only on particular aspects of their compliance with the Convention should serve to lighten the reporting burden placed upon states, and therefore encourage states to submit their reports in a timely manner.

However, despite these efforts on the part of the framers of the Istanbul Convention to make the reporting procedure as effective and efficient as possible, the monitoring mechanisms of the Istanbul Convention nevertheless still bear strong similarities to those of UN instruments such as CEDAW, as discussed in Chapter 5. It is possible that the simple fact that the Istanbul Convention is a regional instrument as opposed to an international instrument may be beneficial as regards enforceability. As Smith remarks:

94 Rehman, op. cit., at pp.538–9.

95 Rehman, op. cit., at p.554.

96 Lacey N., 'Feminist Legal Theory and the Rights of Women', in K. Knop (ed.), *Gender and Human Rights*, 2004, Oxford University Press, Oxford, 13–55 at 54.

97 Egan, op. cit., at p.174.

> Regional systems can be easier to enforce than international systems. There may be a greater political will to conform to regional texts as they are sometimes seen as being of more immediate concern than the international initiatives. Diplomatic efforts may be more successful when pressure is applied by neighbouring States rather than States from more distant regions. Similarly, there will always be more of an incentive with respect to implementation of decisions of regional bodies.[98]

Nevertheless, it is still very possible that the implementation and enforcement difficulties that have arisen for the UN treaties will also occur in respect of the Istanbul Convention. Indeed, it is not easy to see how such problems could be entirely avoided. This is not a difficulty with the Convention itself, but is rather a problem that pervades international and regional human rights law in general. Essentially, when dealing with human rights systems, as Vesa remarks, 'one should remain aware of an overarching issue that straddles all human rights systems; enforceability is still a lingering weakness'.[99]

Conclusion

The adoption by the Council of Europe of the Istanbul Convention is certainly an immensely positive development as regards the use of human rights law to combat domestic violence. This chapter has highlighted a number of the advantages that this development entails. The fact that domestic violence has now been expressly included in a human rights treaty in the European context is extremely important, given that even the use of the language of rights in itself carries significant symbolic weight. However, the fact that the Convention essentially places the recommendations and statements that had previously been made by entities such as the CEDAW Committee and the UN Special Rapporteur on violence against women, its causes and consequences on a secure legally binding footing in the European context is arguably the most important facet of this instrument. In particular, the legally binding nature of these duties is a factor that can be used by non-governmental organisations working in the area of gender-based violence to place further pressure on governments in states that have ratified the Convention to adopt measures to combat domestic abuse, as well as other forms of gender-based violence.

98 Smith, op. cit., at p.88.

99 Vesa A., 'International and Regional Standards for Protecting Victims of Domestic Violence', (2004) 12 *American University Journal of Gender, Social Policy and the Law*, 309–60 at 360. For discussion of the problems relating to the implementation and enforcement of human rights standards in the context of domestic violence, see also McQuigg R., *International Human Rights Law and Domestic Violence*, 2011, Routledge, Abingdon, at pp.10–13. For discussion of potential difficulties for the Istanbul Convention, see also McQuigg (2012), op. cit.

The provisions of the Istanbul Convention that relate to domestic violence build substantially on the duties placed upon states by the European Court of Human Rights as regards this issue, given that the provisions of the Istanbul Convention are much more comprehensive in nature. In addition, there are other benefits entailed in having a Convention monitored primarily by a reporting mechanism, as opposed to placing the onus on victims to take cases to court, as is the situation under the European Convention on Human Rights, particularly when addressing an 'unseen crime' such as domestic violence. Another benefit of using a strategy other than that of litigation is that a substantially more detailed approach can be taken.

However, it is argued that the jurisprudence of the European Court of Human Rights on domestic violence will remain of substantial importance, due largely to the fact that the duties established by this case law apply to all 47 member states of the Council of Europe, whereas the obligations found in the Istanbul Convention apply only to the states that have ratified this instrument. It is possible that a number of states may be reluctant to ratify the Convention, due to the detailed nature of the duties that it places upon states parties. Nevertheless, the large majority of the states within the Council of Europe have either ratified the Convention or have indicated their intention to do so by signing this instrument. Potentially more problematic for the effectiveness of the Convention, however, are the difficulties surrounding implementation and enforcement that are endemic to human rights law. As discussed earlier in the chapter, the framers of the Convention have adopted measures with the aim of reducing the problems surrounding reporting that have created such difficulties for the UN human rights treaty bodies, and it is to be hoped that these measures will be successful.

7 Conclusions

The aim of this chapter is to summarise the key points and conclusions from the preceding discussion as regards the potential held by the Istanbul Convention in relation to the issue of domestic violence. In addition, in 2012 the then UN Special Rapporteur on violence against women, its causes and consequences, Rashida Manjoo, called for the adoption of an international convention on violence against women at the UN level.[1] It is likely that the provisions of any such instrument would have strong similarities to those of the Istanbul Convention. The chapter will therefore contain a number of brief reflections in relation to the question of whether the adoption of a UN convention on violence against women may be a possible development, and with regard to the potential held by such an instrument in the context of domestic violence.

Summary

The Istanbul Convention is certainly a very significant development for the movement to combat gender-based violence. The European Women's Lobby states that the Convention 'is an internationally recognised, visionary treaty with great potential to become an effective tool for ending violence against women and girls'.[2] This book has focused specifically on the potential held by the Convention as regards the issue of domestic violence. As discussed in Chapter 2, historically there was a reluctance to view domestic violence as an issue that required the attention of any form of law, let alone human rights law. Given this reluctance even to view domestic violence as a legal matter, the slowness in recognition of

1 UN Women, 'Needed: specific international legally binding instrument on violence against women', 1 November 2012, available at www.unwomen.org/en/news/stories/2012/11/needed-specific-international-legally-binding-instrument-on-violence-against-women (accessed 18 October 2016).

2 European Women's Lobby, 'A European Women's Lobby Lobbying Kit for a transparent monitoring process of the Council of Europe Convention on Preventing and Combating Violence against Women and Domestic Violence', 2014, available at www.womenlobby.org/EWL-Observatory-on-Violence-against-Women-publishes-Lobbying-Kit-on-the (accessed 18 October 2016), at p.1.

domestic violence as being a human rights issue was unsurprising. In addition, the public/private divide in international human rights law certainly created substantial difficulties as regards the application of human rights law to the issue of domestic violence. However, there have been major developments within human rights law such as the formulation of the concepts of positive obligations and state responsibility, and it is now clearly established that domestic violence constitutes a human rights issue. As was discussed, UN bodies such as the Committee on the Elimination of Discrimination against Women (CEDAW Committee) have now made detailed statements relevant to violence against women and, more specifically, to domestic violence. These developments have not been limited to the UN level. In addition, the Inter-American Convention on the Prevention, Punishment, and Eradication of Violence against Women (the Convention of Belém do Pará) was adopted by the General Assembly of the Organization of American States in 1994, and the Protocol to the African Charter on Human and Peoples' Rights on the Rights of Women in Africa (the Maputo Protocol), a women's rights instrument which encompasses violence against women, was adopted by the African Union in 2003. It was against the background of these developments that the Istanbul Convention was adopted by the Council of Ministers of the Council of Europe.

As seen in Chapter 3, domestic violence has a relatively long history as constituting an issue of concern within the Council of Europe. Attention has been paid to this issue since as far back as 1985 and, more substantively, since the 1990s. These developments gained added impetus with the adoption in 2002 by the Committee of Ministers of Recommendation Rec(2002)5 on the protection of women against violence. The establishment in 2006 of the Task Force to Combat Violence against Women, including Domestic Violence, constituted another important milestone in this respect, as did the establishment in 2008 of the Ad Hoc Committee on Preventing and Combating Violence against Women and Domestic Violence (CAHVIO). The 2007 report of the European Committee on Crime Problems (CDPC) concerning its feasibility study regarding a convention on domestic violence was also of substantial importance.[3]

As discussed in Chapter 4, one of the most striking features of the Istanbul Convention is the comprehensive scope of its provisions. The level of detail in which the obligations of states parties in relation to the issue of domestic violence are described is unprecedented in an instrument of this nature. For example, neither the Convention of Belém do Pará nor the Maputo Protocol contains obligations described in anywhere near this level of precision. The provisions of the Istanbul Convention cover a wide range of important areas, such as criminal justice responses, the provision of social support measures to victims and the raising of awareness within society as a whole of the issues involved in domestic violence. Indeed, the detailed nature of the obligations found in the Istanbul

3 European Committee on Crime Problems, 'Feasibility study for a convention against domestic violence', 12 June 2007, Council of Europe, Strasbourg, CDPC (2007)09 rev.

Convention serves to illustrate the developments in understanding of the phenomenon of domestic violence that have occurred in recent years. In addition, the Istanbul Convention contains recognition that domestic violence may also be perpetrated against men, an aspect of violence in the home that has only recently been investigated to any great extent.

As examined in Chapter 5, the Istanbul Convention incorporates similar monitoring mechanisms to those that exist under the main UN human rights treaties, such as the Convention on the Elimination of All Forms of Discrimination against Women (CEDAW).[4] As with the UN treaties, the primary monitoring procedure is constituted by a reporting mechanism. There are, however, certain innovative divergences from the CEDAW reporting model, such as the selection by the Group of Experts on Action against Violence against Women and Domestic Violence (GREVIO) at the commencement of each round of reporting of specific provisions of the Convention on which the evaluation procedure will be based, and the subsequent preparation by GREVIO of a questionnaire. The adoption of such an approach could well prove to be very beneficial as it will allow the aspect of state compliance chosen for monitoring to be examined in greater detail than would otherwise be possible. Such an approach may also enable GREVIO to carry out its work in a more efficient manner. The monitoring mechanisms of the Istanbul Convention also encompass an inquiry procedure, broadly similar to that found in the Optional Protocol to CEDAW. As with the UN human rights bodies, GREVIO may also adopt general recommendations regarding the implementation of the Convention. However, the lack of an individual complaints mechanism under the Istanbul Convention seems to constitute a somewhat surprising omission, given that individual complaints can be taken under CEDAW, the Convention of Belém do Pará and the Maputo Protocol. Nevertheless, considering the seeming general lack of awareness of CEDAW's Optional Protocol, it is arguable that the omission of a communications procedure from the Istanbul Convention may not lessen the effectiveness of this instrument to any great extent.

Chapter 6 analysed a number of specific advantages that the adoption of the Istanbul Convention entails for the movement to combat domestic violence, and also assessed particular challenges that may be encountered. The fact that domestic violence has been expressly included in a human rights treaty in the European context is extremely significant, given that the use of the language of rights in itself carries substantial symbolic weight. The Convention demonstrates a commitment on the part of the Council of Europe to the adoption of meaningful action as regards the insidious problem of domestic violence, as well as other forms of violence against women. This development demonstrates the impetus that has been built up over a relatively short period of time in relation to the movement

4 CEDAW (1249 U.N.T.S. 13) was adopted by the UN General Assembly on 18 December 1979 and entered into force on 3 September 1981.

to combat domestic abuse. In addition, the inclusion of the principle of due diligence in the Istanbul Convention emphasises the fact that the public/private divide, which has historically created such immense difficulties with regard to the effectiveness of human rights law and in particular the rights of women, has now been surmounted to a substantial extent.

However, the fact that the Convention essentially places the statements that had previously been made by bodies such as the CEDAW Committee and the UN Special Rapporteur on violence against women, its causes and consequences, on a firm legally binding footing in the European context is arguably the most important aspect of this instrument. In particular, the legally binding nature of these duties is a factor that can be utilised by non-governmental organisations working in the area of gender-based violence to place further pressure on governments in states that have ratified the Convention to adopt measures to combat domestic abuse, as well as other forms of gender-based violence.

Prior to the Istanbul Convention, the weightiest statements emanating from the Council of Europe on the issue of domestic violence had been those made by the European Court of Human Rights. However, the provisions of the Istanbul Convention that relate to domestic violence build substantially on the obligations placed upon states by the European Court in relation to this issue, given that the provisions of the Istanbul Convention are much more comprehensive in nature. In particular, although the European Court has placed positive duties upon states to ensure that their criminal justice systems are of a sufficient standard in responding to domestic violence, the Court has not placed obligations upon states as regards other aspects of their responses to domestic abuse, such as the provision of social support measures to victims or the implementation of public awareness campaigns. In addition, having a Convention monitored primarily by a reporting mechanism, as opposed to placing the onus on victims to take cases to court, as is the situation under the European Convention on Human Rights, may well be beneficial, particularly when addressing an 'unseen crime' such as domestic violence. Another benefit of using a strategy other than that of litigation is that a substantially more detailed approach can be taken. Judges must confine themselves to addressing the precise issues in the cases that come before them, whereas a monitoring body such as GREVIO is free to adopt a much wider approach. Essentially, there are limits to the extent to which a litigation strategy can be used effectively to promote change.

Nevertheless, despite the adoption of the Istanbul Convention and the benefits entailed by this development, it is argued that the jurisprudence of the European Court of Human Rights on domestic violence will remain of substantial importance, due largely to the fact that the obligations established by this case law apply to all 47 member states of the Council of Europe, whereas the duties found in the Istanbul Convention apply only to the states that have ratified this instrument. It is possible that a number of states may be reluctant to ratify the Convention due to the detailed nature of the duties that it places upon states parties. Nevertheless, the large majority of the states within the Council of Europe have either ratified the Convention or have indicated their intention to do so by signing this instrument.[5] Potentially more problematic for the effectiveness of the Convention, however, are the difficulties surrounding implementation and enforcement that are endemic to human rights law. The drafters of the Convention have nevertheless adopted measures with the objective of reducing the problems surrounding reporting that have created such difficulties for the UN human rights treaty bodies, and it is to be hoped that these measures prove to be successful.

A global treaty on gender-based violence

As mentioned in Chapter 6, in November 2012, Rashida Manjoo, the then UN Special Rapporteur on violence against women, its causes and consequences, called for the adoption of an international convention on violence against women at the UN level. She stated: 'How do I hold States accountable if there is no specific legally binding instrument on violence against women? . . . It is time to adopt a comprehensive international convention on violence against women at the UN level.' She also referred to the good practices of the Council of Europe and the Inter-American regional systems with regard to their adoption of the Istanbul Convention and the Convention of Belém do Pará respectively.[6] In September 2014, in a report to the UN General Assembly, the Special Rapporteur again called for the adoption of a legally binding instrument at the global level to address the issue of violence against women. In this report she stated: 'The lack of a legally binding instrument on violence against women precludes the articulation of the issue as a human rights violation in and of itself.'[7]

Likewise, the main focus of Manjoo's final report as Special Rapporteur was on the need for the development and adoption of a binding instrument at the UN level on violence against women. In this report she stated:

> Such an instrument should ensure that States are held accountable to standards that are legally binding, it should provide a clear normative framework for the protection of women and girls globally and should have a specific monitoring body to substantively provide in-depth analysis of both general and country-level developments. With a legally binding instrument, a protective, preventive and educative framework could be established to reaffirm the commitment of the international community to its articulation

5 At the time of writing, the Istanbul Convention has been ratified by 22 states, and has been signed but not yet ratified by another 20 states.

6 UN Women, 'Needed: specific international legally binding instrument on violence against women', 1 November 2012, available at www.unwomen.org/en/news/stories/2012/11/needed-specific-international-legally-binding-instrument-on-violence-against-women (accessed 18 October 2016).

7 Report of the Special Rapporteur on Violence against Women, its causes and consequences to the UN General Assembly, U.N.Doc.A/69/368, 1 September 2014, at para. 59.

> that women's rights are human rights, and that violence against women is a human rights violation, in and of itself.[8]

In the light of such a call for action, is it now time for a global treaty on violence against women, encompassing domestic violence, to be adopted by the UN?

As discussed in Chapter 2, the international human rights bodies have made a fairly comprehensive set of recommendations to states in relation to domestic violence (and indeed as regards gender-based violence more generally). States have been urged to improve their criminal justice systems, improve measures of civil protection, provide measures of social support for victims, improve societal awareness, improve the awareness of professionals, develop inter-agency approaches, tackle risk factors associated with domestic violence, develop programmes for perpetrators and undertake research into domestic violence. However, the issuing of all of these statements and recommendations does not alter the fact that CEDAW itself does not expressly mention the issue of violence against women. As discussed in Chapter 2, this 'glaring omission'[9] can be explained by the fact that when CEDAW was adopted by the UN General Assembly in 1979, the issue of violence against women was simply not on the international agenda.[10]

As explained in Chapter 2, General Recommendation No. 19 of the CEDAW Committee[11] had the effect of interpreting CEDAW in such a manner as to encompass violence against women within its scope. However, as General Recommendations are technically 'soft law' and are not therefore legally binding upon states, is such an approach sufficient? The views of commentators differ on this question. For example, although Rashida Manjoo, the former UN Special Rapporteur on violence against women, its causes and consequences, was adamant that a global treaty on violence against women was needed, her successor, Dubravka Šimonović, appears to be less convinced of the necessity for such a measure.[12] Writing in 2014, prior to her appointment as Special Rapporteur, Šimonović questioned 'whether the lack of an express provision on violence against women is an inadequacy of the Convention which requires its revision

8 Report of the Special Rapporteur on Violence against Women, its causes and consequences, Rashida Manjoo, UN.Doc.A/HRC/29/27, 10 June 2015, at para. 64.

9 Edwards A., *Violence against Women under International Human Rights Law*, 2013, Cambridge University Press, Cambridge, at p.8.

10 Chinkin C., 'Violence against Women' in M.A. Freeman, C. Chinkin and B. Rudolf (eds), *The UN Convention on the Elimination of All Forms of Discrimination against Women: A Commentary*, 2012, Oxford University Press, Oxford, 443–74 at 444. See also Šimonović D., 'Global and Regional Standards on Violence against Women: The Evolution and Synergy of the CEDAW and Istanbul Conventions', (2014) 36 *Human Rights Quarterly*, 590–606 at 599.

11 Committee on the Elimination of Discrimination against Women, U.N. Doc A/47/38 (1992).

12 Dubravka Šimonović was appointed as UN Special Rapporteur on Violence against Women, its causes and consequences in June 2015.

by amendment or even an Optional Protocol on violence against women'.[13] This comment seems to reflect the view that the issue does not centre upon the fact that the existing statements made by the CEDAW Committee and by the other UN bodies on violence against women are not technically legally binding, but rather the question to be addressed is whether more detailed guidance should be given to states as regards how they should respond to violence against women.[14] In this vein. therefore, Šimonović suggested the updating of the General Assembly's Declaration on the Elimination of Violence against Women (DEVAW)[15] or the CEDAW Committee's General Recommendation No. 19.[16] Certainly, the updating and revising of documents such as these would be a positive development. Although it is submitted that states have received a substantial amount of detailed guidance from the UN bodies on how they should respond to violence against women,[17] these statements and recommendations have emerged from a variety of sources and are therefore found in a range of documents. Thus it may well be beneficial if all of these documents were merged into a single instrument, such as a revised version of General Recommendation No. 19 or a revised version of DEVAW.

However, this development would not change the fact that such a document would still fall into the category of 'soft law' and would not therefore be legally binding upon states. Essentially, such a document would still be 'guidance' only. It is of course possible to argue that the distinction between 'soft law' and 'hard law' in this context makes little difference in practice. As analysed in Chapter 6, international human rights law as a whole suffers from extensive difficulties relating to implementation and enforcement. For human rights standards to be implemented within states, there must be a political will among governments to do so,[18] and often such a will is lacking. Copelon comments that 'the international human rights system still operates more in rhetoric than in reality'.[19] It is extremely

13 Šimonović, op. cit., at p.601.

14 It is worth noting nevertheless that Dubravka Šimonović has called for submissions from stakeholders on the question of whether there is a need for a separate legally binding treaty on violence against women with a separate monitoring body. For the call for submissions to all stakeholders, see www.ohchr.org/EN/Issues/Women/SRWomen/Pages/InternationalLegalFramework.aspx, Office of the High Commissioner for Human Rights (accessed 18 October 2016). See also 'Statement by Ms Dubravka Šimonović, Special Rapporteur on violence against women, its causes and consequences at the Human Rights Council, Thirty-second session', 17 June 2016, available at www.ohchr.org/EN/NewsEvents/Pages/DisplayNews.aspx?NewsID=20183&LangID=E (accessed 18 October 2016).

15 General Assembly Resolution 48/104 (1993).

16 Šimonović, op. cit., at pp.601–2.

17 See Chapter 2 for discussion of the statements and recommendations made by the UN bodies as regards the issue of domestic violence.

18 Wallace R., *International Human Rights*, 2001, Sweet & Maxwell, London, at p.590.

19 Copelon R., 'International Human Rights Dimensions of Intimate Violence: Another Strand in the Dialectic of Feminist Lawmaking', (2003) 11 *American University Journal of Gender, Social Policy and the Law*, 865–76 at 875.

difficult to compel states to comply with their duties if they are reluctant to do so. As Byrnes remarks, 'The limitations of international law generally when it comes to enforcement of binding standards are well known, and international human rights law is no exception in that regard.'[20] Essentially, the UN has no real method of forcing states to alter their policies. It must instead attempt to persuade nations to comply with their international duties.[21] The effectiveness of human rights treaties therefore depends greatly on the level of commitment of states to give effect to their obligations. These problems apply even to the numerous human rights duties that are articulated expressly in treaties and which are therefore unquestionably legally binding upon states. No definitive data exists on whether states are any better at complying with the international human rights obligations that are expressly found in treaties to which they are party than they are at complying with guidance emanating from UN human rights bodies which falls into the 'soft law' category. Indeed, this would constitute an interesting question for future research. When states do not comply, for example, with statements on the issue of domestic violence that have been made by the CEDAW Committee or the UN Special Rapporteur on violence against women, its causes and consequences, it is debatable whether the fact that such statements are technically 'soft law' standards is considered by the governments in question, or whether framing such statements and recommendations as legally binding treaty provisions would result in increased levels of compliance.[22] As the implementation of human rights law, even as regards 'hard law' provisions, is so heavily dependent upon the political will and the commitment held by individual governments, it is possible to argue that the technical distinction between legally binding obligations and 'soft law' standards may not matter a great deal in practice.

Nevertheless, on the other hand, it can be argued that the distinction between legally binding duties and 'soft law' is of critical importance. Although violence against women constitutes one of the most widespread human rights abuses on the global scale,[23] none of the UN human rights treaties expressly prohibits gender-based violence. Even if only from a theoretical perspective, such a situation is simply unacceptable. However, it seems that the advantages of a global treaty on gender-based violence would not be limited simply to the theoretical benefits

20 Byrnes A., 'Enforcement Through International Law and Procedures', in R.J. Cook (ed.), *Human Rights of Women: National and International Perspectives*, 1994, University of Pennsylvania Press, Philadelphia, 189–227 at 191–2.

21 Ulrich J., 'Confronting Gender-Based Violence with International Instruments: Is a Solution to the Pandemic Within Reach?', (2000) 7 *Indiana Journal of Global Legal Studies*, 629–54 at 638–9.

22 It is also questionable whether such states would indeed ratify a treaty containing such provisions.

23 For statistics on violence against women at the global level, see UN Women, 'Facts and Figures: Ending Violence against Women', February 2016, available at www.unwomen.org/en/what-we-do/ending-violence-against-women/facts-and-figures (accessed 18 October 2016).

of such an instrument. As noted earlier in this chapter, a former UN Special Rapporteur on violence against women, its causes and consequences has herself highlighted the difficulties she faced in holding states to account as regards violence against women in the absence of a specific legally binding instrument on this issue. In her report of September 2014 to the UN General Assembly, Rashida Manjoo stated:

> An international convention on the elimination of violence against women or an optional protocol to the Convention on the Elimination of All Forms of Discrimination against Women would ensure that States are held accountable to standards that are legally binding and that provide a clear normative framework for the protection of women and girls globally, one which would have a specific monitoring body to substantively provide in-depth analysis of both general and country-level developments.[24]

As discussed in Chapter 6, the legally binding nature of the duties contained in the Istanbul Convention is a factor that can be used by non-governmental organisations working in the area of gender-based violence to place further pressure on governments in states that have ratified this instrument. Likewise, a legally binding global instrument on gender-based violence could be utilised by non-governmental organisations in a similar manner. It is therefore argued that the time is ripe for either a new UN treaty on gender-based violence or a new Optional Protocol to CEDAW on violence against women to be adopted. As Rashida Manjoo commented in her 2014 report, 'A legally binding international instrument would provide a function that is protective and preventative, as well as educative. Recognition that women's rights are human rights and that violence against women is a human rights violation demands this measure of commitment.'[25]

Conclusion

The adoption by the Council of Europe of the Convention on Preventing and Combating Violence against Women and Domestic Violence is certainly very much to be welcomed. At the time of writing, 22 states have ratified the Convention,[26] and another 20 states have signed this instrument.[27] It is to be

24 Report of the Special Rapporteur on Violence against Women, its causes and consequences to the UN General Assembly, U.N.Doc.A/69/368, 1 September 2014, at para. 71.

25 At para. 71.

26 Albania, Andorra, Austria, Belgium, Bosnia and Herzegovina, Denmark, Finland, France, Italy, Malta, Monaco, Montenegro, Netherlands, Poland, Portugal, Romania, San Marino, Serbia, Slovenia, Spain, Sweden and Turkey.

27 Bulgaria, Croatia, Cyprus, Czech Republic, Estonia, Georgia, Germany, Greece, Hungary, Iceland, Ireland, Latvia, Lithuania, Luxembourg, Norway, Slovakia, Switzerland, the former Yugoslav Republic of Macedonia, Ukraine and United Kingdom.

hoped that these 21 signatory states will soon substantiate their commitment by ratification of the Convention, and also that the four states that have currently neither signed nor ratified this instrument[28] will do so in the near future. The first round of monitoring of state compliance has now commenced, and the first state reports are due to be submitted in September 2016. It is without doubt an exciting time for the movement to combat gender-based violence in Europe. It will certainly be immensely interesting to observe how implementation and monitoring of the Istanbul Convention develop in the future. Above all, it is to be hoped that this instrument will make a crucial contribution to combating both domestic violence and other forms of violence against women.

28 Armenia, Azerbaijan, Moldova and Russia.

Bibliography

Afsharipour A., 'Empowering Ourselves: The Role of Women's NGOs in the Enforcement of the Women's Convention', (1999) 99 *Columbia Law Review*, 129–72.

Armatta J., 'Getting beyond the Law's Complicity in Intimate Violence against Women', (1997) 33 *Willamette Law Review*, 774–845.

Banda F., 'Blazing a Trail: The African Protocol on Women's Rights Comes into Force', (2006) 50 *Journal of African Law*, 72–84.

Barron J., *'Not Worth the Paper . . . ?' The Effectiveness of Legal Protection for Women and Children Experiencing Domestic Violence*, 1990, Women's Aid Federation England, Bristol.

Bayefsky A.F., *The UN Human Rights Treaty System: Universality at the Crossroads*, 2001, Transnational Publishers, Ardsley.

Becker M., 'Access to Justice: The Social Responsibility of Lawyers: Access to Justice for Battered Women', (2003) 12 *Washington University Journal of Law & Policy*, 63–98.

Beetham D., 'What Future for Economic and Social Rights?', (1995) 43 *Political Studies*, 41–60.

Berry D.B., *The Domestic Violence Sourcebook*, 1998, Lowell House, Los Angeles.

Bettinson V. and Bishop C., 'Is the Creation of a Discrete Offence of Coercive Control Necessary to Combat Domestic Violence?', (2015) 66 *Northern Ireland Legal Quarterly*, 179–97.

Binion G., 'Human Rights: A Feminist Perspective', (1995) 17 *Human Rights Quarterly*, 509–26.

Bishop C., 'Domestic Violence: The Limitations of a Legal Response', in S. Hilder and V. Bettinson (eds), *Domestic Violence: Interdisciplinary Perspectives on Protection, Prevention and Intervention*, 2016, Palgrave Macmillan, London, 59–79.

Bond J.E., 'International Intersectionality: A Theoretical and Pragmatic Exploration of Women's International Human Rights Violations', (2003) 52 *Emory Law Journal*, 71–186.

Bourlet A., *Police Intervention in Marital Violence*, 1990, Open University Press, Milton Keynes.

Bruce E., 'Attitudes of Social Workers and Police in the Select Committee Report on Violence to Women and Children', in *Women and Abused Children: Intricacies of Legal and Administrative Intervention*, 1979, Issues Publications, University of Bradford, 50–61.

Bunch C., 'Women's Rights as Human Rights: Towards a Re-Visioning of Human Rights', (1990) 12 *Human Rights Quarterly*, 486–98.

Burman J.M., 'Lawyers and Domestic Violence: Raising the Standard of Practice', (2003) 9 *Michigan Journal of Gender & Law*, 207–59.

Burnet G., 'Housing: More Than Just Bricks and Mortar. Domestic Abuse Interventions within the Housing Sector', in S. Hilder and V. Bettinson (eds), *Domestic Violence: Interdisciplinary Perspectives on Protection, Prevention and Intervention*, 2016, Palgrave Macmillan, London, 227–48.

Burton M., *Legal Responses to Domestic Violence*, 2008, Routledge-Cavendish, Abingdon.

Burton M., 'The Human Rights of Victims of Domestic Violence: *Opuz v Turkey*', (2010) 22 *Child and Family Law Quarterly*, 131–40.

Burton M., 'A Fresh Approach to Policing Domestic Violence', in S. Hilder and V. Bettinson (eds), *Domestic Violence: Interdisciplinary Perspectives on Protection, Prevention and Intervention*, 2016, Palgrave Macmillan, London, 37–57.

Byrnes A., 'Enforcement through International Law and Procedures', in R.J. Cook (ed.), *Human Rights of Women: National and International Perspectives*, 1994, University of Pennsylvania Press, Philadelphia, 189–227.

Byrnes A., 'The Convention on the Elimination of All Forms of Discrimination against Women' in W. Benedek, E.M. Kisaakye and G. Oberleitner (eds), *Human Rights of Women: International Instruments and African Experiences*, 2002, Palgrave, New York, 119–72.

Byrnes A. and Bath E., 'Violence against Women, the Obligation of Due Diligence, and the Optional Protocol to the Convention on the Elimination of All Forms of Discrimination against Women – Recent Developments', (2008) 8 *Human Rights Law Review*, 517–33.

Cassel D., 'Does International Human Rights Law Make a Difference?', (2001) 2 *Chicago Journal of International Law*, 121–35.

Charlesworth H., 'What are "Women's International Human Rights"?', in R.J. Cook (ed.), *Human Rights of Women: National and International Perspectives*, 1994, University of Pennsylvania Press, Philadelphia, 58–84.

Charlesworth H. and Chinkin C., *The Boundaries of International Law: A Feminist Analysis*, 2000, Manchester University Press, Manchester.

Charlesworth H., Chinkin C. and Wright S., 'Feminist Approaches to International Law', (1991) 85 *American Journal of International Law*, 613–45.

Chayes A., 'The Role of the Judge in Public Law Litigation', (1976) 89 *Harvard Law Review*, 1281–316.

Chinkin C., 'Violence against Women' in M.A. Freeman, C. Chinkin and B. Rudolf (eds), *The UN Convention on the Elimination of All Forms of Discrimination against Women: A Commentary*, 2012, Oxford University Press, Oxford, 443–74.

Chinkin C., 'Addressing Violence against Women in the Commonwealth within States' Obligations under International Law', (2014) 40 *Commonwealth Law Bulletin*, 471–501.

Chinkin C. and Freeman M.A., 'Introduction', in M.A. Freeman, C. Chinkin and B. Rudolf (eds), *The UN Convention on the Elimination of All Forms of Discrimination against Women: A Commentary*, 2012, Oxford University Press, Oxford, 2–33.

Choudhry S. and Herring J., 'Righting Domestic Violence', (2006) 20 *International Journal of Law, Policy and the Family*, 95–119.

Clapham A., *Human Rights in the Private Sphere*, 1993, Clarendon, Oxford.

Connelly C. and Cavanagh K., 'Domestic Abuse, Civil Protection Orders and the "New Criminologies": Is There Any Value in Engaging with the Law?', (2007) 15 *Feminist Legal Studies*, 259–87.

Cook R.J., 'Reservations to the Convention on the Elimination of All Forms of Discrimination against Women', (1989–1990) 30 *Virginia Journal of International Law*, 643–716.

Cook R.J., 'Women's International Human Rights Law: The Way Forward', in R.J. Cook (ed.), *Human Rights of Women: National and International Perspectives*, 1994, University of Pennsylvania Press, Philadelphia, 3–36.

Cook R.J., 'State Responsibility for Violations of Women's Rights', (1994) 7 *Harvard Human Rights Journal*, 125–75.

Copelon R., 'Intimate Terror: Understanding Domestic Violence as Torture', in R.J. Cook (ed.), *Human Rights of Women: National and International Perspectives*, 1994, University of Pennsylvania Press, Philadelphia, 116–52.

Copelon R., 'International Human Rights Dimensions of Intimate Violence: Another Strand in the Dialectic of Feminist Lawmaking', (2003) 11 *American University Journal of Gender, Social Policy and the Law*, 865–76.

Crawford J., 'The UN Human Rights Treaty System: A System in Crisis?', in P. Alston and J. Crawford (eds), *The Future of UN Human Rights Treaty Monitoring*, 2000, Cambridge University Press, Cambridge, 1–12.

Cretney A. and Davis G., 'Prosecuting "Domestic" Assault', (1996) *Criminal Law Review*, 162–74.

Cretney A. and Davis G., 'Prosecuting Domestic Assault: Victims Failing Courts, or Courts Failing Victims?', (1997) 36 *The Howard Journal*, 146–57.

Davidson L.L., King V., Garcia J. and Marchant S., 'What Role Can the Health Services Play?', in J. Taylor-Browne (ed.), *What Works in Reducing Domestic Violence? A Comprehensive Guide for Professionals*, 2001, Whiting & Birch, London, 95–122.

Dennis M.J and Stewart D.P., 'Justiciability of Economic, Social, and Cultural Rights: Should There Be an International Complaints Mechanism to Adjudicate the Rights to Food, Water, Housing, and Health?', (2004) 98 *American Journal of International Law*, 462–515.

Diduck A. and Kaganas F., *Family Law, Gender and the State*, 1999, Hart Publishing, Oxford.

Dobash R.E. and Dobash R.P., *Violence against Wives: A Case against the Patriarchy*, 1979, Open Books, London.

Dobash R.E. and Dobash R.P, *Women, Violence and Social Change*, 1992, Routledge, New York.

Dobash R.P. and Dobash R.E., 'Women's Violence to Men in Intimate Relationships: Working on a Puzzle', (2004) 44 *British Journal of Criminology*, 324–49.

Edwards A., *Violence against Women under International Human Rights Law*, 2013, Cambridge University Press, Cambridge.

Edwards S., *Policing 'Domestic' Violence: Women, the Law and the State*, 1989, Sage Publications, London.

Edwards S., 'New Directions in Prosecution', in J. Taylor-Browne (ed.), *What Works in Reducing Domestic Violence? A Comprehensive Guide for Professionals*, 2001, Whiting & Birch, London, 211–38.

Egan S., *The UN Human Rights Treaty System: Law and Procedure*, 2011, Bloomsbury Professional, Dublin.

Epp C.R., *The Rights Revolution*, 1998, University of Chicago Press, Chicago and London.

Ewing A.P., 'Establishing State Responsibility for Private Acts of Violence against Women under the American Convention on Human Rights', (1995) 26 *Columbia Human Rights Law Review*, 751–800.

Fortin J., *Children's Rights and the Developing Law*, 2003, Butterworths, London.

Fraser A.S., 'Becoming Human: The Origin and Development of Women's Human Rights Law', (1999) 21 *Human Rights Quarterly*, 853–906.

Fredman S., *Human Rights Transformed: Positive Rights and Positive Duties*, 2009, Oxford University Press, Oxford.

Gaer F.D., 'And Never the Twain Shall Meet? The Struggle to Establish Women's Rights as International Human Rights', in C.E. Lockwood, D.B. Magraw, M.F. Spring and S.I. Strong (eds), *The International Human Rights of Women: Instruments of Change*, 1998, American Bar Association, Washington, DC, 1–89.

Goodman R. and Jinks D., 'Measuring the Effects of Human Rights', (2003) 14 *European Journal of International Law*, 171–83.

Goodmark L., 'Symposium: Domestic Violence & the Law: Theory, Policy, and Practice: Law is the Answer? Do We Know That for Sure? Questioning the Efficacy of Legal Interventions for Battered Women', (2004) 23 *Saint Louis University Public Law Review*, 7–48.

Gormley L., 'The Council of Europe Convention on Preventing and Combating Violence against Women and Domestic Violence: A Consolidation of Existing International Law, or a Significant Progression?', (2014) *European Human Rights Law Review*, 606–17.

Grdinic E., 'Application of the Elements of Torture and Other Forms of Ill-Treatment, as Defined by the European Court and Commission of Human Rights, to the Incidents of Domestic Violence', (2000) 23 *Hastings International and Comparative Law Review*, 217–60.

Hafner-Burton E.M. and Tsutsui K., 'Human Rights in a Globalizing World: The Paradox of Empty Promises', (2005) 110 *American Journal of Sociology*, 1373–411.

Hague G., 'Domestic Violence Policy in the 1990s', in S. Watson and L. Doyal (eds), *Engendering Social Policy*, 1999, Oxford University Press, Oxford, 131–47.

Hague G. and Malos E., *Domestic Violence: Action for Change*, 2005, New Clarion Press, Cheltenham.

Hague G., Mullender A., Aris R. and Dear W., 'Abused Women's Perspectives: Responsiveness and Accountability of Domestic Violence and Inter-Agency Initiatives', 2001, Report to the ESRC.

Hale B., Pearl D., Cooke E. and Bates P., *The Family, Law and Society*, 2002, Butterworths, London.

Hall M., 'The Relationship between Victims and Prosecutors: Defending Victims' Rights?', (2010) *Criminal Law Review*, 31–45.

Hanna C., 'The Paradox of Progress: Translating E. Stark's Coercive Control into Legal Doctrine for Abused Women', (2009) 15 *Violence Against Women*, 1458–76.

Harvey C., 'Talking about Human Rights', (2004) *European Human Rights Law Review*, 500–16.

Hasselbacher L., 'State Obligations Regarding Domestic Violence: The European Court of Human Rights, Due Diligence, and International Legal Minimums of

Protection', (2010) 8 *Northwestern Journal of International Human Rights*, 190–215.

Hathaway O., 'Do Human Rights Treaties Make a Difference?', (2002) 111 *Yale Law Journal*, 1935–2042.

Hathaway O., 'Testing Conventional Wisdom', (2003) 14 *European Journal of International Law*, 185–200.

Heisecke K., 'Raising Awareness of Violence against Women: Article 13 of the Istanbul Convention', 2014, Council of Europe, Strasbourg.

Hester M., Hanmer J., Coulson S., Morahan M. and Razak A., *Domestic Violence: Making it through the Criminal Justice System*, 2003, University of Sunderland and Northern Rock Foundation, Sunderland.

Hester M. and Lilley S., 'Domestic and Sexual Violence Perpetrator Programmes: Article 16 of the Istanbul Convention', 2014, Council of Europe, Strasbourg.

Hester M. and Lilley S., 'Preventing Violence against Women: Article 12 of the Istanbul Convention', 2014, Council of Europe, Strasbourg.

Hester M. and Westmarland N., 'Tackling Domestic Violence: Effective Interventions and Approaches', 2005, Home Office Research Study 290.

Hilder S. and Freeman C., 'Working with Perpetrators of Domestic Violence and Abuse', in S. Hilder and V. Bettinson (eds), *Domestic Violence: Interdisciplinary Perspectives on Protection, Prevention and Intervention*, 2016, Palgrave Macmillan, London, 273–96.

Hirschl R., '"Negative" Rights vs. "Positive" Entitlements: A Comparative Study of Judicial Interpretations of Rights in an Emerging Neo-Liberal Economic Order', (2000) 22 *Human Rights Quarterly*, 1060–97.

Hughes B., 'Can Domestic Violence Be Considered a Violation of Human Rights Law?', (2006) 14 *British Journal of Midwifery*, 192.

Isa F.G., 'The Optional Protocol for the Convention on the Elimination of All Forms of Discrimination against Women: Strengthening the Protection of Women's Human Rights', (2003) 20 *Arizona Journal of International and Comparative Law*, 291–322.

Johnson M.P., 'Conflict and Control: Gender Symmetry and Asymmetry in Domestic Violence', (2006) 12 *Violence Against Women*, 1003–18.

Johnstone R.L., 'Feminist Influences on the United Nations Human Rights Treaty Bodies', (2006) 28 *Human Rights Quarterly*, 148–85.

Kalin W., 'Examination of State Reports', in H. Keller and G. Ulfstein (eds), *UN Human Rights Treaty Bodies: Law and Legitimacy*, 2012, Cambridge University Press, Cambridge, 16–72.

Keller H. and Ulfstein G., 'Conclusions', in H. Keller and G. Ulfstein (eds), *UN Human Rights Treaty Bodies: Law and Legitimacy*, 2012, Cambridge University Press, Cambridge, 414–25.

Kimmel M.S., '"Gender Symmetry" in Domestic Violence: A Substantive and Methodological Research Review', (2002) 6 *Violence Against Women*, 1332–63.

Khaliq U. and Churchill R., 'The Protection of Economic and Social Rights: A Particular Challenge?', in H. Keller and G. Ulfstein (eds), *UN Human Rights Treaty Bodies: Law and Legitimacy*, 2012, Cambridge University Press, Cambridge, 199–260.

Knop K., 'Introduction', in K. Knop (ed.), *Gender and Human Rights*, 2004, Oxford University Press, Oxford, 1–12.

Kuennen T.L., 'Analyzing the Impact of Coercion on Domestic Violence Victims: How Much is Too Much?', (2007) 22 *Berkeley Journal of Gender, Law and Justice*, 2–30.

Lacey N., *Unspeakable Subjects*, 1998, Hart Publishing, Oxford.

Lacey N., 'Feminist Legal Theory and the Rights of Women', in K. Knop (ed.), *Gender and Human Rights*, 2004, Oxford University Press, Oxford, 13–55.

Lewis R., 'Making Justice Work: Effective Legal Interventions for Domestic Violence', (2004) 44 *British Journal of Criminology*, 204–24.

McQuigg R., 'The Responses of States to the Comments of the CEDAW Committee on Domestic Violence', (2007) 11 *International Journal of Human Rights*, 461–79.

McQuigg R., *International Human Rights Law and Domestic Violence*, 2011, Routledge, Abingdon.

McQuigg R., 'The Victim Test under the Human Rights Act 1998 and its Implications for Domestic Violence Cases', (2011) *European Human Rights Law Review*, 294–303.

McQuigg R, 'What Potential Does the Council of Europe Convention on Violence Against Women Hold as Regards Domestic Violence?', (2012) 16 *International Journal of Human Rights*, 947–62.

McQuigg R., 'A Contextual Analysis of the Council of Europe's Convention on Preventing and Combating Violence against Women', (2012) 1 *International Human Rights Law Review*, 367–81.

McQuigg R., 'Domestic Violence and the Inter-American Commission on Human Rights: *Jessica Lenahan (Gonzales) v United States*', (2012) 12 *Human Rights Law Review*, 122–34.

Martin L., 'Debates of Difference: Male Victims of Domestic Violence and Abuse', in S. Hilder and V. Bettinson (eds), *Domestic Violence: Interdisciplinary Perspectives on Protection, Prevention and Intervention*, 2016, Palgrave Macmillan, London, 181–201.

Merry S.E., 'Constructing a Global Law – Violence against Women and the Human Rights System', (2003) 28 *Law and Social Inquiry*, 941–74.

Meyersfeld B., *Domestic Violence and International Law*, 2010, Hart, Oxford.

Miles J., 'Domestic Violence', in J. Herring (ed.), *Family Law: Issues, Debates, Policy*, 2001, Willan Publishing, Devon, 78–124.

Mowbray A.R., *The Development of Positive Obligations under the European Convention on Human Rights by the European Court of Human Rights*, 2004, Hart Publishing, Oxford.

Mullender A., *Re-thinking Domestic Violence*, 1996, Routledge, London.

Mullender A. and Hague G., 'Women Survivors' Views', in J. Taylor-Browne (ed.), *What Works in Reducing Domestic Violence? A Comprehensive Guide for Professionals*, 2001, Whiting & Birch, London, 1–33.

Mullender A. and Morley R., 'Context and Content of a New Agenda', in A. Mullender and R. Morley (eds), *Children Living with Domestic Violence*, 1994, Whiting & Birch, London, 2–16.

Murdoch J., 'Unfulfilled Expectations: The Optional Protocol to the Convention on the Elimination of All Forms of Discrimination against Women', (2010) *European Human Rights Law Review*, 26–46.

Ocran C., 'The Protocol to the African Charter on Human and Peoples' Rights on the Rights of Women in Africa', (2007) 15 *African Journal of International and Comparative Law*, 147–52.

O'Hare U., 'Realising Women's Human Rights', (1999) 21 *Human Rights Quarterly*, 364–402.

Oloka-Onyango J., 'Reinforcing Marginalized Rights in an Age of Globalization: International Mechanisms, Non-State Actors, and the Struggle for Peoples' Rights in Africa', (2003) 18 *American University International Law Review*, 851–913.

Radford L., 'Legalising Woman Abuse' in J. Hanmer and M. Maynard (eds.), *Women, Violence and Social Control*, 1987, Macmillan, London, 135–51.

Randall M., 'Symposium: Domestic Violence & the Law: Theory, Policy, and Practice: Domestic Violence and the Construction of "Ideal Victims": Assaulted Women's "Image Problems" in Law', (2004) 23 *Saint Louis University Public Law Review*, 107–54.

Rehman J., *International Human Rights Law*, 2nd edn, 2010, Pearson Education, Harlow.

Rishmawi M., 'The Developing Approaches of the International Commission of Jurists to Women's Human Rights', in R.J. Cook (ed.), *Human Rights of Women: National and International Perspectives*, 1994, University of Pennsylvania Press, Philadelphia, 340–8.

Risse T. and Sikkink K., 'The Socialization of International Human Rights Norms into Domestic Practices: Introduction', in T. Risse, S.C. Ropp and K. Sikkink (eds), *The Power of Human Rights: International Norms and Domestic Change*, 1999, Cambridge University Press, Cambridge, 1–38.

Ritz K.L., 'Soft Enforcement: Inadequacies of Optional Protocol as a Remedy for the Convention on the Elimination of All Forms of Discrimination against Women', (2001) 25 *Suffolk Transnational Law Review*, 191–216.

Robinson A. and Payton J., 'Independent Advocacy and Multi-Agency Responses to Domestic Violence', in S. Hilder and V. Bettinson (eds), *Domestic Violence: Interdisciplinary Perspectives on Protection, Prevention and Intervention*, 2016, Palgrave Macmillan, London, 249–71.

Robinson M., 'Making Human Rights Matter: Eleanor Roosevelt's Time Has Come', (2003) 16 *Harvard Human Rights Journal*, 1–11.

Romany C., 'Women as Aliens: A Feminist Critique of the Public/Private Distinction in International Human Rights Law', (1993) 6 *Harvard Human Rights Journal*, 87–125.

Romany C., 'State Responsibility Goes Private: A Feminist Critique of the Public/Private Distinction in International Human Rights Law', in R.J. Cook (ed.), *Human Rights of Women: National and International Perspectives*, 1994, University of Pennsylvania Press, Philadelphia, 85–115.

Rosenberg G.N., *The Hollow Hope: Can Courts Bring About Social Change?*, 1991, University of Chicago Press, Chicago.

Rudolf B. and Eriksson A., 'Women's Rights under International Human Rights Treaties: Issues of Rape, Domestic Slavery, Abortion and Domestic Violence', (2007) 5 *International Journal of Constitutional Law*, 507–25.

Scheingold S., *The Politics of Rights: Lawyers, Public Policy, and Political Change*, 2004, University of Michigan Press, Ann Arbor.

Schneider E., *Battered Women and Feminist Lawmaking*, 2000, Yale University Press, Connecticut.

Schopp-Schilling H.B., 'Treaty Body Reform: The Case of the Committee on the Elimination of Discrimination against Women', (2007) 7 *Human Rights Law Review*, 201–24.

Schriver T., 'Establishing an Affirmative Governmental Duty to Protect Children's Rights: The European Court of Human Rights as a Model for the United States Supreme Court', (2000) 34 *University of San Francisco Law Review*, 379–408.

Šimonović D., 'Global and Regional Standards on Violence against Women: The Evolution and Synergy of the CEDAW and Istanbul Conventions', (2014) 36 *Human Rights Quarterly*, 590–606.

Smart C., *Feminism and the Power of Law*, 1989, Routledge, London.

Smith L.J.F., 'Domestic Violence: An Overview of the Literature', 1989, Home Office Research Study 107.

Smith R.K.M., *Textbook on International Human Rights*, 6th edn, 2014, Oxford University Press, Oxford.

Stanko E.A., *Intimate Intrusions*, 1985, Routledge & Kegan Paul, London.

Stark B., 'Symposium on Integrating Responses to Domestic Violence', (2001) 47 *Loyola Law Review*, 255–82.

Stark E., 'Rethinking Coercive Control', (2009) 15 *Violence Against Women*, 1509–25.

Starmer K., *European Human Rights Law, the Human Rights Act 1998 and the European Convention on Human Rights*, 1999, LAG, London.

Sullivan C.M., 'Using the ESID Model to Reduce Intimate Male Violence against Women', (2003) 32 *American Journal of Community Psychology*, 295–303.

Tadros V., 'The Distinctiveness of Domestic Abuse: A Freedom Based Account' in A. Duff and S. Green (eds) *Defining Crimes*, 2005, Oxford University Press, Oxford, 119–42.

Thomas C., 'Domestic Violence', in K.D. Askin and D.M. Koenig (eds), *Women and International Human Rights Law*, Vol. 1, 1999, Transnational Publishers, New York, 219–56.

Thomas D.Q. and Beasley M.E., 'Symposium on Reconceptualizing Violence against Women by Intimate Partners', (1995) 58 *Albany Law Review*, 1119–47.

Ulfstein G., 'Individual Complaints', in H. Keller and G. Ulfstein (eds), *UN Human Rights Treaty Bodies: Law and Legitimacy*, 2012, Cambridge University Press, Cambridge, 73–115.

Ulrich J., 'Confronting Gender-Based Violence with International Instruments: Is a Solution to the Pandemic within Reach?', (2000) 7 *Indiana Journal of Global Legal Studies*, 629–54.

Van Alebeek R. and Nollkaemper A., 'The Legal Status of Decisions by Human Rights Treaty Bodies in National Law', in H. Keller and G. Ulfstein (eds), *UN Human Rights Treaty Bodies: Law and Legitimacy*, 2012, Cambridge University Press, Cambridge, 356–411.

Van Leeuwen F., *Women's Rights Are Human Rights*, 2010, Intersentia, Antwerp.

Van Schaack B., 'With All Deliberate Speed: Civil Human Rights Litigation as a Tool for Social Change', (2004) 57 *Vanderbilt Law Review*, 2305–48.

Vesa A., 'International and Regional Standards for Protecting Victims of Domestic Violence', (2004) 12 *American University Journal of Gender, Social Policy and the Law*, 309–60.

Wallace R., *International Human Rights*, 2001, Sweet & Maxwell, London.

Williamson E., 'Living in the World of the Domestic Violence Perpetrator: Negotiating the Unreality of Coercive Control', (2010) 16 *Violence Against Women*, 1412–23.

Wiseberg L.S., 'The Role of Non-Governmental Organizations (NGOs) in the Protection and Enforcement of Human Rights', in J. Symonides (ed.), *Human Rights: International Protection, Monitoring, Enforcement*, 2003, Ashgate, Aldershot, 347–72.

Youngs J., 'Domestic Violence and the Criminal Law: Reconceptualising Reform', (2015) 79 *Journal of Criminal Law*, 55–70.

Index

For Product Safety Concerns and Information please contact our EU representative GPSR@taylorandfrancis.com Taylor & Francis Verlag GmbH, Kaufingerstraße 24, 80331 München, Germany